HIDDEN
CODES
&
GRAND
DESIGNS

HIDDEN CODES & GRAND DESIGNS

Secret Languages from Ancient Times to Modern Day

Pierre Berloquin

STERLING

New York / London
www.sterlingpublishing.com

For my dear wife, Marie-Thérèse

STERLING and the distinctive Sterling logo are registered trademarks of
Sterling Publishing Co., Inc.

Library of Congress Cataloging-in-Publication Data Available

10   9   8   7   6   5   4   3   2   1

Published by Sterling Publishing Co., Inc.
387 Park Avenue South, New York, NY 10016

© 2008 by Pierre Berloquin

Distributed in Canada by Sterling Publishing
c/o Canadian Manda Group, 165 Dufferin Street
Toronto, Ontario, Canada M6K 3H6
Distributed in the United Kingdom by GMC Distribution Services
Castle Place, 166 High Street, Lewes, East Sussex, England BN7 1XU
Distributed in Australia by Capricorn Link (Australia) Pty. Ltd.
P.O. Box 704, Windsor, NSW 2756, Australia

Sterling ISBN 978-1-4027-2833-4

For information about custom editions, special sales, premium and
corporate purchases, please contact Sterling Special Sales
Department at 800-805-5489 or specialsales@sterlingpublishing.com.

Contents

Introduction 1

CHAPTER 1 5
The Dawn of Code

CHAPTER 2 33
Pythagoras's Codes

CHAPTER 3 73
The Knights Templar

CHAPTER 4 99
The Vitruvian Saga

CHAPTER 5 129
Freemasons from Guilt to Free

CHAPTER 6 157
Homophones and Vigenère

CHAPTER 7 197
Washington 108°

CHAPTER 8 225
Turing Turing

CHAPTER 9 253
Migrating to Code Land

CHAPTER 10 273
The Cipher Gallery

Solutions 329
Bibliography 363
Index 367
Acknowledgments 376
Picture Credits 377

Introduction

Writing about hidden codes is a paradox. Secret activities traditionally are concealed behind codes and ciphers. However, time passes. Secrets eventually float up from the dark waters of occult groups and mystical communities. However secret their activities are, people love to leave traces behind. They hope to survive through their actions and creations. They want to keep their actions secret, but their grand designs have to be public so that they can amaze the universe.

We humble curious historians can only stand outside their secret worlds and gaze at their achievements or explore whatever archives reach us. In that sense, their code is both their most intimate and most vulnerable secret. It can be the code of their secret ciphered exchanges or the aesthetic code of their achievements. Breaking and entering their codes leads us to knowledge of their daily arcane life as well as to understanding of their great achievements.

We now live in codes. The world we have developed and live in is more coded every day.

We use codes to open and close our houses, cars, computers, cell phones, e-mails, and bank accounts. These codes are strangely similar, not to say identical, to the magic formulas of fairy tales, in which wealth and life depended on the knowledge of one word. An open sesame would open caverns or stop armies. Today, digital keyboards everywhere await our codes, and amulets we call credit cards generate money from ATMs. We live in a fantasy writer's dream. No wonder fantasy books and films are so successful—they depict our daily lives.

Coding becomes a virtual extension of our skin, defining what we are and what we are not: "I code, therefore I am."

All this magic relies on computers to manage the business of delivering, remembering, and checking codes. Computers work from programs, which are codes, the critical links between human thought and nonhuman machinery. Codes within codes within codes, as formerly there were wheels within wheels, but the watchmaker's world has given way to the more subtle programmer's world. Subtle or complex? Should we fear the day when one more code will gridlock the whole system or the day when codes carry on their business without caring about us?

With codes managing security, we don't have to carry physical keys anymore. We carry codes in our heads. Is that how society protects itself against the insane? Lose your mind, lose your memory, and you are shut out of your house, your car, and the rest of your life. Remember your codes and you are back in your world. Or is that how we progressively give the keys of our universe to memoryproof, absolutely logical machines that will never fail to remember the codes?

As you'll see in Chapter 2, "Pythagoras's Codes," that must be how an ancient Greek named Pythagoras felt before the universe two and a half millennia ago. He intended to break the codes of nature. Knowing the codes, he could become a player instead of a bystander indefinitely played by the world. The pentagram, the right angle, and perfect numbers were Pythagoras's mystical set of keys. With those keys, he could start creating, assured that his creations would be as valid and beautiful as the original creation. Ever since Pythagoras, mystical societies have revered Pythagorean codes and strived to transmit them. Architects, builders, and artists have lived by his codes to guarantee the aesthetic value of their works.

This book explores how codes—both cipher and aesthetic—have come to exist and develop parallel to common open writing and speech. Coding is probably as old as humanity. We follow the developments of code from the ancient world of Pythagoras and Aeneas the tactician (Chapter 1, "The Dawn of Code") to the present.

Code is a rich and ambiguous word. It can be a reference: a moral code, an aesthetic code, a code of honor, or a dress code. It also can be the key to a cipher in which one purposely hides a meaning that someone else can read by using the same code. This means it can be a key to being true to your surroundings or a key to treacherous diplomacies aimed at your brothers. We follow these two threads throughout the book because they cannot be separated.

Codes have been a concern of "pure" mathematicians such as Pythagoras (600 B.C.E.) and Alan Turing (1940), who believed in being true to one's surrounding but who also had to take part in wars.

Ciphers are fascinating subjects because cipher making and cipher breaking are like puzzles applied to real life. The contest between the cipher maker and the cipher breaker is the ideal contest between two minds. Coders and codebreakers keep outwitting one another. "It may be roundly asserted that human ingenuity cannot concoct a cipher that human ingenuity cannot resolve," Edgar Allan Poe wrote in 1840. Indeed, the history of cipher has proved that no secret writing resists breaking forever. Some codes have taken several centuries to break into, but eventually all of them were broken. We see in Chapter 6, "Homophones and Vigenère," that the Vigenère method was renowned for three centuries as an absolutely unbreakable cipher, only to be broken by a simple solution.

Although it looks like a puzzle, it is important to stress that a cipher is not a puzzle. What is the difference? A real cipher is a conversation. It involves three persons: the sender, the receiver, and the breaker. The sender writes a text, turns it into a "cipher-text" with a code, and sends it to the receiver. The "ciphertext" is supposed to be unreadable by the breaker. Later, the receiver, knowing the code, is able to get back to the original "clear" text. However, this is not happening in the virtual world of games and puzzles; it is happening in real life, and that has two consequences. First, the coding method has to be practical and as foolproof as possible: the coder needs be sure that the receiver will read the message easily and correctly under stress and in difficult conditions such as a combat environment or a diplomatic mission in a hostile country. Also, the sender and the receiver know that the codebreaker's success or failure is a matter of time: time, ingenuity, or plain intelligence information will bring clues and crack the code wide open. A cipher can always be made harder to break by coding and recoding a message several times, as one would put a safe in a safe in a safe, but chances are that it will become unbreakable for its very users. The risks of error will be high, not to mention the time lost in coding and uncoding. A simple mistake in one of the steps will render the code useless.

In practice, the choice of a cipher code is an acceptable risk as long as a workable code will protect the message at least as long as its content is useful. But this requires walking a thin line. For instance, historians say that Napoleon was defeated in Russia because his code was too easy: The Russians often uncoded and read his ciphered orders before his generals could read them. In contrast, the Vigenère code was used in World War I and World War II, a century after everybody knew how to crack it. In a combat environment, it held up long enough to protect short-lived information.

Aesthetic codes are the other, brighter side of coding, as the Vitruvian saga teaches us. Unlike cipher codes, they are meant to be obvious. They are meant to touch the heart before the brain. Aesthetic appreciation should come before logical analysis. Paradoxically, though, the aesthetic value is more intense when a strong hidden logic supports the code. Ever since the Pythagoreans, an aesthetic code has been considered perfect when it has been based on perfect mathematics or perfect logic yet reaches the heart directly even though the logic is hidden. With aesthetic codes as with cipher codes, we have to compromise. The code has to be refined enough to be aesthetically perfect and simple and versatile enough to be usable in all situations. Pythagoras's genius produced that rare combination with the golden mean 25 centuries ago.

If this book were a novel, its main character would be code wearing varied masks, whether appearing in communications, aesthetics, or morals. In this epic, we humans are codes' partners. We pride ourselves on being codes' masters, with an inborn right to create code and to use it, disregard it or discard it. However, the reality of our relationship with code is more complex. We do create code rather easily, but code eventually gets the better of us. We often find ourselves inextricably bound by code to the point of being paralyzd in double- or triple-bind situations (our quest for freedom, our need for security, and our curiosity about new technologies, each with its own exclusive code).

Even worse, a new situation arose in the twentieth century: code underwent a quantum leap, acquiring independence and autonomy. Today code still depends on people to create and develop it, but this acquired autonomy already lets code spread and act beyond the possibility of human control. Millions of little frankencodes are out there, swarming in the virtual sphere of the Internet and electronic communication. Are these ultimate grandchildren of Pythagoras's codes a help or a danger greater than global warming?

A note about the content and design of this book. In addition to pictures and graphics, this history of code features many examples of ciphers and codes, both old and new. They can be seen as challenges by the puzzle-minded reader, exercises by the industrious reader, or eye-catching illustrations by the aesthetic-minded reader. Who wants to read about codes without seeing some? To satisfy the aesthetically minded reader, Chapter 10, "The Cipher Gallery," is a portfolio of codes. Some of the coded texts contain collateral data on the subject but do not influence the general course of the story.

CHAPTER 1

The Dawn of Code

A few centuries before our Common Era (C.E.), the Greeks and Romans explored basic principles of cipher that, with progressive refinements, would remain in use for two millennia. The basic human need for network communication and ciphers as a necessary counterpart was so strong that it emerged and was developed even before an appropriate technology was available. For centuries, optical telegraphy with torches, mirrors, smoke, flags, or semaphore established the basis for our current digitized networking civilization.

Polybius

	1	2	3	4	5
1	A	B	C	D	E
2	F	G	H	I	J
3	K	L	M	N	O
4	P	Q	R	S	T
5	V	W	X	Y	Z

The innocent-looking matrix of figures and letters at the left was a major breakthrough in the second century B.C.E. (Before Common Era). Twenty-two centuries ago, Polybius, a Greek soldier and historian, designed it to create the first efficient, sturdy all-purpose code for sending optical messages over a distance.

In this chapter you will see how this "Polybius code" works and how it might have become the essential communication tool in the Roman Empire. As a result of technologies such as this, Roman armies had a serious advantage over their opponents. They could exchange orders and information directly without having to send horseback messengers who might be captured by the enemy.

The Romans built the first information network and used it to exchange messages across western Asia and Europe in hours or days instead of weeks or months. For want of definite documentation, my hypothesis to date is that this system was based on the Polybius code.

Decode:

This adage of Scipio Africanus became a proverb. Can you read its meaning before learning more about the code? In the Latin alphabet, U and V are the same letter. (All answers are at the back of the book.)

21 35 43 45 51 34 15   21 11 51 35 43 44   45 23 15   12 35 32 14

The discovery and development of this code, along with the communication technologies that supported it, are vital to understanding what a code is and how it works. This history leads us to our present-day codes.

From Greece to Rome

In the second century B.C.E., Rome was in the process of conquering Greece, the last independent civilized region in the area. The Romans were pursuing their grand design of *Pax Romana*—a local "world peace"—by surrounding Italy with friendly countries that were run by Romans and that followed the Roman legal system.

Polybius resisted Roman domination by trying to create a federation among the Greek cities of the Peloponnese, the southern part of the Greek mainland. That effort failed when he was captured by the Romans and sent to Rome, where he spent 17 years.

Although technically a captive and then a slave of the famous Scipio family, he was able to participate in Roman culture. He wrote books bearing witness to this important period when Rome was destroying its strongest enemies: Carthage and Corinth. We know of Polybius through his books on history, in which he also wrote about military strategy and technology.

As a strategist, Polybius was acutely aware of the importance of communications, and he researched methods of communicating across long distances. As a historian, he recorded the use of a sort of telegraph that had been invented and described two centuries earlier by another Greek, Aeneas the Tactician. Aeneas's text is lost, but Polybius's description of it is precise enough to allow us to understand the system and what he did to improve it.

Aeneas used what we now call a codebook. This is a list of possible messages—"Advance," "Halt," "Engage," and so forth—in which each message is numbered. When two parties who have the list need to communicate, they need only send and receive these numbers.

Although Aeneas's codebook listed only a few items, modern codebooks, such as those used by navies during World War I, are thick. They contain thousands of items and refer to names, places, weapons, and even specific words and sentences.

A codebook might look like this:

Advance	1
Retreat	2
Halt	3
Camp	4
Hide	5
Engage	6

With this codebook, the message 1–4–6 would mean "Advance, make camp, and then engage in battle."

More important than his codebook is the way Aeneas sent messages. Although he was not the first to use optical signals, Aeneas invented the first optical telegraph. Well before him, the Babylonians and others had used smoke signals or mirrors to reflect the sun's rays, but those messages were limited to very basic content such as "we win" or "we lose." For any information beyond "yes" or "no," the Babylonians had to resort to using messengers on foot or on horseback. Aeneas moved beyond such "either-or" signals and toward a defined list. Thus, his invention may well be called a telegraph, although that word was coined much later. Claude Chappe, the Frenchman who made up the word in the eighteenth century, knew about Aeneas and had so much respect for him that he created a Greek-sounding word for the device by combining graph, which means "writing," and tele, which means "at a distance."

How did this telegraph work in practice? Aeneas had to synchronize the sender and the receiver. To do that, he used the only time device that was available to him: a water clock. A clepsydra, or water clock, is a vessel of water in which the water drips out regularly so that its level displays the time.

Each party had an identical vessel with a tap at the bottom. The codebook was written on both vessels, with each word or phrase corresponding to a certain level of the water. The technique involved starting with both vessels full of water, opening the taps together, letting the water flow from both vessels at the same speed, and closing the taps at exactly the same time. When the water was level with the intended message in both vessels, the receiver would read the correct message on his vessel.

Two synchronizations were thus essential: the start and the stop of the flow of water. Here's how that was done:

1. Party A would raise a torch, meaning "ready to send."
2. Party B would raise his torch, meaning "ready to receive."
3. Party A would lower his torch, meaning "I am opening my tap; open yours." Party B then would lower his torch and open his tap, and the water would flow from both vessels.
4. Party A would raise his torch again to signal "Let's close the taps."

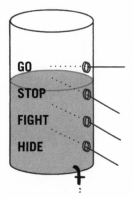

Reading level of water inside the vessel was not as simple as it would be today. At that time, no transparent large glass vessels were available, and so Aeneas's telegraph had to work with opaque earthenware vessels. Aeneas drilled holes in those vessels so that one hole was level with each message item and put corks in the holes. He stuck wooden rods through the corks, half inside and half outside the vessel (see the illustration at the left). When the vessel was full of water, the inner parts of the rods would float up in the water, causing the corresponding outer parts to flip down. When the level of water was between the top and the bottom, some rods would be up and others would be down. This arrangement made it possible to know the level of water inside a vessel by looking at the outside rods. Many other systems could be used to display the water level. For example, a float on the water could activate an outside marker with a string-and-pulley system.

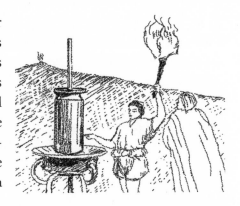

Much of Greece is hilly enough to make an optical system practical, but the Greeks had to compensate for distance and bad weather. To do so, they used an early version of telescopes—simple hollow tubes—to concentrate the image. Modern lens telescopes were still 2,000 years in the future.

Theoretically, the torch and water clock system was a definite improvement on smoke signals, but there is no proof that it ever was used. It could convey only a dozen or so fixed messages, and every military situation meets with unforeseen events that call for a wider range of communication, or a larger bandwidth, as we say today. When he studied the system, Polybius felt that a finite list of items would never be sufficient: they needed a way to send the full range of real language. In other words, he needed a simple way to code language and a method for sending that code. His five-by-five array (see page 6) satisfied both requirements. His brilliant idea was to switch from a code-book to a code and send letters instead of items on a list.

Polybius's telegraph used 10 torches. The sending party had five torches on the left and—well separated from them—another five on the right, arranged so that that the receiver could count them easily. When they were not being used, they were hidden behind a wall.

To send a single letter, a specific number of torches was raised on the left-hand side, corresponding to the row in the code matrix; simultaneously, a number of others were raised on the right-hand side, corresponding to the column. The receiver needed only one torch to indicate when the letter corresponding to the intersection of row and column had been received and understood. The sender then would display the next letter.

The torch code for the letter L would look like the illustration at the right, with the taller symbols in the first sequence representing the raised left-hand torches and the taller symbols in the second sequence representing the raised torches on the right.

"Hello" would be torch coded in Latin like this:

Here we are coding Polybius with numbers instead of torches.

Decode:

Cato the Elder's message to the Senate.

13 11 43 45 23 11 22 15   33 51 44 45   12 15   51 45 45 15 43 32 54

14 15 44 45 43 35 54 15 14

Decode:

Scipio Africanus's paradoxical confidence.

24   11 33   34 15 51 15 43   32 15 44 44   11 45

32 15 24 44 51 43 15   45 23 11 34   52 23 15 34   11 45

32 15 24 44 51 43 15   35 43   32 15 44 44   11 32 35 34 15

45 23 11 34   52 23 15 34   11 32 35 34 15

In the 1980s, students at the RWTH Aachen University, a technical school in Germany, tested Polybius's technology by using traditional torches to send signals between two hills. After some practice, they succeeded in sending an average of eight letters a minute. Let's compare that rate with present-day computer transmission. If a letter is transmitted in 8 bits, the students succeeded in transmitting 64 bits a minute, or roughly 1 bit a second. This may seem low even to a pre-DSL Internet subscriber enjoying 48,000 bits a second, but it was a considerable improvement over systems.

Decode:

Suppose Polybius had adopted a slightly different coding logic in his matrix. What would the poet Virgil be saying here?

45 42 51 23 41   43 53 54   54 53   33 42 44 12 53 34 54 15 43 51 44

21 15 54   11 41 15 11 43 31 51   11 23 23   54 32 51   33 53 34 51   21

53 23 41 23 45   11 22 11 42 43 44 54   54 32 51 33

Here, the first number is the column and the second number is the row.

Julius Caesar

In 55 B.C.E., Julius Caesar leaped from his ship onto the British shore before his soldiers had a chance to do it. That act of bravery, which he carefully recorded in his own book, celebrates Caesar the first Roman to set foot on British soil. Two millennia later, Napoleon considered invading Britain but never made up his mind to do it. Because his physical strength and skill were no match for Caesar's, he would not have jumped ashore ahead of his men. He always took part in combat from a tent on a hill with his spyglass, maps, and couriers. As we'll see later, on this occasion he had his own telegraph ready to communicate across the channel.

Decode:

Here are Caesar's legendary words upon hitting British soil:

OHDS, IHOORZ VROGLHUV, XQOHVV BRX ZLVK WR EHWUDB BRXU HDJOH

WR WKH HQHPB. L, IRU PB SDUW, ZLOO SHUIRUP PB GXWB WR WKH

FRPPRQZHDOWK DQG PB JHQHUDO

Of course, Caesar's words were not sent as ciphered messages as we know them today; they were shouted in the middle of action and probably were different from what he recorded in his *Commentary on the Gallic Wars*. However, as you'll see, Caesar played an important role in the development of codes, in more ways than one.

Like other powerful men, Caesar had a team of servants, called *speculatores* in Latin, devoted to an ambiguous function. They were employed as both carriers and gatherers of information; they acted as couriers as well as spies. Every politically active person had his *speculatores* to inform him on and dispatch letters to his friends and enemies. Caesar went further. Knowing all too well that they could be bribed by his adversaries, Caesar did not trust his speculatores to safely deliver his important letters. He devised the code that bears his name to hide the content from them as well as from other parties.

Here is how Caesar's method works. You replace each letter by the letter three places farther down the alphabet: D stands for A, E for B, and so on. Conversely, when you receive a message, you replace each letter by the letter three places up the alphabet.

X, Y, and Z are coded by going "around the corner." Think of the alphabet as being written on a circle, with A following Z, and so on. Then X is coded as A, Y as B, and Z as C. When you are decoding, A is decoded as X, B as Y, and C as Z.

There is no proof that Caesar knew about Polybius's code, but it seems likely that he did. Torch telegraph towers were still in use well beyond Caesar's time, several centuries later, under the emperor Trajan (98–117 C.E.). They were such an important means of communication that Caesar must have known about their basic code. However, he might not have realized the power of Polybius's code as an enciphering method and considered it a simple telegraphic device, never imagining that its use with a keyword could transform messages into secrets (see the section on Marie-Antoinette in Chapter 6).

Today Caesar's code may seem too simple to provide adequate secrecy, but in the first century B.C.E. it was a major innovation and probably defeated all attempts to break it.

Legend says that Caesar excelled in everything. As a teenager, he was an excellent swordsman and an indefatigable horseman. He was an outstanding strategist with a continuous record of success. He had a direct relationship with his soldiers, who loved him. He was an excellent writer and poet, a quality recognized even by his enemies. As a politician he could be dishonest, capable of bribing any opponent to achieve his goals, but he was also a visionary, passing excellent laws that became the foundation of modern republics. We owe to Caesar the rule that all debates in senates and congresses must be public. This rule is the essential difference between democratic assemblies and secret societies. Yet secrecy is a basic need of all societies for two reasons. First, democracies always need to keep an eye on government agencies. Second, in democracies, the most prominent citizens and members of the government often belong to secret societies in which laws are discussed and developed before becoming public.

Decode:

This is a saying of Publius, often quoted by Caesar, that may account for Caesar's outstanding record of successful strategies:

EDG LV D SODQ ZKLFK FDQQRW EHDU D FKDQJH

Caesar's death took place exactly as he wished. He had said many times that the best possible death is an unexpected one. However, his famous last words express his surprise, for he never expected to see his adopted son slay him.

Decode:

Caesar's last words at seeing his son Brutus ready to kill him.

BRX WRR PB VRQ?

Even in death Caesar could not escape singularity: Indeed the Senate immediately voted for his deification. As if to validate that act, a comet appeared that evening over Rome and remained in the sky for several days. Would a god make this his personal motto?

Decode:

Caesar's cynical advice to politicians (coded with a different leap and broken into five-letter groups to increase the challenge).

ROHXD VDBCK ANJTC QNUJF MXRCC XBNRI NYXFN ARWJU UXCQN ALJBN

BXKBN AENRC

Breaking Caesar's Code

The main weakness of Caesar's code is that there are only 25 possible jumps. If you try all of them successively, you are bound to find the right one. However, there is a much more elegant way to break the code. We'll see in Chapter 6 that in English the letter E is used much more often than any other letter. Knowing this, the codebreaker can compute the statistics for all the letters in the message. The most frequently used one is likely to represent E, which suggests the secret leap.

Here N stands out, with 9 occurrences, followed by the 6 occurrences of C and X. This suggests that N represents E and that the code thus uses a leap of 9.

Augustus, who after a period of civil war became Caesar's successor as head of state, felt the need for a better tool for managing the empire than private speculatores. He created the cursus publicus carried by oxen for ordinary mail and the cursus velox carried on horses for express messages, public communications, and messenger services run by the state. We'll see that this technology survived until the nineteenth century, when optical telegraphs appeared in Europe and America switched from the Pony Express, a service very similar to the cursus velox, to the Morse telegraph.

These details of Caesar's life are not just entertaining anecdotes. They represent the parameters of an aesthetic and political code in that Caesar has been magnified into a fundamental code of reference: that of outstanding political leader. Caesar's name is used in many languages to designate a political leader who has absolute power. For example, it is the basis of *kaiser* in German, czar in Russian, and possibly Gesar in Tibetan.

Whether Caesar-like leaders are actually called *Caesar* or not, the code of reference addresses at least four elements of those leaders:

- They excel in physical as well as mental achievements.
- They are makers of good laws yet stand above them and may break them.
- They are excellent strategists, seeing ahead and leading the nation to conquer new territories.
- They stand as mediums between common mortals and the spiritual world.

The last element creates a link between political leadership and secret societies, in which Caesars are created and/or belong and that symbolize their access to a mythic world. Moreover, paradoxes such as simultaneously making and breaking the laws add to their mythical status and strengthen their image. Ambiguously, such leaders stand between several worlds, drawing power from all of them (see the discussion of mythical journeys at the end of Chapter 5).

The Scytale

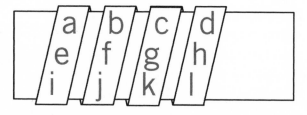

Another encryption technology was invented by the Greeks as early as the seventh century B.C.E. Using a radically different approach, this method does not replace the letters of a message with other letters, figures, or arcane symbols. Instead, it simply works on the order of the letters, setting them in a new coded order. Technically, this is referred to as transposition rather than substitution.

The Greek scytale system is technically very simple: the sender wraps a leather band around a stick and writes the message on the band, line after line. When the band is unwrapped, it bears a meaningless string of letters. In the example above, "abcdefghijk" becomes "ieajfbkgclhd." One can read the content only by wrapping the band around a stick with the same diameter. The loop used here is three letters long. In the following ciphers you will have to guess the length of the loops. The ciphers are broken into groups of five letters, something professionals usually do to limit transmission errors.

Decode:

A wise remark by Aesop.

ANACD DEIOR SUTWB AOTIR FNSUE ELNTF EHRMA IYNE

Decode:

A cynical remark by Aristotle.

NNLIA RTAAI NNEHS RFGTN ELEEO HOVEA FNEBI ELOEL EGPIR HATOK
AAZTR ELLYE OWLFD RUHMO UTSEE FRHA

Decode:

A practical remark by Sophocles.

DAITL TOTIC OSOIT NMHCP EEAMA RELTR TGIHO TEOOT DFRNA UEGTW
EHSNA ENR

The mindset involved here must have been advanced, for transposition codes were only rediscovered and developed in the nineteenth century.

Trajan's Network

In the first centuries of our Common Era, the Roman Empire seems to have made extensive use of optical communications to transmit data throughout Europe, the Near East, and North Africa. According to Ottavio Bianco Zanotti in *Telegrafia optica (Torino, 1887)*, a network of small towers was spread over thousands of miles, with each tower guarded and managed by two soldiers. Zanotti mentions 1,200 towers in Italy, 1,200 in Gaul, and 500 in Asia.

We know what those towers looked like from pictures on Trajan's Column, the monument the emperor Trajan erected to record episodes of his wars against the Dacians.

The monument is a 98.5-foot (30-meter) marble column on which scenes from the wars are displayed on a spiraling frieze, with very precise details of the characters and their clothes, weapons, and tools. At the start of the strip, which you can see above, five small towers, each enclosed in a wooden fence, could be interpreted as signal towers. Three of the towers display a burning torch, and two have no torches. Two straw huts stand between the towers on the left and the right.

Between the two types of towers a rectangular object forms a sort of 5-by-12 matrix. This could be a pyre made of very precisely piled logs, but there is no flame or

anything on it to be burnt. Furthermore, the carver used a perspective that makes the towers look as if they were being viewed by an observer standing in front of the matrix.

The interpretation of the first spiral as a depiction of a network system is credible, but it would be much more convincing if there were written documentation. Its situation at the very start of the strip underlines its importance. Of course, a system of information and communication would have been essential to the management of war and of the empire as a whole. Moreover, the buildings are not fortified, and that precludes interpreting them as defensive structures such as forts and watchtowers.

There are several ways this system might have functioned. The carver took such care with other parts of the frieze that we have to assume that he took the same care with this part.

One possibility is that the network is a series of stations, each consisting of a single isolated tower. This tower may or may not display a torch. The system would employ a code that used only one possible signal; this would be like Morse code with only the dots. This seems feasible, but it would not have been reliable.

Let's base another hypothesis on the matrix between the towers. The fact that that object is placed by perspective at the very center of the scene means that it must play a central role. Indeed, it shows five lines, reminding us of the Polybius code, which is based on a 5-by-5 matrix. Since there are five towers, we might imagine that the Romans used a five-torch system in which every station was a set of five small towers, each one displaying or not displaying a torch and with the towers sufficiently far apart to be seen as distinct from a distance. Like the array of shutters later used by Claude Chappe and Nicola Edelcrantz that we will discuss later in this chapter, this would enable a 5-bit binary system with 32 ($2 \times 2 \times 2 \times 2 \times 2 = 32$) possible signals; that is sufficient to transmit an alphabet and even more information.

This hypothesis would stand on firmer ground if the nodes of the matrix were readable. Unfortunately, the marble of the original tower has been eroded by acidic air pollution. The plaster mold ordered by Queen Victoria for the Victoria and Albert

Museum in London is not precise enough. The bronze copy ordered by Napoleon III and displayed in the moats of the Saint-Germain castle is in better shape but offers no more detail except that the array of unknown objects does look like a pile of logs.

We may be engaged in an impossible quest here. Would the Romans carve their network code in stone for everybody to see and thus give away their secrets? If we choose the matrix hypothesis, we may consider that the log pile is there for no other purpose than to symbolize a matrix.

The Chappe Brothers' Telegraph

After the fall of the Roman Empire, the telegraph system was all but forgotten, with no physical trace of it remaining. If ruins still exist today, they are not known as such. The system was rediscovered by scientists in Europe in the eighteenth century. As was the fashion, research started by looking for good ideas in ancient texts. Scientific work in those days required knowledge of Latin and Greek. Research papers and books were often written in Latin so that they could be read in every country. New concepts or machines often were given names formed by combining elementary Latin or Greek words. This naming strategy worked as a universal code. Anybody with a standard education could analyze a new name and know what the concept or machine was about.

In 1791, Claude Chappe read a book by Polybius. With the enthusiastic aid of his four brothers, he started a series of experiments. Quickly setting aside the use of torches or smoke signals, he looked for other types of indicators. He also excluded electricity, which was still only a toy: nobody really knew how to put it to practical use. As is almost always the case in research, he did not go straight to the simpler solutions but first worked at improving Aeneas's system.

The Tachygraph

The system that Chappe called a *tachygraph* ("fast writing") involved the synchronization of two clocklike pendulum devices (see the illustration at the right). Each one displayed a quadrant bearing symbols and had a needle powered by a falling weight. Since the devices were synchronized, the needles moved at the same speed and pointed to the same symbols. The sender would transmit symbol after symbol by signaling to the receiver whenever the needle passed over the desired symbol. Referring to his own quadrant, the receiver would note only those symbols.

The signals had to be clear and instantaneous so that sender and receiver were pointing to the same symbol. Chappe experimented with several possibilities. He first tried sounding a bell or striking a pan, but in that case the two posts had to be within hearing distance, no more then a thousand feet apart, not mentioning the time lag due to the speed of sound. Strangely enough, among other things, he did experiment with an electric wire, which put him close to beating Samuel Morse's invention of the electric telegraph by a half a century. He abandoned electricity for lack of good insulation for such a long wire and finally opted for a rotating shutter with black and white sides above the quadrant. Opening and closing the shutter could be done almost instantaneously, and the display could be seen over long distances with the aid of a telescope.

Modern telescopes with lenses had been in use for more than a century. They played an essential role in all optical telegraphy and allowed for greater distance between posts.

Chappe demonstrated his clock and shutter mechanism to a group of official witnesses, including a notary, a priest, and a mayor, on March 2, 1791. The witnesses were impressed and testified that the message was sent and received correctly.

It is not known whether that machine sent letters, numerals, or symbols, but however quaint and unnecessarily complex it may look today, it did work. The signed affidavits of the witnesses are on display in the small museum of the village of Brûlon where the event took place. The tachygraph was not developed further, but its success encouraged Chappe to continue his work.

The Shutters

Chappe went on to do experiments with different technologies. He tried an array of five wooden shutters that displayed a 5-bit binary system, with 32 (2 × 2 × 2 × 2 × 2) possible signals. By opening or closing shutters with pulleys, he could display 32 different codes, 26 of which are shown below.

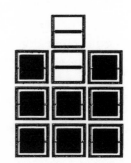

Chappe also experimented with an array of 10 shutters, which allowed for a much greater range of codes: 1,024 different signals. This better suited his goal of working not only with an alphabet but with an extended codebook, letters, symbols, and a dictionary of common words, as we'll see shortly.

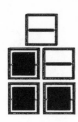

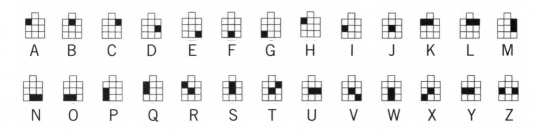

Decode:

The message sent by the first—and short-lived—tachygraph is coded here in the 10-shutter system.

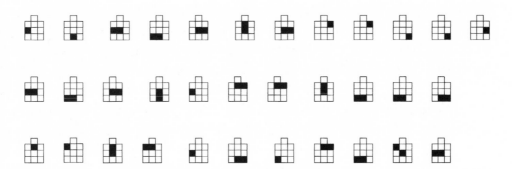

Absorbed in this scientific work, Chappe did not realize that he was risking his life. During the French Revolution, the people of Paris were in dread of the armies of neighboring countries and were not informed of Chappe's real purpose. Seeing his machine set up on the hill of L'Etoile (the path leading up the hill was not yet the Champs Elysées), they imagined that he was exchanging signals with the enemy armies. An angry mob soon gathered to lynch him. He fled in a hurry, leaving his nearly destroyed machine behind.

After that misadventure, Chappe abandoned the shutter system. His main reason for doing that was that the signals were not sufficiently visible at a long distance in all types of weather. An array of open and closed shutters requires a very clear sky behind it to display the black and white squares clearly.

The Beam System

In 1792 Chappe finally came closer to actually writing in the sky with the system of articulated wooden beams that made him famous. A long beam—the regulator—was mounted at the top of a pole. Two shorter beams—the indicators—were attached at the ends of the regulator, as is shown in the illustration at the right. All three of the beams could rotate on axes. Each indicator was balanced with a counterweight so that the whole system could easily be manipulated into and then hold a large number of positions. With little effort, a man using ropes and pulleys could set the system into 196 of those positions. Inside the tower, a small repeater or telltale showed the operator the exact position of the beams.

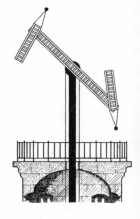

However, Chappe's mind was set on a grander design than the signal machine itself. Chappe saw beyond the elementary mechanism of transmission; his real goal was the creation of a communications network. That vision set him apart from his contemporaries, who were proposing clever mechanisms for one-to-one communication. None of them had seen beyond that limited scope.

With the ultimate goal of creating a practical network, in August 1793, the French National Convention (that nation's parliament or congress) appropriated enough money to build a line of 15 telegraph stations between Paris and Lille. They were not promoting a new device; rather, they were promoting modern communication.

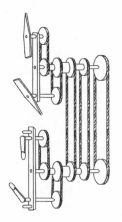

Because of his breadth of vision, Chappe was awarded the new title of "telegraph engineer" with full official powers to use existing high buildings or build towers and cut down trees wherever necessary.

The line formally opened in July 1794. It cost the Chappe brothers a year of hard work. They had to overcome all kinds of difficulties, the least of them being constant conflict with local interests. In spite of government support, few people understood the national scope of the project. Fortunately for the project, the first transmitted message bore excellent news: victory over the enemy. The town of Condé-sur-l'Escaut had been won back from the Austrian Army.

The Codebook

Chappe then set his mind to improving the speed of communication. Since breaking messages up into letters sent one by one was too slow, he developed an extended codebook, a rich dictionary of common words and expressions that could be sent as simple signals.

Theoretically, the main beam could assume four positions and each indicator could assume seven, allowing for 96 ($4 \times 7 \times 7$) different signals. For the sake of clarity, only 92 of the signals were used, and they were sent in pairs. The codebook thus contained 92 pages of 92 codes. When a pair was sent, the first signal pointed to a page and the second pointed to a code, word, sentence, or symbol on that page.

Among the 92 pages, there was one that contained only letters, both uppercase and lowercase, and another devoted to network use, with signals for breakdown, end of day, poor visibility, error, lunch break, and so on.

Chappe also had to deal with the fact that his signal could be seen by everyone. His telegraph was never put to public use but was reserved for official matters that had to be kept secret. To ensure security, aside from an absolute minimum number of people at both ends of the lines, no one had the codebooks or knew the codes. A message was encoded by a director and then sent and relayed from tower to tower by operators who copied what they saw without understanding the content. At the other end, another director would decode the message and deliver it.

A tower usually had two operators. A "glassman" read the incoming signals from the preceding tower with a field glass and then informed the "ropeman," who reproduced the signal. The glassman then would observe the next tower to make sure the signal was read and transmitted correctly. A specific position of the beams signaled that everything had been done correctly.

Soon, all over France and Europe, Chappe towers were waving their beams and broadcasting indecipherable and puzzling contents. Understandably, frustrated bystanders wondered about the meaning of the signs, which became a common subject of conversation. It also stimulated the imagination of poets. Victor Hugo, for example, wrote hundreds of angry or ironic verses about it. Although he was fond of séances in which he talked to great people of the past, including Christ, and recorded the conversations in French alexandrines, Hugo resented the contemporary telegraph, which eluded his understanding.

⌣	⟩	⌐	✓	[	⌣	⟍	⌠	Γ	Γ	Γ	L	⌐
A	B	C	D	E	F	G	H	I	J	K	L	M

⌐	⌞	⟩	⌐	Γ	⟩	⟋	⟍	⌐	⌐	⟩	Γ	⟍
N	O	P	Q	R	S	T	U	V	W	X	Y	Z

Decode:
The first Chappe "victory" message.

⌐ ⌞ ⌐ ✓ [Γ [⟩ ⟋ ⌞ Γ [✓ ⟋ ⌞ ⟋ ⌠

[Γ [⟩ ⟍ ⟋ L Γ ⌐ Γ [✓ ✓ Γ ⟋ Γ ⌞ ⌐

⟋ ⌠ Γ ⟩ ✓ ⌞ Γ ⌐ Γ ⌐ ⌞ ⌣ ⟋ ⟩ Γ ⟩

At its peak, before closing in 1854, the Chappe network operated hundreds of towers and could link Amsterdam to Venice.

Military Developments

The first country to follow France in developing an optical telegraph network was Sweden. King Karl XIII, who feared an invasion by the Russians, commissioned the young poet and engineer Abraham Niclas Edelcrantz to build a line of telegraph stations from the shore to the roof

of the royal castle. Edelcrantz had studied many forms of technology in depth and had written the only book on optical telegraphy available at that time. For Sweden, he chose the 10-square shutter system shown at the right.

When Napoleon seized power, he closed the French telegraph line, fearing that it might be used against him. Not long afterward, realizing that it was a useful tool for the exercise of power, he not only reopened the line but extended it in all directions across France and parts of Europe.

That triggered the development of an optical telegraph in England. The London Admiralty was concerned about the possibility of an invasion by the Napoleonic armies and wanted to be informed as rapidly as possible if that occurred. Indeed, on his own side of the English Channel, Napoleon had built a giant telegraph adapted to the 20-mile-wide (32.2-kilometer) gap and had assembled all the elements of a second one to be constructed on the British side to send back signals as soon as his armies landed there.

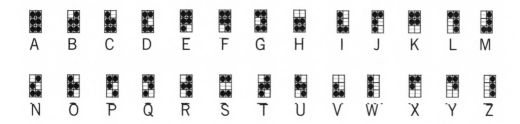

Napoleon's invasion never took place, but a British telegraph system was deployed from the shore to London. The British Admiralty chose a shutter system with a code similar to the alphabet shown above.

The British shutter system must have been unreliable or perhaps it had other shortcomings, for the Admiralty closed and dismantled it the day Napoleon was removed from power. Lord Popham then chose one of the beam systems described by Edelcrantz in his 1796 *Treatise on Telegraphs*.

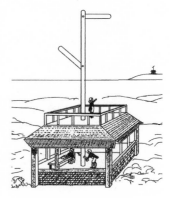

The First Network Virus

The first documented network virus appeared on the Chappe telegraph in 1834. It persisted until 1836. Like present-day computer viruses, it took advantage of a specific weakness in the code and the network. Far ahead of its time, it worked perfectly and brought its hacker creators a fortune.

The hackers exploited the way the system managed errors. Unavoidably, the operators sometimes would make a mistake when trying to send a code. When a tower operator realized he had sent an incorrect code, he had no alternative but to send a "cancel" code immediately, before sending the correct one. The incorrect code, together with its cancellation code, would be transmitted down the line, tower by tower, with the error "tagged" for eventual correction. At the end of the line, where the messages were translated, the director would simply erase every code that immediately preceded a cancel signal.

Thanks to this procedure, it was easy for dishonest directors to introduce a virus code into a message as long as they followed it with a cancel code. At the end of the line, the code and the cancel code would be suppressed like any other mistake, and no one would be the wiser. All that was needed to complete the scheme was an accomplice near any tower, watching the wooden arms with field glasses and waiting for the right code-and-error combination. Of course, the most important weakness of the system was the fact that the wooden arms of the towers could be seen by anyone.

The hackers who used the scheme were the Blanc brothers, who were bankers in Bordeaux. They made money by playing the local stock exchange. The Bordeaux stock exchange used on Paris stock prices, but only after those prices reached Bordeaux. That involved a delay of three days, the time it took the horseback postal service to deliver a letter containing the details. Every evening a letter would leave Paris with the prices, and Bordeaux would display them when the letter arrived three days later. The Chappe telegraph could have carried the data in a matter of hours but was restricted to government use. As with all stock exchanges, anyone in Bordeaux who knew in advance whether the rates were going up or down could make easy money by buying before they rose and selling before they fell.

The Blanc brothers were persuaded to use the Chappe telegraph error system to make huge profits. However, first an obstacle had to be overcome. The telegraph line did not go straight from Paris to Bordeaux. It stopped at a substation in Tours, where the messages were decoded and written down and then sent over the line to Bordeaux. Any code-error virus sent from Paris would be routinely canceled in Tours and would not reach Bordeaux, and so the real hacking had to start in Tours.

The final solution worked like this: the Blanc brothers bought the services of the telegraph director and his assistant in Tours. In Paris, an accomplice visited the stock exchange daily, concentrating on a particular government bond that was the most popular investment at that time. Whenever the rate changed significantly, he would send a small parcel to the director's wife in Tours: socks if it was going down, gloves if it was going up. This was not likely to arouse suspicion because the director's wife ran a haberdashery shop where she sold those articles. Immediately after receiving the parcel, the director would insert the corresponding code into a message and his assistant accomplice would send it. The Blanc brothers had another accomplice in Bordeaux, a former telegraph manager from Lyon. Knowing the codes, he spent his days in a rented a room with a view of a Chappe tower. Watching for the right codes, he immediately reported the corresponding information to his banker friends, thus beating the postal service by two days.

Of course, the Blanc brothers' extraordinary streak of luck aroused suspicion, but a discreet inquiry found nothing. The hacking was discovered only when the assistant to the Tours director who was in on the scam died. Before passing away, he confided in a friend, suggesting that he ask the director to take him on in his place. The director refused, and the dead man's friend went to the police.

The hackers were obviously guilty, but they were breaking no law. Their lawyers easily won the case, arguing that although the telegraph was used only by the government, no law actually forbade private use of it. The hackers were acquitted and paid only the legal costs. The Tours director was fired.

During the trial the government came to see the danger of that loophole. A new law was drafted hurriedly that forbade personal use of a means of communications without government approval, and it was passed on the day of the verdict. Thereafter, the broadcasting of information remained a state monopoly in France until January 1, 1998, when European Community liberal laws forced a change.

It was the former director from Lyon who had watched from outside and knew everything about the Chappe codes who was the real hacker. It was he who had conceived the scheme and taken it to the Blanc brothers to put into operation. His name was Pierre Renaud. Should his name be honored or cursed?

The British network was never linked to the continental one. It connected London to strategic sites on the shore: Yarmouth, Sheerness, Deal, Portsmouth, and Plymouth. It was later replaced with a network supplied by the railroads.

Optical Telegraphy in the New World

True to the spirit of private enterprise, American telegraph systems were never government-run centralized networks. Instead of being reserved for administrative and military affairs, they were created by businessmen and used for commercial matters. Except for the Philadelphia–New York line, which was used by stockbrokers, the optical telegraph functioned mainly in ports, sending information on sea traffic. Telegraph systems of this sort were erected in Baltimore, Boston, Charleston, New York, Portland (Maine), and San Francisco.

Americans adopted the wooden beam rather than the shutter system but also developed a system of their own: the simple and sturdy "yard-and-ball" (see the illustration above).

The Martha's Vineyard–Boston Line

As early as 1801, the Massachusetts line was transmitting information over 72 miles (116 kilometers) between an observatory on the island of Martha's Vineyard and Boston. The first station on the mainland was in Woods Hole. Thirteen other stations, most of them on hills that still are called Telegraph Hill, relayed the messages to Boston. The line was created, patented, and run by Jonathan Grout, a lawyer from Belcherstown. It was used by the merchants of Boston and Salem, who were eager to know about the cargoes of ships arriving in their harbors as early as possible. Conveniently, the information was delivered at post offices or was received there originally. Several successive owners then developed the line further.

There is no surviving detailed description of the system, but it was close to that of Chappe's wooden beams. Grout named his project a *telegraphe*, with the terminal e indicating the French origin. Grout's offer was business-oriented: clients applied for information on specific ships and paid if and when information about those ships was announced.

John Rowe Parker, who took charge of the system in 1822, adapted it to make it universal. He used a higher beam placed on top of the mast to indicate which code was in use, allowing the system to accommodate a variety of codes. Among others, he used the so-called Elford numbers to identify American ships precisely.

From New Jersey to Staten Island to Manhattan

New York built its first telegraph, of which we know very little, in 1812. It seems to have been based on the "yard-and-ball" or "barrel signal" principle. Black balls or barrels glided up and down vertical cables, replacing the European shutters or beams. At night the balls could be replaced with lamps, a definite improvement on European systems.

Later a line of wooden beam semaphores was deployed from Wall Street to the Sandy Hook lighthouse and to the Navesink Highlands on the New Jersey coast.

At its peak, the operation of that telegraph seems to involved the coordination of several actions and technologies. When a vessel was approaching the coast, a canoe would row out to it, get information about its cargo, and send pigeons carrying that information to the Sandy Hook or Navesink telegraph station. From there the sema- phores would relay the data to Wall Street via the Staten Island and Battery stations.

The system worked with numbers in a cor- responding codebook that was divided into five parts with a thousand lines each. The first part dealt with compass points and positions, the second with nautical phrases, the third with words and expressions, the fourth with vessel names, and the fifth with countries and port names.

The San Francisco Semaphore

Telegraph Hill in San Francisco got its name from the installation of a wooden beam telegraph on its summit. This was the last one built in the United States, and it started operations in 1849, two years after San Francisco abandoned its earlier name Yerba Buena and began to expand. The code described ships and where they came from. It worked between the Outer Station, beyond the Golden Gate, and Telegraph Hill.

The San Francisco semaphore (see the illustration at the right) was short-lived: the fog that sets in at any time of the day or year made transmission impractical. In 1853 it was replaced by an electromagnetic telegraph. The mast on Telegraph Hill later was used for another code: the "time-ball." Each day exactly at noon, a large hollow ball was dropped from the top so that ship captains could synchronize their watches, allowing them to position their ships on the high seas. Time-balls were in operation in many harbors until 1900.

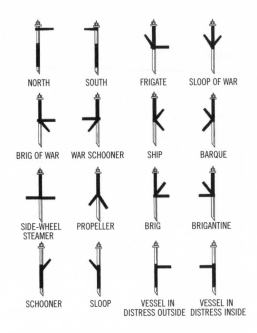

Morse Code

While articulated beams and switching shutters were chatting away to each other, many inventors had not given up hope of harnessing electricity to carry information. The essential breakthrough was the invention of the electromagnet by William Sturgeon in 1825. Sturgeon had shown that he could use electricity to strike a bell a mile away. Five years later the magnet was refined by Joseph Henry into a more powerful version that could work over greater distances.

But progress is seldom simple at the start. The first real electric telegraph was devised by the physicist Charles Wheatstone, who filed a joint patent with William Fothergill Cook in 1837. This was an apparatus with five magnetic needles pointing to a matrix of 20 letters. Despite the fact that six letters of the alphabet could not be sent and the system required six wires to run it, it was the first electric telegraph to be used successfully. The first experiment was conducted on July 25 of that year over a distance of one and a half miles in London, between Euston terminus and Camden Town station. It surprised the British Parliament, which at the start of the nineteenth century had banned "useless" debates on "electric toys."

Samuel Morse was a portrait painter whose hobby was electric machines. His interest in communication was triggered during a trip to France when he saw the Chappe telegraph in operation. Back home, he toyed with batteries, wires, and electromagnets until he came up with an idea that was distinctly different from all previous attempts: he sent simple bursts of electricity over a wire and used an electromagnet at the far end to write on or punch dots on a paper tape. This method was simpler than Weatstone's and left a material trace of the transmission. No trained personnel were needed at the receiving end for interpretation or recording of the message. Groups of dots represented numbers, and those numbers yielded letters in a code similar to that of Polybius.

Only later did Morse and his assistant Alfred Vail invent the combination of dots and dashes that constitute Morse code as we know it today. The debate is still open as to which of the two men actually added the essential dashes that turned the clumsy dots-only system into the practical dot-dash code. According to some historians, it was Vail alone who came up with the decisive concept, but Morse persuaded him that the commercial success of the system depended on its being marketed under a single name.

Morse first tried to raise money in the United States to put his invention into production. When that failed because American investors were not yet on the lookout for new technologies, he turned his hopes to the French and went and presented his project to the Academie des Sciences in Paris. Unfortunately, at that time, the young republic that had sponsored the optical telegraph had collapsed. Following Napoleon, France was ruled by kings who were not concerned with the advancement of the sciences. The academicians congratulated Morse on his unusual and fascinating project but dismissed it. They were happy with the Chappe telegraph, unaware that it was already outdated. Since the beginning of research on the telegraph, the French had feared that electric wires might be cut too easily; they were not sufficiently conscious of the threat posed by the fact that anyone could see their optical signals.

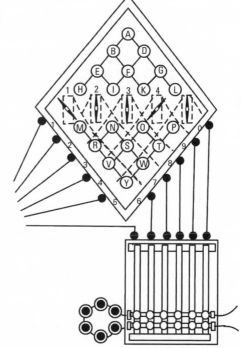

Back in the United States, Morse made another try and finally found government funding for a full-scale experiment between Baltimore and Washington. On March 3, 1843, Congress passed a bill to spend $30,000 for the line. Morse set it up with insulated wires on chestnut poles. On May 24, Baltimore was linked to Washington and Morse successfully sent a message.

Decode:

Samuel Morse's first message (Numbers 23:23).

Morse rapidly went on to create an industry, the Magnetic Telegraph Company. Ten years later he was making plans for an international link between Newfoundland and Ireland. However, his competitor Western Union proved more successful in the long run and is now recognized as the telegraph company.

From Morse Dot to Dot-Com

> *Effective January 27, 2006, Western Union will discontinue all Telegram and Commercial Messaging services.*

This message marked the definitive end of the 155-year era of Morse code. When Western Union sent it, the Morse-based telegraph was so obsolete that the message was not coded in Morse, and the millions of people who read it received it over the Internet, the very technology that supplanted it.

Until the middle of the twentieth century, when computer codes became more efficient, the Morse code was essential. Computer coding brought faster transmission, and computer-managed time superseded Morse's slow, hand-managed time. With the disappearance of Morse code, humanity lost its last direct hold on its information network. Thereafter, only machines would be fast enough to manage and conduct the communication process. With satellite communication we have gone, within two centuries, from wooden beams to laser beams.

Accordingly, during the era of Morse code, all traditional forms of cipher survived and even blossomed (see Chapter 8). Such is the speed of history, however, that nowadays the Morse code and all refinements of traditional cipher coding have become the toys of Girl Scouts and Boy Scouts. However, they are fascinating in and of themselves and are central to an understanding of the history of secret societies, hidden diplomacy, and open warfare.

CHAPTER 2

Pythagoras's Codes

Pythagoras assembled an aesthetic codebook that is still used. His secret brotherhood served as a precursor to most of the later sects and secret societies that dominate popular culture and the collective imagination today.

The First Coder

Pythagoras, who lived in the sixth century B.C.E., was the first conscious "coder"—the first person to envision and to put to practice codes as the logical structure of art, music, science, and even religion.

Because of Pythagoras's extraordinary personality and achievements, the term *code* now takes on a wider meaning than it has so far in this book. From now on we deal with codes in all their diverse meanings. That is, we will look at code as more than a communication tool. By following the Pythagorean thread, you will see how code moves from the aesthetic to the logical in mathematics, science, and mythology.

Pythagoras had such a powerful vision of code that he succeeded in using it to reconcile science and religion. His achievement did not resolve the conflict between science and religion that is still going on—as in the current debate over evolution versus creation—but it gave science an acceptable base.

From Cookbook to Codebook

Pythagoras is the father of a coding tradition that has successfully survived for 25 centuries. His codebook is still the yardstick and "pocket calculator" for many builders, artists, and critics. For those who believe in it, his "golden mean"—a ratio comparing a whole to its parts: $B/A = A/(A + B)$—is indeed the golden tool. Believers would never draw a door, window, or altar that is not a golden rectangle. They would never paint a canvas that does not include the layout of the buildings and characters as a golden ratio. The sacred ratio is the magic wand that turns any creation into gold.

As critics, these adherents' first reaction when looking at a work of art is to search for the numbers and geometric codes. Of course, there are creators and critics who abhor the golden mean and do everything they can to ensure that their work is a statement against it, but working against the golden mean is another way of using it as a reference.

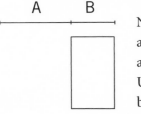

Pythagoras was not the first to deal with numbers and geometry. Numbers and geometry had been common knowledge for millennia and were used throughout the ancient world by builders, merchants, and travelers. The pentagram, for instance, dates back to at least the Uruk IV period in ancient Mesopotamia, around 3500 B.C.E. It is believed that the pentagram was a "heavenly body" that roughly

represented a star. Later, during the cuneiform period (see the illustration to the left), around 3000 B.C.E, the pentragram also might have meant "region" or "direction." The pentagram was used in Babylon (see the illustration to the right), around 900 B.C.E., and the Babylonians might have been the first to realize that it could be inscribed in a circle.

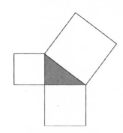

Pythagoras crystallized that knowledge into hard science. He turned whole numbers, rational numbers, squares, and pentagons into pure mathematical entities that obeyed logic instead of following practical usage. Recipes became theorems. Pythagoras began writing a modern codebook from earlier cookbooks.

Pythagoras's theorem of the right-angle triangle, for example, presents triangles in a different light. Pyramid-building Egyptians several millennia before him might have had a theoretical knowledge of geometry and mathematics, but it was lost by Pythagoras's time. Contemporary Egyptian geometers used a rule-of-thumb technique to create a right angle on the spot whenever one was needed. Every year, when the Nile finished flooding the valley and returned to its bed, boundaries between fields were erased. As the peasants worked to reconstruct the limits of their properties, they established right angles, whenever necessary, by using a rope and two sticks. They would knot the rope to mark off equal segments, plant the sticks with a space of exactly five knots between them, and bring the ends of the cord together to meet at the junction of three and then four knots. The angle between the two smaller segments was a right angle.

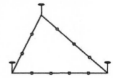

The Jeweler's Son

Pythagoras's life is a mystery. In spite of his immense fame, he left almost no writings from which to learn of his life. We do have the works of authors who wrote about him, but how does one distinguish between fact and legend? More often than not, it's impossible to do so.

Some scholars take the extreme position that Pythagoras is a myth and never really existed. They argue that although he is supposed to have lived in the sixth century B.C.E., the first detailed biographies of him were written five centuries later, in the first century C.E. Worse, the closer those texts are to his supposed lifetime, the fewer the details concerning him they have, whereas the farther they are from it, the more details they contain. This would cast serious doubt on his existence in the absence of the writings of contemporary rivals such as Heraclitus. They did not leave us biographical facts, but they did write extensively against Pythagoras. Surely that much energy spent contradicting him indicates that he existed.

According to current research, Pythagoras was born around 582 B.C.E., roughly 40 years after the Buddha's birth in 624 B.C.E (some scholars place his birth at least 100 years later). From the point of view of codes and their history, the historical facts of Pythagoras's life have little importance. Myth or reality, the character of Pythagoras plays such a central role in our culture that for all practical purposes we may take him as real. The continued transmission of his character and works through several millennia makes him a reference worth exploring.

The best we can do is give credit for his production to the "Pythagoreans." Pythagoras did not wish to be distinguished from the community of followers he created. According to that brotherhood, the outcome of any person's work belonged to the community. The members believed in, practiced, and developed a Pythagorean way of life in which they all were equal and shared everything.

Pythagoras's father was a jeweler, and that probably stimulated Pythagoras's interest in geometry and mathematics. As a teenager working in his father's shop, he was in direct contact with precious stones. The magic of their purity and their crystals must have impressed his young imagination. Jewelers deal with crystals that are made of smaller elementary crystals arranged in geometric arrays. They know that crystals have cleavages, or weak angles in their structure, that separate easily if struck in the right place, leaving perfectly smooth planar faces. By repeating this process over and over, jewelers transform raw minerals into precious stones. Thus, a jeweler reveals the perfection hidden within the stone.

Seeing and handling those shapes, Pythagoras envisioned a universe in which everything was composed of perfect simple elements and could be explained in terms of perfect structures. He thus grew up with a spontaneous yet intimate knowledge of perfect geometry.

Cutting and assembling gems into jewels is not a common, everyday experience. The world around us is not usually perfectly shaped. Compared with the everyday unorganized world, crystals seem to be somehow mystical—magic doors into a hidden order of the universe. They suggest that there are basic laws governing the architecture of the world that people can discover if they make an intelligent effort.

Pythagoras's father also gave him a taste for travel. They frequently left their home island of Samos to sell jewels in other Greek cities. Pythagoras's biographers have him traveling continuously as a young man. Some writers record him visiting all the religious and cultural centers of that time: Chaldea, Persia, India, Egypt, Arabia, Thrace, Phoenicia, and Judea. In those places, they say, he met the greatest priests and stayed long enough to acquire their knowledge. However, all those trips, added together, would fill several lifetimes, and so we have to take those claims as symbolic of the way Pythagoras inherited all the wisdom and religious knowledge of his time and integrated that knowledge into his own system.

Among his early travels, a visit to Egypt is certain. He saw and studied the pyramids, some of which were two millennia older than he was. They affirmed for him that humanity could undertake grand projects that rivaled the beauty of the natural world and that geometry could support impressive works of art. The pyramids of Giza, especially the pyramid of Cheops, are expressions of pure geometry. Pyramids also are perfect examples of artifacts that need no written or spoken commentary: they "radiate" meaning. A pyramid need only stand there; no discourse or theory is necessary to reveal its importance. A pyramid is obviously coded and invites decoding by its presence alone.

Pythagoras spent some time in his father's birthplace, Tyre, where he studied the teachings of the famous scholar Pherekydes. He also attended the school of Anaximedes, a researcher famous for his ideas on astronomy.

All this took place several centuries before Socrates' and Plato's practice of teaching through dialogue and irony. In Pythagoras's time, a disciple never challenged the master or engaged in dialogue with him, humbly receiving the teachings without questioning them. When he became a master, Pythagoras adopted that tradition. His brotherhood demanded total respect for the master and

his knowledge. "The master said" was a fundamental rule of the brotherhood (the picture on page 37 shows a master and a pupil in the Porta Maggiore Pythagorean underground basilica in Rome, which is discussed later in this chapter).

It may seem strange to see such respect for authority and tradition in a school renowned for its daring thoughts and quest for new knowledge. How can one respect the teachings of the masters yet come up with new and creative inventions? There is no real contradiction. Pythagoras was not looking for a newfangled freedom of thought; he was seeking new master principles. He was in search of the master laws governing the world so that he could explain its creation. He was discarding older laws and principles, but only to find better and more powerful ones. His view of the world was based on the absolute authority of numbers and geometry. Authority was his guideline in life as well as in science.

History—or legend—places Pythagoras in the forty-eighth Olympic Games, winning prizes as a pugilist. Pugilism is an ancient form of boxing. Becoming a champion would have required spending a considerable amount of time training, along with a high degree of pugnacity and a taste for violence. This hardly seems to fit a young "philosopher" unless his biographers wished to stress the aspect of authority in his character. They might have wanted to emphasize that Pythagoras was an active philosopher with enough energy to create a school and impose his ideas.

The Brotherhood

Pythagoras founded a brotherhood on Croton. According to legend, he used an innovative technique to advertise himself. Unknown as a teacher, he chose a disciple and paid him to listen to his teachings. The scheme was successful: the disciple was so fascinated by what he learned that he soon begged Pythagoras to let him pay to hear more. As the story spread, other disciples came.

The school rapidly became crowded with would-be disciples. Pythagoras was obliged to impose strict rules for joining and living within the brotherhood, based on successive steps.

The first step was a test on physiognomy, the science of guessing someone's character by looking at that person's face, body, and posture. If successful, the disciple was tested for a period of three years on his or her social behavior and moral fortitude. If the disciple passed that test, he or she became a novice for five years, during which time he or she learned to listen. Called an auditor, or "hearer," when on the brotherhood's premises, a novice was allowed only to listen and had to observe complete silence. A novice was not permitted to see the initiates and certainly not the master, who spoke to novices from behind a curtain.

After this initiation, a brother became an "esoteric." Esoterics could meet with the master, ask questions, and express their own thoughts. Yet their education was never complete, and they continued learning geometry, music, astronomy, medicine, and other sciences according to their tastes and abilities.

Parallel to the esoterics who followed the strict rule of the brotherhood within its premises, Pythagoras accepted "exoterics," who followed the same ideals but lived a normal life in the city with their families and businesses. Some exoterics were influential people who made the brotherhood famous. Both men and women could be esoterics or exoterics. An exoteric might even be a married woman whose husband was not a member of the brotherhood.

Neither esoterics nor exoterics were cloistered within the community like later Christian monks. Even the esoterics could go out at night to private houses. Nor was there a fundamental difference between them, and they all exchanged ideas freely. Esoterics were not considered better Pythagoreans; they simply had chosen a different way of life.

What made the brotherhood so distinctive was a deep sense of comradeship among its members. Pythagoreans looked at that friendship as mathematical harmony applied to social life, a mutual love that united all the members. The logic that bound all true theorems in mathematics was equivalent to the friendship that united all the members of the brotherhood. As a result of the equivalence between the two codes, the rules of the community, however strict, were easy to follow because a general feeling of closeness pervaded all activities, human and scientific. Freemasons frequently refer to this idea of comradeship as the cement of their brotherhood.

Esoterics followed an austere daily agenda in the brotherhood. They rose with the sun and meditated on the previous day and the present day. Then they put on clothes of white linen and went out to walk in quiet places far from the noise and turmoil of the city. Then there were sessions of education in which they were taught in groups, followed by gymnastics, bodily exercises, and massage. After those activities they ate a quick, simple lunch.

The afternoon began with debates on the politics of the brotherhood and the city. That was followed by informal discussions and walks in small groups and then a common bath in the community pool. Bathing was seen as purification of the soul and body and as a liquid representation of the community's bonds. After ritual libations on religious altars, dinner was taken at small tables that never were occupied by more than 10, the sacred number of the *tetraktys* (see page 44).

For moral and philosophical rather than medical reasons, the food was vegetarian. In their desire to live as simple a life as possible, the Pythagoreans refrained from any use of fire for cooking and ate only raw vegetables, honey, and milk.

One reason for their vegetarianism was their belief in life after death and the transmigration of souls. According to that belief, after death the soul is freed from the body and remains free or moves on to live in another body, possibly that of an animal. This explains the avoidance of bloodshed, whether involving animals or people. The sole exception was that the Pythagoreans sacrificed and ate suckling pigs and goats, possibly because those animals were too young to host a soul.

Pythagoras imported that Egyptian belief into Greece, and it was this action that his enemies criticized most. A common joke was that Pythagoras recognized the voices of his dead friends in the barking of dogs. Pythagoras, however, said: "As long as mankind massacres animals, men will likewise continue to massacre each other."

As a result of that lifestyle, the brotherhood was a perfect combination of church, school, open monastery, and research center. It was so remarkable that it became a template for later brotherhoods and secret societies such as the Essenes at the time of Christ, Christian monks (including the Knights Templar), and the Freemasons. Although none of those societies retained every aspect of the original Pythagorean brotherhood, they all were informed by the essential principles of harmony and mutual love.

Humans by Numbers

Pythagoreans were so fascinated by numbers and geometric figures that they identified themselves and their fellow humans with them. They were so attracted by the beauty of mathematics that they felt that a certain form of mathematical structure should apply to humans, raising them to the perfection of mathematical objects. Then a logical friendship would bind the brotherhood.

Looked at from that angle, Pythagorean science and brotherhood fit together quite well. The rules of the brotherhood facilitated the integration of a logic similar to that of mathematics into the members' lives, with the ultimate goal of sharing in and actually experiencing the harmony of the mathematical universe. The years of silence required of novices helped them go beyond the loose language and posturing of ordinary human existence as they progressively adopted a more logical style of life. The uniform of white linen erased undesirable marks of difference between brothers.

The final aim was to generate a symbiosis between humans and mathematics. If they were sufficiently close and similar, humans would have a perfect understanding of mathematics and thus of the mathematically coded universe.

Before Pythagoras, the Greeks had had gods, but they were a violent gang of heavenly beings who were modeled on humans and displayed all their random and violent passions. Pythagoras presented a different heavenly world of pure entities pursuing ideal goals in which logic replaced passion, in contrast to the romantic characters traditionally found on Mount Olympus.

This pursuit of an ideal structuring of human behavior has survived both within and beyond the boundaries of Christianity. Convents and monasteries still practice a secluded and structured way of life. Though their faith does not refer to mathematics as an ultimate goal, they feel that observing strict, logical rules is a powerful way to reach mystical goals. Beyond Christianity, as we'll see in the following chapters, Masonic and craft brotherhoods that make more obvious reference to Pythagorean symbols believe in structuring their lives to reach higher levels of understanding and integration with the universe.

Moreover, the leading of a life coded by a set of rules generates its own dynamics. Coding the mundane daily details of life frees the mind from the petty choices of the normal human day. There are no questions concerning food or clothing; everything is determined by the brotherhood or order. The group's structure thus reinforces its own energy, and the adept's mind, freed from the bother of choosing, is able to invest itself in study and mystical contemplation. Coding oneself on a lower level liberates energy to those above it and gives easier access to understanding the high-level codes of science and philosophy.

A Number World

Pythagoreans worked at revealing the specific personalities of numbers. According to the Pythagoreans, numbers are not, as they seem to be, a series of dots along an infinite line. In spite of their uniform creation—1 plus 1, plus 1, and so forth—each number is a different object with different properties. Adding 1 to a number doesn't just create another, similar number. Rather, it presents a new number that has hardly any relation to the number before it and may possess totally opposing qualities. The Pythagoreans considered this set of "numerical personalities" to be the ultimate code of the universe, the code the gods had used to create the world, piling number bricks on number bricks.

Let's take a look at the first 10 numbers from both the arithmetic and the symbolic point of view. As we do so, keep in mind that Pythagoras did not have access to the decimal system. He represented numbers either symbolically with letters or practically with sets of tokens. Token sets are much less handy than the modern decimal system, but they have one advantage: the display of tokens suggests a natural bridge to geometric figures.

This brief exploration covers only what will be useful later in this book. It does not do justice to the vast body of knowledge and symbolism concerning numbers. We should note also that Pythagoras did not know the number 0 (zero) or the negative numbers, which appeared a millennium later in India.

ONE (1)

The fundamental number is 1, the essential cement, the tool used to create other numbers. By adding 1 indefinitely to itself, we can generate the infinite series of integers.

Symbolism: The number 1 is the principle of identity, equality, unity, and sympathy.

TWO (2)

Pythagoreans and Chinese philosophers agree that 2 is the feminine principle in that it can separate to give birth to new numbers; as an even number, it can be halved to make two numbers. Pythagoras could not foresee the importance and potential of 2 in the development of logic, binary arithmetic, and electronic computing, but 2 and its powers have come to dominate our culture. In line with the thesis of *The Da Vinci Code*, we might say that the modern development of computing, led by 2, is the true revenge of the feminine principle.

Symbolism: The number 2 embodies the ideas of duality, of true and false, friendship and enmity, and the difference between oneself and the universe.

THREE (3)

The first "triangular" number, 3, is linked to triangles, the backbone of geometrical logic.

Symbolism: The number 3 is the first masculine number beyond fundamental unity. The three points and the triangle figure are central in the symbolism of the Freemasons.

FOUR (4)

The number 4 is even and the first real square (1 is only its own square).

Symbolism: The number 4 is feminine and represents the four directions, a key to understanding our environment.

FIVE (5)

The number 5 is prime and the sum of two other prime numbers (2 + 3).

Symbolism: The number 5 represents the wedding of the feminine 2 and the masculine 3; hence, it is the number of love. It is also the number of vertices in a pentagram, which makes it all the more sacred. Finally, 5 distinguishes the human being, with five fingers and five toes, from most other animals.

SIX (6)

The number 6 is the first "perfect number," equal to the sum of its divisors:
$6 = 1 + 2 + 3 = 1 \times 2 \times 3$

Symbolism: The number 6 represents harmony and the perfection of the whole.

SEVEN (7)

The number 7 is prime and the sum of a triangle and a square.

Symbolism: You can't divide a circle into seven equal segments with a rule and compass; for Pythagoreans, that is a sure sign that it represents virginity.

EIGHT (8)

The first cube is 8, equal to 2 multiplied by itself three times.

Symbolism: The number 8 represents a high degree of femininity because it can be halved three successive times to yield 4, 2, and 1.

NINE (9)

The number 9 is the square of 3 and contains three triangles.

Symbolism: Representing all the sciences is the number 9, which also evokes the arts of the nine Muses of Greek mythology.

TEN (10)

The sum of the first four numbers is 10.

Symbolism: The number 10 is the all-important tetraktys, the "quartet" cumulating the symbolic powers of 1, 2, 3, and 4. The Pythagoreans considered it too sacred to be spoken of, viewing it as worthy of profound meditation over a lifetime. The Pythagoreans had no decimal system giving 10 the importance it has today. Yet it was still one of their most important numbers arithmetically and symbolically. Such was their respect for 10 that only the gods were allowed to use it. Pythagoreans would never seat more than 10 people around a dinner table.

The Families

Arranging numbers in families provides a link with geometric figures and generates series of regular polygons. With this graphic presentation, elementary arithmetic properties become visually obvious.

Triangular numbers are generated by adding successive integers. In turn, they become bricks that can generate all the numbers. Karl Gauss proved that any integer is the sum of at most three triangulare numbers.

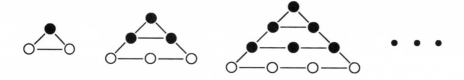

The number of the beast, 666, is a triangle number.

Square numbers are generated by odd numbers. The geometrical representation below clearly shows that successive squares differ by an odd number.

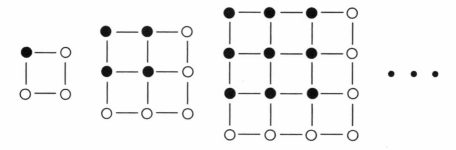

Pentagon numbers progress uniformly by 4.

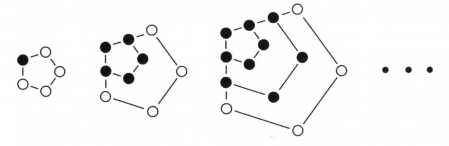

Hexagon numbers progress uniformly by 5.

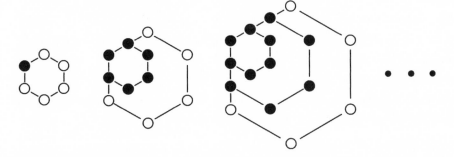

Spatial Perfection

The Pythagoreans extended their exploration of geometric objects to the so-called Platonic solids: the five convex polyhedrons with equal vertices and equal angles. Pythagoras's interest in their perfection was in keeping with his childhood interest in his father's crystals and jewels. These solids were known by neolithic civilizations well before the sixth century B.C.E.: the Ashmolean Museum exhibits early examples of them cut in stone, but Pythagoras apparently was the first to prove that there were five and only five. Working on those perfect gems of geometry made Pythagoras a virtual jeweler, in continuity with his father's trade.

We'll see that the five solids later interested Leonardo da Vinci for the challenge they provided in perspective drawing and Salvador Dali for their symbolism of perfection in a world beyond.

An Irrational Codebook

The originality and success of the Pythagoreans stemmed from their simultaneous study of numbers and geometry. If they had remained in the peaceful realm of numbers alone, they might have been content simply to explore the qualities of whole numbers, or integers, and the pure ratios of integers divided by other integers. That would have brought them a lifetime of easy pleasure analyzing arithmetic and numerical symbolism. However, they chose to deal also with geometric figures and their measurements, and that unexpectedly confronted them with shocking situations that challenged their logic. Their genius is shown by the fact that they accepted the challenge instead of refusing to acknowledge a failure.

The Pythagoreans encountered an unsolvable problem as soon as they began to study the square and tried to express the length of its diagonal in terms of its sides. Up to that point, they had followed the principle that integers and rational numbers (integers divided by integers) are the only numbers that will ever exist or be necessary for mathematics.

Unfortunately, the diagonal of the square, which we now know is the square root of 2, is not a rational number. Pythagoras was able to prove that the division of two integers would never yield the exact length of that diagonal.

The blow was severe, and the Pythagoreans feared that their entire philosophy had collapsed. Legend has it that a brother made this discovery while sailing at sea and that his fellow brothers threw him overboard. To save the brotherhood and its reputation, the discovery had to remain secret, and so disciples were absolutely forbidden to let it be known outside the fold.

Later, the Pythagoreans realized that they had made a fundamental discovery. When Pythagoras had asserted his central principle that "all is number," the numbers he was referring to were the integers and their ratios. Music supported that limited view, because integer ratios are enough to explain musical harmony. However, that limited world was too small for the newfound numbers. The Pythagoreans had met with new characters in the mathematical saga, and even though they did not obey the traditional laws, the new numbers would have to be included as a new family in the set of mathematical entities. New laws would have to be established to allow them into the mathematical universe and reestablish harmony.

Of course, pi is not rational either, but neither Pythagoras nor the Egyptians knew that. Their mathematics did not possess the tools to prove it. They used pi extensively with approximate values, imagining that it was a ratio they eventually would be able to calculate.

Practically speaking, the new "irrational" numbers gave spice to Pythagoras's aesthetic codebook. They forced his geometry to display quantities that went beyond simple, direct proportion. It may be that this is where the human eye perceives beauty: in proportions it cannot readily apprehend.

The Golden Mean

The Pythagoreans' star irrational ratio is the golden mean. It is less mathematical and more philosophical and aesthetic than pi or square roots. Its definition links Pythagoras to Eastern philosophies that claim that the whole is in the part. It states that the division of a segment into two parts is "golden" when the ratio of the larger part to the smaller part equals the ratio of the whole to the larger part.

$$\frac{Phi}{1} \qquad \frac{}{Phi \qquad 1}$$

Ratios of this sort stem from the aesthetic problem that confronts architects in choosing the proportions of a building. Is it possible to please the eye while making a choice that is philosophically sound? Ideally, if proportions are mathematically sound, they embody mathematical beauty and the intelligent eye is able to detect this intuitively. For example, the human eye may find it agreeable to see a whole that relates to its greater part in the same way the greater part relates to the smaller part. It is possible that the simultaneous display of both ratios makes manifest a harmony that is satisfying to people's need for symmetry.

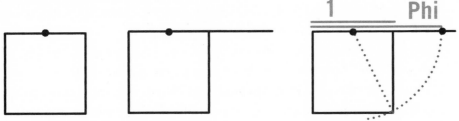

The most practical method for constructing a golden mean utilizes a square and a compass (see bottom of page 47).

Start with a square and mark the middle of a side. Extend this side roughly the same length. Draw a circle that is centered on the middle of the side and passes through an opposing angle. The circle will intersect the side at the golden mean. The new point is 1.616 from the first angle on the top left.

However, there is no need to construct the golden mean. It can be found in the convex pentagon and the crossed pentagram, as shown in the pictures below.

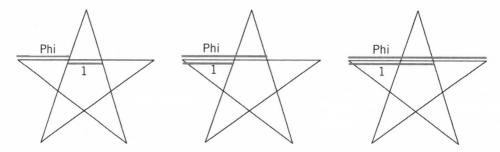

These were central symbols for the Pythagorean brotherhoods. The pentagram was called "health"; it represented the harmony of the human body. It was also the secret key with which disciples from different cities could identify themselves. Showing a pentagram would open the doors to the local brotherhood.

One may wonder how a simple geometric figure has such fascination for the human mind. It has played an essential symbolic role in most secret societies and cults since Pythagoras: the Knights Templar, the Freemasons, the Rosicrucians, and innumerable witchcraft cults, among others.

The pentagram is simply the culmination of all the riches of its different origins. As a representation of the stars, it evokes the celestial bodies from which it draws its energy, mystery, and unreachability. As a symbol of the wholeness of the human body and its fivefold nature (five fingers and five toes, a rarity in the animal world), it draws energy from life and the living. As a geometric figure with extraordinary properties, it draws energy from science as a realization of the mysterious power of logic. In short, the pentagram is perceived as a link to the stars that is filled with human life and intelligence.

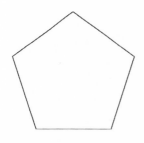

The pentagram has an interesting competitor: the heptagram. Next in the series of crossed polygons with an odd number of vertices, the heptagram can be drawn with a single line as a continuous chain of seven segments (see the illustration to the left). Like the pentagram, it evokes the stars and relates to the seven planets that were known in the Middle Ages. It was used at that time by esotericists who needed a more complex symbol than the pentagram. Heptagrams abound in the coded Voynich manuscript (see Chapter 10) as bullet markers for the paragraphs of that cryptic text.

The heptagram lacks the all-important living and logical references of the pentagram. No living creature displays seven fingers or seven toes. The pentagram thus remained the essential symbolic bridge between the stars, the human body, and the mind. It was a virtual rocket that reached the celestial universe millennia before humankind achieved a material link. Symbolically, humanity needed to experience space travel in the imagination before it was ready to face its realities.

If you are more comfortable conceptualizing algebraic symbols than geometric figures, you may prefer to see the golden mean as a purely algebraic object independently of its connection with pentagrams. The golden mean is the ratio that is used to divide a segment into two parts in such a way that the ratio of the whole to the larger part equals the ratio of the larger part to the smaller part.

In algebra, if the whole is divided into 1 and x, the golden mean is written as follows:

$1/x = x/(1 - x)$

or:

$x2 = 1 - x$

Phi is the solution of the equation $x2 + x - 1 = 0$, and this gives phi the value of

$$\frac{-1 + \sqrt{5}}{2}$$

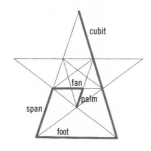

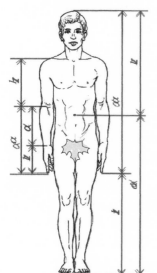

Thus, phi is equal to 0.6180339 plus an endless and unpredictable series of decimals.

The golden mean also may be observed as a series of ratios in the extended pentagon, where the vertices of the original pentagram are joined to form a five-sided figure, the sides of which are also extended to form a pentagram, and so on, as in the illustration to the left. If we mark the same segments, but in a continuous series, we get five golden means.

Traditional masons found this same series in their own bodies, as shown in the illustration to the left. Palm width, finger span (from thumb to little finger, see illustration below), span, foot, cubit: these were their basic measuring tools, their metric aesthetic codebook. Some of these measurements, however approximate and different from one individual to another, have survived until today. Many wise craftspersons know exactly the length of their span in inches or centimeters and use it as a portable measuring tool for all occasions. When one is designing anything—a piece of furniture, a garden bed, or a temple roof— the set of five body lengths comes in handy to ensure the project's aesthetic value.

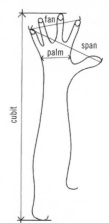

Pythagoreans theorized that the human body is made up entirely of various combinations of the golden mean. The golden section indeed can be found in several other parts of the body with greater or lesser exactness, and these ratios may serve as a reference for drawing or sculpting a body. However, their real measurements are so inexact that they cannot be used to prove or disprove the basic value of the golden mean ratio.

The 108° Signature

A discreet yet obvious signature of a building's Pythagorean mason or architect is provided by the use of 108° angles. This angle is the geometric DNA of the sacred pentagon: the angle of its five vertices. It often is seen in the angle of the roof of a temple or

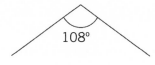

private house, and from that angle alone the trained eye immediately imagines the remainder of the pentagon and becomes aware of the symbolism placed there by its creator.

A similar Pythagorean signature is 36°, the smaller angle of the pentagram. This angle is too sharp to be displayed easily in normal architecture, and only certain cathedral steeples show it.

The 108° angle is an essential part of the Pythagorean heritage that was integrated into their symbolism by the Freemasons. We'll see that it plays a central role in many Masonic projects, notably the design of Washington, D.C. Architects of the Pythagorean or Masonic persuasion still use it as a hidden yet provocative signature.

Music

Musical harmony is another codebook that complements Pythagoras's harmonic world. Here the human ear and eye can directly perceive and observe the aesthetic quality of purely rational ratios. Precise lengths of strings or pipes produce harmonious combinations of sound. Experimentation with these lengths of strings and pipes is so easy and pleasant that it may have been the starting point of reflection on ratios and aesthetics.

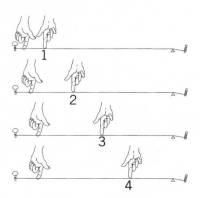

How Gilded Is the Golden Mean?

Pictures and shapes do not react spontaneously to ratios the way strings and pipes do. Cut to the right lengths, two strings will resonate when either one is played and vibrate in harmony. However, nothing like that happens when a door and a window are cut in the correct ratios. No physical phenomenon supports the aesthetic emotion sensed by the observer's faculty of sight.

A fundamental question thus arises: is the golden mean inherently pleasant to the human eye, or has appreciation of it been forced on us by artists, critics, and our culture in general?

Many psychologists have addressed this question, and subjects of every type have been tested in psychological laboratories. Alas! When subjects are shown rectangles of all dimensions, carefully divested of all context, their reactions have always been the same. The golden rectangle has no special significance, and this contradicts the usual assumption. We do not select it spontaneously as manifesting more aesthetic beauty than any other shape. Thus, we have to face the truth: the golden mean is not particularly gilt.

However, whether it is viscerally beautiful or not, the fact remains that the very concept of the golden mean appeals to our intellectual sense of beauty, if only from a logical and mathematical point of view.

Perfection's Tragic Fate

In spite of their wisdom, the reign of the Pythagorean brotherhood ended tragically. When Pythagoras died around 500 B.C.E., the Pythagoreans ruled most of Sicily and southern Italy. Their political power lasted for another half century, but, for all their science and philosophy, they became increasingly estranged from the people and ended up facing rebellion. They lost one city after another. Finally, Metapontum, where most of the brothers had taken refuge, was besieged, and the majority of the remaining brothers died in a fire.

Among the very few initiates who survived Metapontum, Philolaos is said to have fled with the sacred books of the brotherhood, only to sell them to the local tyrant, Denys of Syracuse. That act of treason was beneficial because those books seem to have fallen eventually into the hands of Plato, who included Pythagorean philosophy in his teachings.

Later, in the second century C.E., Pythagoreanism flourished for a while in Alexandria and then in Rome.

The Star Gods

A word is needed here to describe the Pythagorean religion and how it differed from the general beliefs of the Romans when Pythogoreanism flourished briefly in Rome. Before Pythagoras, astronomers had noted that the vast majority of celestial bodies—the stars—followed precise and constant paths in the sky. They also had noticed that certain bodies, called by them planets—meaning "vagrants" in Greek—followed erratic, apparently random paths. Unable to explain the behavior of the planets yet persuaded that everything in the sky had a purpose, they believed that the planets were cast like dice to determine the destiny of the world and the fate of human beings. That led to the "science" of astrology, which posited that the positions of the planets at the time of a person's birth reveal what is to be expected in that person's life. In other words, the planets were a coding of human destiny.

Pythagoras reversed that proposition, stating that the planets cannot code people's lives because they themselves are coded. Using geometry, he speculated that the paths of the planets were not erratic, but, on the contrary, follow paths as precise as those of the stars except that they are more complex. The planets move in circles the way the stars do, but their circles turn on other circles. With this, Pythagoras became the first coder of the stars rather than someone who was coded by them.

He was on the right path, of course, but was slightly wrong. Unfortunately, he had too much respect for the stars and celestial bodies to imagine that they could move along anything but perfect circles, and this invalidated his geometrical astronomy. It took 2,000 years for Kepler to be able to go beyond that preconceived idea and propose ellipses rather than circles, thus coming closer to the truth.

Because the planets are coded and do not code us, we cannot hope to find knowledge about ourselves in the study of their behavior except perhaps to observe that the universe is perfect and that all celestial bodies, including planets, obey logical laws.

From a religious point of view, this implied that the stars and planets, moving by themselves and according to perfect laws, possessed a perfect intelligence and were thus the true gods. Pythagoras rejected the humanlike traditional gods who were invented by Homer and other poets and were said to live on Mount Olympus. He placed paradise, which until then had been the underworld Elysian Fields, in the sky, and, more particularly in the Milky Way. Unless they were not sufficiently pure to deserve it and fell back to earth to be born anew in another body and progress toward purity, the souls of the dead rose up to the sky and remained there as stars.

The door to Paradise was the moon, mistress of the closest celestial sphere. This led to the further spheres of the sun, the planets, and the stars. The stars and the planets were on different spheres and could not interact with one another as the astrologists supposed. Pythagorean poets elaborated on these principles, opposing our "sublunar" world, the earth, enclosed within the sphere of the moon, to the celestial world of the sky above and beyond it. The soul is imprisoned in the image of a body, immersed in sublunar disorder, and aspires to free itself and reach the eternal order of the celestial realms.

The Pythagoreans marked an essential difference between the two worlds. On the sublunar earth the spontaneous path of a body is a straight line, whereas beyond the moon it is a circle. We tend to move along straight lines, whereas stars move effortlessly along circles, on spheres. This principle contributes to the confrontation of circle with square (made of straight lines) exhibited all along the Pythagorean geometrical heritage. The Vitruvian man (see Chapter 4) fights for his freedom between straight earth and spherical heaven.

More importantly, from a scientific point of view, this cult of the stars founded a geometrical and dynamic astronomy as a bridge to religion. Science and religion did not have to be opposed. The more we applied our intelligence to the study of the stars, the more we honored the gods. The more we honored the gods, the more we sought to study the sciences of astronomy and mathematics.

The Porta Maggiore Missing Link

In the April–June 1920 issue of the *American Journal of Archaeology*, the archaeologist C. Densmore Curtis announced: "one of the most important discoveries of the modern era: the so-called underground basilica just outside the Porta Maggiore in Rome. In April 1917, a large room was found 50 feet beneath the Naples railroad line, with a nave and side aisles of exactly the form of an early Christian basilica. It dates from the first century C.E. and was evidently a pagan place of worship".

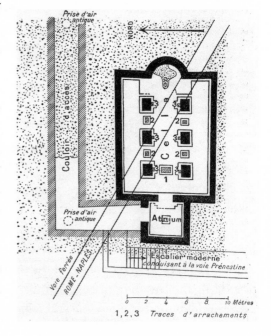

Indeed, the construction of the railway line from Rome to Naples led directly to the discovery of an underground temple near the gate called the Porta Maggiore. It dates from the first century c.e. and thus is pagan, for Christianity did not come to Rome until several centuries later. However, it is not built on the traditional plan of Greek or Roman temples. On the contrary, it follows the more Christian building code of three parallel sections with a nave and two aisles.

It is obvious that the construction was carried out as secretly as possible by a group intent on remaining unnoticed both during and after the building of the temple. The masons first dug shafts for the walls and the roof and filled them with concrete. Only after the concrete had set did they dig out the earth inside the church beneath the concrete roof; up to that point the earth had played the role of the scaffolding. Finally, they decorated the interior with white stucco.

The Medusa Door to Paradise

The Pythagorean beliefs were not those of the Romans at the start of the Common Era. Replacing Greek names with Roman ones, the Romans honored the gods of Olympus and did not regard the stars as deities. When a comet appeared in the sky at Caesar's death, for instance (see Chapter 1), it was not considered to be showing his soul being transformed into a star but a celestial body coding the meaning of his death: an announcement of his transformation into a deity.

The Pythagorean connection with the basilica is demonstrated at length in the 400 pages of Jérôme Carcopino's *La Basilique Pythagoricienne de la Porte Majeure (The Pythagorean Basilica of the Porta Maggiore)*. This book, first published in 1927, 10 years after the site's discovery, was reprinted 20 years later by another publisher and points out the many relationships between the Pythagorean religious worldview and the basilica's frescoes.

Among many clues, an important one is the presence of Medusa heads—several on the walls and even one over the entrance. The Medusas (Medusa was one of the three Gorgons in Greek mythology) are no longer the scary faces of ancient times that turned mortals into stone and petrified Eurydice when Orpheus looked back at his beloved. They often appear on tombs and have become strange but helpful guardians of the other world who welcome souls onto their new path. They evoke a face that the imagination easily decodes into the details of a full moon, and they guard the mythical door to the celestial paradise. Their former power of fascination is not entirely forgotten: they retain enough of the charm of their former powers to soften the difficult passage from life to death.

Certain poets, under Pythagorean influence, shifted the Elysian Fields from their ancient subterranean location to faraway isles at the very limits of the mythical ocean surrounding the earth. Indeed, those "Fortunate Isles" could easily be imagined at sunset as mythical steps toward the sun or the moon, toward the Milky Way.

The abundance of scenes evoking those myths marks the basilica as a place of initiation designed to lead the faithful to the Pythagorean paradise. This means that the church stands out as a link between the religions of Pythagoras and Christ. This is of great importance for the history of codes: it proves that the Pythagorean code was not mere intellectual knowledge passed on through books by scholars but remained alive and was transmitted as an actual religion. At some time in its history, people believed in it strongly enough to risk their lives by building a secret church to honor it.

Historical analysis of the architectural style, stucco technique, motifs, and even type of concrete used for the walls situates the building in the first 50 years of our Common Era. The sand used for the concrete, for example, is pure, whereas in the years of the Roman Empire that followed, sand was increasingly mixed with fragments of brick and marble.

It is also clear that hasty looters did not vandalize the building. On the contrary, whereas looters would have left broken objects and defaced frescoes, the furniture and tapestry were removed carefully and methodically. It looks as if an administrative decision was made to shut the temple forever by filling it with rubble. Historical analysis suggests that it was closed up and sealed during the reign of Emperor Claudius, shortly after its construction and opening.

Fortunately for us, that manner of closing preserved the temple in exceptionally good condition until its rediscovery in the twentieth century, making the site by far the best Pythagorean remains in the world. Somehow, the rubble of Emperor Claudius played a similar role to that of the ashes of Etna in Pompeii, preserving an exceptional site for future generations.

There is another hypothesis that is compatible with the findings. The shutting down of the temple might have been decided on and enacted by its builders, perhaps for security, in the hope of using it later. They might have removed the furnishings and filled the basilica as secretly as they had built it and then vanished, perhaps retreating to another, safer place. This possibility—that the temple was left intact as a Pythagorean heritage for the future—provides a more plausible explanation for the state of the building and the stucco decoration and might account for the lack of references in classical literature.

Researchers have made an even more challenging discovery. They have determined that not all the rubble filling the basilica came from the first century. Part of it is more recent, probably from the sixteenth or seventeenth century. This brings up another mystery: who dug up and then refilled the basilica at that time? Digging up such a place requires time and effort, and refilling it requires even more time, effort, and determination. True, at that time, wealthy people from Western Europe had started traveling to Italy to rediscover the ruins of the Roman Empire, but an early tourist would have paid local workers to dig the place up and would have examined the art and removed some of it to take back to his "cabinet of curiosities." He would not have bothered to fill it up

again. Here the diggers carefully sealed and resealed the place, successfully hiding it again for several more centuries.

With only these facts at our disposal, let us allow our imaginations to build other hypotheses. The seventeenth century is the period when the Masonic societies began to reappear and reorganize themselves in the Western world. They claimed to be the heirs of the Pythagoreans. Did they possess some old texts that led them to the underground basilica to fulfill the will of its builders? Did Freemasons dig up the site, understand how to read the sacred frescoes, make copies of the art and possibly take some remaining sacred objects, and then seal it up again with great care? That would make the basilica a message from the Pythagoreans to the Masons.

The hypothesis would be stronger if we could find a perfect connection: some elements in Masonic art or ritual objects that reference decorations or artifacts found in the basilica. Then the basilica could be considered a "missing link" on two counts: between the Pythagoreans and the Christians on one hand, and between the Pythagoreans and the Freemasons on the other.

Throughout the last two millennia of Western civilization, two parallel creeds have developed, one secret and one open. Whereas Pythagoreans tend to hide and conceal their knowledge in cults, brotherhoods, guilds, and secret societies, Christians openly evangelize and spread their beliefs. Why the Pythagorean secrecy and the Christian openness? It seems that each creed appeals to different aspects of the human mind that sometimes are opposed and sometimes are complementary. Pythagoreanism relates more to the analytical and logical left brain, and Christianity more to the emotional and intuitive right brain. Christians share their faith spontaneously and enthusiastically, whereas Pythagoreans discourage easy sharing and see a need to conceal themselves while they study and develop new knowledge. Depending on the occasion and situation, each may see the other as a threat or a necessary complement.

A classical cathedral is the perfect example of Pythagoreans and Christians working together. Desired and financed by Christian orders, it is planned and built by Pythagorean guilds according to Pythagorean code and then used by Christians to gather and pray and to attract the faithful.

Today, the basilica rarely is mentioned in guidebooks and visits are difficult to arrange.

Pythagoras's Heritage

The Pythagorean movement was so rich and powerful that it outlived Pythagoras and even the Pythagoreans and is still in existence.

Let's follow the developing thread of the Pythagorean aesthetic codebook through a few of its landmarks.

Vitruvius

Whether his fame rests only on an accident or is based on real accomplishments, Vitruvius is renowned as the author of the only book on architecture to have come down to us from the Roman era. His writings and drawings are our only record of the way architects and engineers thought and worked in the first century B.C.E. It could be that the survival of the book is not entirely due to chance but rather to the continuing interest of generations of readers who took care of and copied them again and again until the Renaissance. In 1414 the manuscript was rediscovered and then circulated among artists in Florence, eventually to be printed in Rome in 1486 and have a decisive influence on Renaissance architects (see Chapter 4).

Vitruvius was very much concerned with beauty as it relates to geometry. Admiring and making use of the works of Pythagoras, he apparently didn't coin the term the golden mean, as legend has it, but more generally emphasized proportions as essential artistic tools. In the writings that have come down to us, we have his descriptions of and specific advice concerning all types of buildings: private, public, and religious. He treated the city as a whole—with buildings, streets, gardens, and inhabitants all interacting with one another—and also wrote on contemporary technology, from clocks and sundials to siege engines.

However, Vitruvius was cautious about the more advanced findings of the Pythagoreans. He was wary of using irrational numbers and even the irrational golden mean itself beyond the square root of 2. Backing away from Pythagoras's audacity, his architecture relies on squares, half-square rectangles, and circles. Unconscious of his importance as a link with the future, he was unaware of the extraordinary preciousness of the cultural content he was transmitting.

Fibonacci's Expanding Code

Pythagoras would have loved Fibonacci and his numbers, for Fibonacci created a new family of numbers that fit perfectly with and extended the Pythagorean universe.

Leonardo of Pisa, usually called Fibonacci, lived from about 1170 or 1180 to 1240 to 1250. A Franciscan monk, he was also a great mathematician. His greatest achievement was the introduction to Europe of a code that now is taken for granted: the system of decimal numbers. Until that time, Europeans were still using the old and unwieldy Roman numeral system. For all activities involving numbers, they had to juggle with the awkward set of letters I, V, X, L, C, D, and M. In retrospect, one wonders how the Romans managed to run an empire with such a cumbersome code in which addition was difficult and multiplication—not to mention division—required specialists. The Romans were efficient in developing our alphabet of practical letters, a legacy nobody questions today, but failed to develop a correspondingly useful number system.

Fibonacci knew Arabic culture, for he had traveled to Algeria, Morocco, and Tunisia with his father, an exporter of the products of the republic of Pisa. The Arabs had developed the modern system consisting of the 10 digits 0, 1, 2, 3, 4, 5 6, 7, 8, and 9, still unchanged today. This resulted from their contact with India, where they had learned the concept of zero, and, more especially, their intense cultural activity. Like the Europeans, they had access to the legacy of Greek and Roman culture, but unlike the Europeans, they started as early as the ninth century to develop Greek and Roman science. In 1202, Fibonacci's book *Liber abaci* (*The Book of Calculation*) described the decimal system and explained how to use it to make calculation easier. On its publication, mathematicians of that time began to be persuaded to adopt the new and advanced system. The decimal system spread slowly, but no one who tried it ever went back to the Roman numerals, which persisted only as an alternative way of numbering series such as hours or book pages.

Decode:

Here, as an homage to their long history, is a cipher using Roman letter-numerals.

XXI XII IX   XXIV XXII XIII VII VI IX XVIII XXII VIII

VII XIX XXII   V XXVI VIII VII   IX XII XIV XXVI XIII

XXII XIV XI XVIII IX XXII   IV XXVI VIII   IX VI XIII

XXVI XXIV XXIV VI IX XXVI VII XXII XV II   XXV II

XX XII V XXII IX XIII XIV XXII XIII VII VIII

XXVI XIII XXIII   XIV XXVI XIII XXVI XX XXII IX VIII

VI VIII XVIII XIII XX   IX XII XIV XXVI XIII

XIII VI XIV XXII IX XXVI XV VIII

Fibonacci's other passion, the one for which he is famous today, was all but ignored during his lifetime: the reproduction of rabbits. It stemmed from a practical problem: how many rabbits he would have by the end of a year if he started with one couple and eventually each couple produced a new couple every month. Each month, for each couple of rabbits, it's as if one rabbit is multiplied by 2 and the other is kept in reserve until the next month. In the long run, this produces a series of numbers in which each step is the sum of the two preceding steps:

1   1   2   3   5   8   13   21   44   65   109...

Later researchers found that this series describes many other biological phenomena in animals and plants, such as cell division and the growth of leaves on a branch.

As a code, the Fibonacci series translates readily into the language of the Pythagorean "figured numbers." As a new number family, it joins the triangles, squares, cubes, and so on, studied by the Pythagoreans.

On the Pythagorean plane, the Fibonacci numbers appear naturally when one draws a spiral of squares. Start with two single unit squares, side by side. A 2 × 2 square comes next to them, then a 3 × 3 square, then one of 5 × 5, one of 8 × 8, and so on. The Fibonacci numbers increase through the simple act of adding a new square to the previous two. The diagram at the right depicts the sides of the squares assembled in a spiral. When one adds an arc passing through each square, one gets the beautiful "golden spiral." Note how this growth of a series of squares is similar to the growth of a living body that generates a new cell beyond those which precede it. Compare the shell above with the graphic at the right.

This opens the door to "dynamic symmetry." In this context symmetry does not mean the property of two parts of a figure being alike across a line or a point, as in a mirror, but has the more general meaning of the harmony of a figure or shape as a whole. In that sense, the golden mean imparts symmetry by its mere presence. The symmetry becomes dynamic when it appears in the form of a series that can develop itself indefinitely. An aesthetic code of this nature seems to propagate itself as if it were alive and even seems capable of growing or moving across time. When used in decoration or architecture, it is a striking way of producing an impression of rhythm and life.

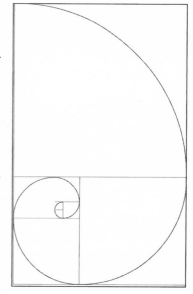

Dynamic symmetry was the first clue in the history of codes that a code could become somewhat independent and have a life of its own. This will become clearer when we discuss computer coding and fractals of the twentieth century, later in this chapter.

Fibonacci numbers also are related to the golden mean in a different and surprising way: they provide a method for calculating the golden mean simply, with pencil and paper or a pocket calculator. The ratio of two consecutive Fibonacci numbers gets closer and closer to the golden mean as you move along the series.

Let's see how this works. As you recall, the golden mean is phi = 0.6180339.... The successive ratios of the Fibonacci series are as follows:

$$1/1 = 1$$

$$2/1 = 2$$

$$3/2 = 1.5$$

$$5/3 = 1.666...$$

$$8/5 = 1.6$$

$$13/8 = 1.625$$

$$21/13 = 1.615...$$

$$34/21 = 1.619...$$

$$55/34 = 1.617...$$

$$89/55 = 1.618181...$$

We don't need to go very far in the series to get an excellent approximation of the golden mean. Indeed, this progressive approximation is not a coincidence but a mathematical fact. In 1843 Jacques Binet, a French mathematician who worked mostly on astronomy and matrices (not to be confused with Alfred Binet, who invented the IQ test), published a formula for the Fibonacci numbers that accounts for this result. The nth Fibonacci number is:

$$F_n = \frac{(1+ \sqrt{5})^n - (1+ \sqrt{5})^n}{2^n\sqrt{5}}.$$

If you know anything about limits, you would certainly agree that the greater the number n, the closer $Fn/Fn - 1$ gets to the formula for phi:

$$\frac{-1 + \sqrt{5}}{2}$$

In other words, the formula approaches 1.6180339...

Two other apparent coincidences are logical facts for lovers of mathematical oddities. There are two other methods of writing and computing the golden mean. The first is with "continuous square roots," using the following formula:

$$\alpha = \sqrt{1 + \sqrt{1 + \sqrt{1 + \sqrt{1 + \ldots}}}}$$

The second is with "continuous fractions," using this formula:

$$\alpha = 1 + \cfrac{1}{1 + \cfrac{1}{1 + \cfrac{1}{1 + \ldots}}}$$

In each case, the farther you go along the progression of the formula, the closer you approximate the golden mean.

Adolf Zeising's Gold Rush

In a strange fit of digital vandalism, modern critics have imposed the golden code on Renaissance and classical artists and forced them back into the aesthetic chains from which they had so painstakingly freed themselves. This trend can be traced to Adolf Zeising, a German art critic who published *Neue Lehre von den Proportionen des menschlichen Körpers (New Laws on the Proportions of the Human Body)* in 1854.

Zeising's thesis was that all nature, including the human body, exhibits the golden mean at all times and that a work of art is beautiful only if it is structured according to those laws. Zeising was followed in his hypothesis by a host of art critics from the second half of the nineteenth century until the end of the twentieth. With no respect for the creations and wishes of artists and no regard for elementary logic, Zeising's disciples drew arbitrary lines across the greatest paintings, imposing silly grids on their shapes and lines. It did not matter that the grids did not correspond to exact details in the works; it seems that their eyes could not appreciate beauty without those grim geometric lines. Although no artist since Villard de Honnecourt (see Chapter 4) had drawn such lines, their aesthetic principles required them. Those critics felt a need to impose the code craze that was sweeping art criticism at that time.

So influential were the golden fundamentalists that many contemporary artists, including Georges Seurat, who prided himself on producing "scientific art," included the golden mean in their works, giving more strength to their creed. It became legitimate to look for the golden means these artists had put in their works.

This unfortunate trend did not actually relate to the golden mean, which was conceived as one of several spontaneous means of dealing with proportions, one philosophy among others linking art and numbers. Indeed, Renaissance artists were far more moderate, advising care in all proportions instead of imposing a central one.

Georg Cantor's Infinity Code

A Russian mathematician in the second half of the nineteenth century, Georg Cantor put an end to family quarrels in the realm of numbers, proving that all families have an equal number of members. Cantor went beyond all his predecessors and successfully tackled the arithmetic of infinity. That won him the hatred of most researchers of his time, who tried to block his career and prevent the publication of his papers. His discoveries constitute an essential step in the exploration of numbers and cast another light on Pythagoras's problems with integers, ratios, and irrational numbers.

To compare infinities, Cantor first devised a tool so simple and straightforward that nobody could challenge it. Two sets are said to have an equal number of members if each member of one set can be lined up exactly with one member of the other set, and conversely. For example, there are an equal number of chairs and diners at the dinner table when each diner is sitting on a chair and each chair has a diner sitting on it. This is common sense, but the rule yields interesting results when it is applied to infinitely large sets. For example, it proves that there are an equal number of squares and integers in general. Indeed, each integer has one and only one square, and each square has one and only one integer as its square root. This is apparent in the sequences below:

1 2 3 4 5 6 7...

1 4 9 16 25 36 49...

This is also true of all other families, for instance, the pentagons we saw above:

1   2   3   4   5   6   7...

1   5   9   13   17   21   25...

This rule also implies that there are identical numbers of integers and ratios. The proof is graphical. Imagine a matrix with all the whole numbers on the first horizontal row and in the first vertical column. The squares of the infinite matrix contain all possible fractions, which are created by placing the number of the column on the number of the row. Yet they can all be reached with a broken line. Numbering along all the squares as the broken line reaches them, we find that there is a single fraction for each number and a single number for each fraction. Thus, there are as many fractions as there are integers. Pythagoras could have drawn that on sand.

This, of course, defies common sense, which dictates that there should be half as many even numbers as there are integers as a whole. Yet Cantor's work shows that all infinities, though not equal in the sense of equality as it is applied to finite numbers, are comparable and thus equal as far as infinities are concerned. All such infinities belong to the same class and have the same infinite number of components, referred to as "aleph-zero."

Pushing ahead, Cantor made the philosophical leap that Pythagoras had made when dealing with the square root of 2. In a famous proof, Cantor established that there was at least one infinity that was superior to aleph-zero: aleph-one, the set of decimal or so-called real numbers.

The demonstration does not call for high mathematics, but its precise description is beyond the scope of this book. Roughly, it consists in pretending to list all the irrational numbers and numbering them with the integers and then showing that there remains at least one irrational number that is not in the list. Even though we add it to the list, there is still another one not in the list, indefinitely; this proves the absurdity of the list.

Hence another infinity, different from and greater than aleph-zero, does exist.

Pythagoras had a glimpse of the complexity of the realm of numbers when he encountered such items as the square root of 2. He believed that his revered whole numbers and ratios were the code of the universe, give or take a few notable exceptions. He was far from imagining the extent of the numbers hidden from his vision, the importance of the infinity that hides behind and beyond the aleph-zero he knew.

But it gets worse.

Like Euclid with his principles of geometry, Pythagoras placed his trust in the most basic code of all: truth and falsehood, the binary code of logic. When Euclid or Pythagoras envisioned a theorem, he must have been confident that he could prove that it was true or false.

However, aleph-zero and aleph-one bring with them an end to that simple mental universe where everything is either proved or disproved. Cantor's discovery of aleph-zero and aleph-one left mathematicians wondering whether there are other infinities between the two. The question was solved—or indefinitely unsolved—in 1963 by Paul Cohen, who demonstrated that the existence of other infinities could be held as both true and false without negative consequences for the rest of mathematics.

In other words, the question is "undecidable," a concept that would have baffled Pythagoras and that we'll encounter again in Chapter 8.

The Gödel Code

Gödel numbers, in yet another direction, illustrate the power of numbers as a coding device.

Kurt Gödel did not have this particular illustrative purpose in mind when he devised his numbering system. Instead, he was addressing the very problem whose solution later made Alan Turing famous (see Chapter 8). Gödel built his system around and applied it to what are called "undecidable" questions.

Gödel numbers provide a way to associate a unique number with every possible written statement. Within this scheme any statement will correspond to one and only one integer in such a way that every integer conversely corresponds to only one statement. This is done in three steps.

Step 1: We number all symbols used in writing with odd integers greater than 2. For instance:

a   Z   2   b   n   =   +...
3   5   7   9   11   13   15...

Step 2: We replace any statement with a unique sequence—the odd integers of its symbols. For instance:

"n = a + 2" would be: 11, 13, 3, 15, 9

Step 3: We replace that sequence with a single unique integer, product of the powers of the successive prime numbers. For example:

$$N = 2^{11} \times 3^{13} \times 5^3 \times 7^{15} \times 11^9$$

As a result of the basic property of prime numbers, which are indivisible, a Gödel number is easy to decipher. N can be broken down into the product of prime numbers. Their powers stand out, giving us the sequence of integers and eventually the original statement.

Gödel numbers rapidly become very large, but size is not a problem in the infinite world of integers.

We can go further and code whole series of statements, such as mathematical demonstrations or even books. Each statement has a Gödel number: n1, n2, n3, and so on. We then code the whole as before, and the Gödel number of the book or the demonstration is the product:

$$N = 2^{n1} \times 3^{n2} \times 5^{n3} \times 7^{n4}\ldots$$

This technology is so powerful that the entire set of all the books ever written in all languages could be coded and stored by this method as *one* possibly cumbersome and certainly mind-boggling large integer.

To experiment with Gödel coding, let's number the letters of the alphabet with odd integers:

a	b	c	d	e	f	g	h	i	j	k	l	m	n	o	p	q	r	s	t	u	v	w	x	y	z
3	5	7	9	11	13	15	17	19	21	23	25	27	29	31	33	35	37	39	41	43	45	47	49	51	53

Decode:

What message is coded in this Gödel number?

152,339,935,002,624

Mondrian's Portrait of the Mean

In his early works, Mondrian researched several possible styles, among them cubism. In the picture *Tableau I: Lozenge with Four Lines and Gray* (1926, Museum of Modern Art, New York), in a typically cubist manner, Mondrian gathers on the same canvas several points of view of his model, the golden mean. However, unlike other cubist works, the points of view are mathematical. The thicknesses of his lines are proportionate to 3, 4, and 5, a conspicuous way of evoking Pythagoras and his right triangle.

The four lines also invite the eye to complete their formation into a square, which is suggested with three vertices outside the canvas, and to compare that square to the square of the canvas itself. As Charles Bouleau demonstrates in his 1963 book *Painter's Secret Geometry*, the diagonal of the small square intersects the large square and its diagonal at the golden mean and conversely, the diagonal of the large square intersects the diagonal of the small square at the golden mean too. This clever construction yields two presentations of the golden mean.

This "portraiting code" appears in retrospect as the last step in the integration of the golden mean into art. The canvas displays its own generation process. Like mathematical recursive functions that address themselves, the work includes its own "makeup."

Not everybody agrees with this point of view. In a correspondence with the author, Mondrian's estate writes: "An even more serious problem is the implication that Mondrian deliberately used the golden mean/rectangle/triangle in his work, Mondrian was an intuitive artist who arrived at his compositions through trial and error, re-adjustment and erasure, revised them many, many times until he felt the balance of lines and planes was harmonious. This interpretation of his work is popular among mathematicians; however, we do not give copyright permission for reproductions which infer that he used this principle." In this situation it's best you form your own opinion by visiting the Museum of Modern Art in New York or its Internet site.

Le Corbusier's Concrete Gold

Charles-Édouard Jeanneret-Gris, who called himself Le Corbusier, was a prominent mid-twentieth-century architect who was famous for his use of concrete. He celebrated concrete as a material that is as noble as wood or stone. He compensated for the austerity of that material with a systematic use of his own adaptation of the golden mean: the "Modulor" (the gold module) that places the human body as a central reference. He contended that with the correct aesthetics we can live in bare concrete and do without paint or wallpaper. He wanted to trade material comfort for geometric comfort.

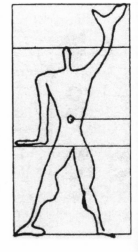

Le Corbusier's work does offer some aesthetic appeal beyond the use of the Modulor. His concrete is rugged, displaying the mold of the wooden planks used to pour it. This brings a naturally wild tone to his bare walls.

The picture on page 68 is from the codebook Le Corbusier published as a manual for architects and urbanists: *Le Modulor*. With that book, Le Corbusier became the latest competitor of Vitruvius (see Chapter 4), with a full set of references for all occasions, from interior decoration to city planning and even world peace. The tiny detail of the left foot stepping out of the frame hints at the fundamental freedom of the creator even in a concrete environment.

Salvador Dali's Transcendental Devotions

In the middle of the twentieth century, two paintings by Salvador Dali celebrated Pythagoras in yet other dimensions: the pentagon and the perfect solid.

Dali's *Last Supper* takes place both above and within a pentagonal dodecahedron. Moreover, Christ's arms encompass the scene in a key 108° triangle, the Pythagorean symbol we've already seen and will see again in Chapter 7.

In the 1954 *Crucifixion*, Dali goes beyond Leonardo da Vinci and the Pythagoreans in the quest for perfect geometry by adding to the Platonic solids. He evokes the imaginary world of the fourth dimension with a tesseract, or hypercube, the equivalent of a

cube in an imaginary four-dimensional world. Dali's cross is a projection of a four-dimensional hypercube in our three-dimensional world. The hypercube is represented as a set of cubes, the same way we represent a cube as a set of squares when we open it on a piece of paper. This yields a striking rendering of Christ as the link to a world beyond ours, just as the hypercube links us to a world beyond our three-dimensional world.

Along with Mondrian's final paintings, these works form a sort of obituary for the golden mean—a portrait and summary of its achievements—before its resurrection in fractals, a transmigration of the code that Pythagoras would have approved.

The Fractals' Active Code

The ultimate advance in aesthetic codebooks is the fractal code. With fractals, aesthetic coding makes a jump from static to dynamic coding, a jump that aesthetic researchers had always hoped for and aimed at. A sort of Fibonacci series gone wild, fractal coding was achieved in the twentieth century through the work of mathematical geniuses and the power of graphic computing.

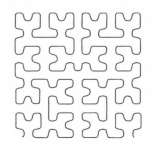

Rather than being a simple static reference, fractals are codes that actually generate pictures. Left to itself, a fractal code will do the complete job of creating the graphic rendering. The human hand need only type an equation, and the equation will draw a complex picture. A fractal code can be seen as a virtual art robot that produces art without any action by its creator other than pressing the right keys.

The development of fractals is due largely to Benoît Mandelbrot, who worked on the earlier findings of Gaston Julia. Julia published the first paper on fractal equations

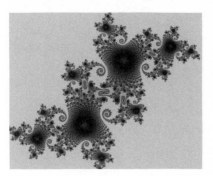

in 1918, a few months after being wounded in the face during the World War I. Having lost his nose, he had to wear a facial mask for the rest of his life. Fortunately, his brain was intact, and he continued his research while in bed in the hospital.

Julia was dealing with mathematical monsters, and his work required courage. He was treading on dangerous ground and venturing into territories usually frowned upon by serious mathematicians. Giuseppe Peano before him had studied an unspeakable curve that filled the entire plane and had no slope anywhere. That defied the precepts of analytical geometry and was derided by the mathematical community.

Julia became instantly famous for his work, and some of the first fractals actually were drawn. Unfortunately, drawing fractals by hand is such a painstaking job that it attracted little interest outside mathematical circles in the 1920s and soon was forgotten. Mathematician specialists are able to envision and appreciate the beauty of a curve merely by looking at its equation, but few people share that talent. For most people, fractals need to be drawn. They have had to wait to see the drawing until a researcher with the adequate technology could do that.

Benoit Mandelbrot was born in Poland in 1924. He immigrated to France, where he had to hide during World War II, and it was there that he received his education, including a college degree. He later immigrated to the United States, mostly because he disagreed with the French school of mathematics, which he perceived as being too involved in the foundations of mathematics to welcome research in the blossoming new area of applied mathematics and its relation to computers.

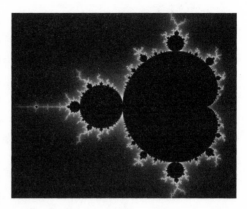

His first contact with Julia's work was in 1945 at the suggestion of his uncle, who presented it as a subject rich in potential. It did not suit Mandelbrot's taste at that time, however, and he rejected the idea of working on fractals. Retrospectively, his intuition was right: It was far too early to have had the aid of computers. The UNIVAC was still struggling with addition and subtraction, and its programmers had not dreamed of computer graphics.

By the 1970s, though, computers had developed into more versatile tools. Mandelbrot became an IBM fellow, meaning that IBM paid him to work in total freedom on the projects of his choice. He had access to the facilities of the advanced IBM laboratories at Yorktown Heights in New York State, where the company built and kept its best computers. There he developed the theory and practice of an entirely new geometry. It is probably the first time software code and mathematics were used together to develop new concepts.

Fractals pay a surprising tribute to Pythagorean principles. Just as the microcosm of the human body was similar to the macrocosm of the world for Plato and Pythagoras—the part is similar to the whole, a concept close to the golden mean— every part of a fractal, however tiny, is similar to the whole fractal. This results from the way a fractal works. When set on its course, it goes on indefinitely, eventually filling the space of the plane. In doing that, it continues to draw the same complex shape over and over, but smaller and smaller, never covering the previous drawings but nesting within them.

Fractals, however, go much further. They open a new door beyond the world of Pythagoras, breaking up the Pythagorean codebook and extending it.

In this geometry, for example, dimensions take on a different life. The three-dimensional frame we are used to loses its rigid traditional limits. Dimensions are split into an indefinite number of subdimensions. Because of the versatility of nano-geometry, fractals can render all of nature's capriciousness, a feat traditional geometry can't accomplish.

Pythagoras and Fibonacci took the first steps toward a workable description of nature. With the new geometry created by Julia and Mandelbrot we have taken another decisive step toward a perfect description. Although Pythagorean geometry remains a splendid exhibit of classical beauty, fractals explore the wild beauty of nature. Whereas Pythagoras dealt with crystals, fractals deal with sunsets. Pythagoras can inspire temples and cathedrals, but fractals can create landscapes the eye cannot distinguish from the real world. Pythagoras speaks to our sense of formal perfection, but fractals speak to our love of unpredictable nature, living or mineral. We started the new millennium with more than one aesthetic codebook.

We'll see in Chapter 9 that fractals are only one aspect of the autonomy of code becoming "active code."

CHAPTER 3

The Knights Templar

Brotherhoods existed long before the Knights Templar, some centered on philosophy or religion and some on a specific craft such as carpentry or masonry, and continued to exist long afterward. However, the Templars—an exceptional union of Pythagoreans and Christians engaged in an armed attempt to maintain peace—are an essential milestone marking the importance of secret societies in history.

Besides the glamour surrounding their history, the Knights Templar represent an essential step in the development of Western civilization on an impressive variety of points. They were a link to the remote past of Christianity as well as a link to the East, beyond Christianity, with the "infidel" Muslims. As the Pythagoreans had done in ancient Greece and the Freemasons would do later, the Knights Templar lived openly as a secret brotherhood. They were created from scratch by the Roman Catholic Church to act as the armed force of a faith yet devoted to peace and "offering the other cheek." They were the first group to experiment successfully with the "obedience" code that would later structure the Freemasons. They applied the Pythagorean code of art in innumerable buildings across Europe and the Near East and developed and practiced cryptographic code to conduct their international business.

In spite of the obvious artificiality of this group of men—living a coded life and wielding code in so many different ways—they were the first group after the fall of the Roman Empire to structure a network of communication across Europe.

A Sacred Link to Jerusalem

Before being wiped out virtually overnight at the beginning of the fourteenth century by the joint powers of the Pope and the king of France, the order of the Knights Templar played an essential role in the history of Christianity, opening up and then securing the road to the birthplace of Christ. To understand this phenomenon, some historical background knowledge is helpful.

Throughout the first millennium, European Christians maintained their link with Palestine, where their religion had been born, by means of art and pilgrimage.

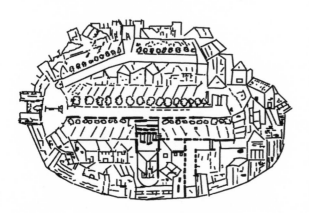

Jerusalem, its surroundings, and the various places mentioned in the Bible were revered and depicted in religious art, and travelers often journeyed to see them firsthand. Reaching Palestine was time-consuming, difficult, and dangerous. Some travelers went there for business purposes and to exchange goods with the East; most went on religious pilgrimages.

The journey to Jerusalem was an important option in a Christian's life, much like going to Mecca for contemporary Muslims. It ranked far higher than shorter pilgrimages such as the popular Saint James pilgrimage to Compostela in Spain. As early as the fourth century, the trek was made mostly by wealthy Christians intent on redeeming themselves from outstanding sins. The picture on page 74 shows a sixth-century mosaic map of the sacred sites that was discovered in Mabada, Jordan.

The pilgrimages were better organized than one might imagine. The pilgrims had manuscript guidebooks like the ones modern-day tourists use that explained how to find one's way to important places in Jerusalem as well as to landmarks such as Rome or Constantinople along the route. The high point of the trip, its most sacred goal, was the Church of the Holy Sepulcher maintained by local Christians; this was the place that held the tomb of Christ, and preserving it was thought to be paramount.

The Christians of those times had an absolute belief in the divine power of the bodies of holy figures. That power was so potent that even a small part of a body exposed in a church as a relic would attract crowds. People who came home after making pilgrimage and having direct contact with the remains of a sacred body felt that they carried part of that sacred power with them for the rest of their lives. They would sew the sign of the pilgrimage on their clothes, and people would come to them for blessings, healing, or advice.

Christians also believed in the physical transmission of faith. The system went so far that in nearby European places such as Compostela, where the crowds were so large that people would trample and sometimes kill one another to touch the relics, they resorted to using glass signs of pilgrimage. The relics were out of reach, and a pilgrim would carry a small piece of glass that became sacred once the relic had been reflected in it. The glass worked as a quaint forecast of laser transmission of data.

This explains why maintaining a link with the sacred birthplace was essential. The physical and spiritual links to the faith's origin could not be separated. First-millennium Christians needed direct contact with holy places and objects to support the strength of their faith. The True Cross, for instance, which Christ had carried and died on, was discovered by the emperor Constantine's mother, Saint Helena. It was revered so intensely that thousands of small parts of it became the prize possession of countless churches and monasteries. Thus, the presence of the cross, the central code of the religion, was both spiritually and physically needed. It was in this tradition that the Knights Templar would display the cross on their garments and use it as the graphic basis of their cipher.

The Millennial Dead Line

Toward the end of the first millennium, during the tenth century, the millennialist aspect of Christianity became all-important. Today most Christians read the passages in the Bible concerning the Last Judgment as a metaphor, a poetic description that will not necessarily happen exactly as written. Before the year 1000, however, Christians believed the very letter of the Apocalypse and expected the events described in the Bible to come true. They read it as announcing the end of this world in the year 1000. People prepared for Judgment Day, as they saw it as a day when the good would go to heaven and the bad would be sentenced to hell. To prepare for the worst, rich people gave their wealth to the Church and the poor became more devout. However, the second millennium arrived and nothing happened.

Disappointment over the absence of the expected Apocalypse was not focused on a specific day or year. Year counting was not precise enough at that time; in addition, people were unsure whether to count the thousand years from the birth of Christ or from His death. In any case, it became clear toward the end of the eleventh century that the world was not going to come to an immediate end and probably would continue to exist much longer. As if to compensate for the loss of Judgment Day and express their faith through another channel, Christians became more concerned with physical achievements symbolizing their beliefs. Locally, they launched ambitious projects for building cathedrals and monasteries. They also undertook the development of the physical and sacred aspects of the faith, which centered on the tomb of Christ that they needed to see and touch. You'll see in later chapters, especially when you read about the compagnons and the Freemasons, the importance of a symbolic journey for the human mind, whether coded, ritual, or mythic.

In the eleventh century Christianity was already divided between the Roman Christians in the West and the Orthodox Christians in the East, centered on Byzantium (now Constantinople). Both revered the same holy place, but an important difference between Western and Eastern Christians was that the former identified that place as the Holy Sepulcher, emphasizing the tomb and thus the death of Christ, whereas the latter chose to call the place Holy Anastasia (*anastasia* means "un-dead," or "resurrection"), and thus putting more emphasis on His rebirth. This is one of the reasons Western Christians later frowned upon the rites of death and rebirth in the brotherhoods of the compagnons and Freemasons (see Chapter 5).

The Crusades

At the beginning of the second millenium, concerns about Jerusalem became more acute because contact between the pilgrims and the local authorities had become difficult. Three centuries earlier the Moslems had invaded Europe through Spain and had been stopped and defeated in the middle of France. In the ensuing centuries, both religions and civilizations coexisted peacefully in Spain, enjoying the advantages of extended commercial and cultural exchanges. The Moslems had preserved a large part of the Greek and Roman legacy; later this would help trigger the Renaissance (see Chapter 4).

Despite this prolonged period of peace between Moslems and Europeans in the eleventh century, relations between pilgrims and the people in the Middle East devolved into open war. In 1009, Caliph Al-Hakim bi-Amr Allah of Cairo, the ruler of Egypt and its surroundings, destroyed the Church of the Holy Sepulcher and sacked the pilgrimage hospice in Jerusalem. He was a rigorous religious leader who was intent on purifying and imposing the Muslim faith. He considered Christ to be neither the son of God nor a reincarnation of God, only one prophet among many before Mohammed and thus one who should not be given too much importance. Because on his side of the world, only the word of Mohammed was to be followed, he also actively persecuted local Christians and took over the Holy Land.

When news of that disaster reached Western Europe, the Christians were devastated. Their reaction went far beyond the actual situation, which quickly found its own temporary solution. Caliph Al-Hakim bi-Amr Allah died soon afterward, and his successor made peace with the Byzantine Empire in Constantinople and with the Eastern Christians, who also were concerned about the Holy Land. The Byzantines quickly rebuilt the Church of the Holy Sepulcher and restored the pilgrimages.

Nevertheless, Western Christians remembered the disaster and considered that such a thing could happen again. However, they were so poorly organized that almost a century would elapse before crusade was preached and they were able to assemble an army to conquer Palestine and secure the Holy Land. In the meantime, the political and military situation grew extremely complex. There was a general conflict between Christians and Moslems in Spain and the Near East, and chaos reigned within each camp. Neither the Christian princes and kings on one side nor the Moslem emirs on the other got along with their fellow local rulers. The result was conquests and losses on both fronts, with no decisive victory. Struggles for power were so intertwined with religious fervor that historians find it difficult to present a clear picture of the eleventh century.

Because of the chaotic situation and its multiple cultural aspects, the history of the Crusades is extremely controversial. Depending on their personal philosophy, culture, or faith, most historians stress only the political, religious, military, or commercial aspects of the period. All those viewpoints are valid in that every human enterprise is determined by several causes. Here we are interested in the history of codes and symbols. The Crusades and their offspring, the Knights Templar, represent the major symbolic actions by which Christianity expressed its paradoxical need to establish a durable, if conflicted, link with Eastern culture.

Christians could not ignore the East or permanently defeat it and could not come to terms with it, although all three options seemed feasible. They could easily have stopped bothering with the Holy Land and the Moslems and peacefully developed their faith in their own lands. Christian princes also could have united to form a considerable force that might easily have wiped out the Muslim powers and spread Christianity in the Near East. Or they could have negotiated a lasting truce with the Muslims, bringing about commercial and cultural benefits for all. Instead, they started a conflict and fed it. This conflict is still going on a whole millennium later.

The Knights Templar may be considered the leading riders of the Christian shock wave. That was a prestigious yet unstable position that won them both honor and destruction.

Creating the Knights

Pope Urban II formally called for the first crusade at the Council of Clermont in 1095. Officially, the Pope was responding to the Byzantine Empire's demand for help against the Turks to regain the kingdom of Jerusalem on a long-term basis instead of making temporary arrangements. The council took place at a time when the Pope was establishing his authority over the Western princes and kings. As a reward to those who joined the effort he offered indulgences: full remission of their sins if they died during their mission. His preaching was first relayed by a charismatic preacher called Peter the Hermit, who led an unorganized crowd of poor people on a first crusade that ended in a total disaster, with the few survivors being converted to Islam. Then Bernard de Clairvaux (later canonized as Saint Bernard) preached the first real crusade, composed of a majority of better organized princes and militaries, which reached Jerusalem.

Indeed, Peter the Hermit well represented the first hope to restore and found Jerusalem anew just as Saint Peter had symbolically founded Christianity a millennium before. The symbolism of Peter's name was reinforced by its double meaning both in Latin, the sacred language of the Church, and in French, the language of the Crusaders, in which *petrus* and *pierre* mean "a stone." The apostle Matthew has Jesus say in his all-important verse 16:18 that He consecrated the apostle Peter as the first Pope of the Christian Church: "And I say also to thee, That thou art Peter, and upon this stone I will build my church; and the gates of hell shall not prevail against it." Pierre L'Hermite started preaching close to Vézelay Cathedral in a village now called Saint-Pierre, where he had been a hermit. Saint Peter traditionally holds the keys to Paradise. The symbol was so strong that Bernard de Clairvaux had to be in the same place to preach the second crusade.

The Knights, from Poor to Templar

Eventually, after a chaotic period of travel, starvation, looting, and mixed military success in Europe and Asia Minor, a motley crowd of rich barons and poor people conquered the kingdom of Jerusalem. Most of them considered their pilgrimage to the Holy Land to have been accomplished successfully and immediately began on the journey home. A few were concerned about the defense of the site and the survival of the Christian kingdom. For that reason, they created two local religious orders: the Knights of the Hospital, or "Knights Hospitallers," who were devoted to the accommodation and care of pilgrims, and the Poor Knights of Christ, who would defend the kingdom and protect pilgrims physically on the dangerous journey to the holy sites.

The Order of the Poor Knights of Christ was founded by nine crusaders in 1118. King Baudouin II of Jerusalem, if only for his own protection, lodged them in his palace on Temple Mount. Several years later the king moved to David's tower and gave the knights a place in what was considered the ruins of King Solomon's temple (see the

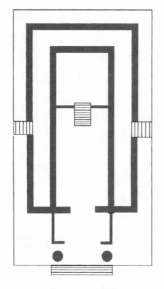

schematic of the temple on the left). Then came a surprising event: The "Poor" Knights decided to change their name to Knights Templar.

What motivated the change from *poor* to *templar*? Was it the influence of the site? Why abandon the strict Christian reference to Christ? Why not refer to the Holy Sepulcher? Difficult as it may be to understand today, apparently no one at the time objected to the change. On the contrary, the Knights' new name was adopted spontaneously, as if the real goal of the Crusades was to secure a bridge to the more ancient religious code of King Solomon and his father, David, who lived a thousand years before Christ. The apostles Matthew and Luke claimed that Jesus was descended from King David. The reference to a common ancestor may have been made to give the Templars more credit with the Muslims.

The Knights Hospitallers stuck to their less romantic, more matter-of-fact name and quietly assumed their role of providing unobtrusive assistance. Their cross was a white one, in contrast with the red cross of the Templars. Because of the hostile environment, like the Templars, the Hospitallers rapidly became warriors and fought side by side with the Templars in many battles. However, the Knights Hospitallers never became as renowned and were awarded far fewer privileges. Their nonobtrusive strategy proved successful in the long run, for they eventually absorbed the Templars when that order was suppressed two centuries later. Unlike the Templars, with their Old Testament reference to King Solomon, the Hospitallers lived on the site of the monastery of Saint John the Baptist and adopted the New Testament reference of Saint John. Their order also could be considered older, because Christians began operating a hospital in Jerusalem in the year 600. Only the twelfth-century Crusade, after half a millennium of persecution, gave the Hospitallers the strength to become a real order.

A third order, the Teutonic Knights, played an important role in northern Europe and the Holy Land. The Order of the Teutonic House of Saint Mary in Jerusalem was founded in 1190 in the strategic Galilean harbor of Acre for the care of German pilgrims. Those knights wore a black cross on a white coat and were created by the merchants of Bremen and Lübeck but soon became a military tool of the Holy Roman emperor Frederick II, who also used them locally in European conflicts.

The tragic fate of the Knights Templar might have been due partly to their association with an Old Testament symbol more ancient than Christ. Their "templar" dimension creates a Christian link to the Jewish tradition, going beyond the gospel of the New Testament to the Old Testament, the sacred book they also shared with Muslims. Indeed, their roots in the often violent Old Testament were appropriate for soldiers of the faith. However, that direct link to Solomon bypassed Christ and the Apostles and made the Templars not quite "Christian," a perilous situation in an era when Christians were deeply concerned with material links to Christ and the sacred places of their faith. As their fundamental and symbolic root, the Knights Templar had traded the Holy Sepulcher for Solomon's Temple. Placing Christ in a historical perspective, they challenged His central place in Christianity.

In the late twentieth century, conflict between Israelis and Palestinians was triggered by a visit of the Israeli leader Ariel Sharon to Solomon's Temple that wiped out years of peace negotiations. It's important to note the extraordinary force of the symbolism here. The spontaneous negative reaction of the Palestinian people surprised officials on both sides, who had planned and agreed on the visit in advance. The symbol proved more powerful than the governments. Several holy places in Jerusalem— among them the Temple Mount, the Church of the Holy Sepulcher, the Har HaBayit/ Al-Haram Al-Sharif Mosque—touch one another. At the turn of a new millennium, instead of providing a venue for meetings and exchange, the multiple holiness of the Jerusalem is an active and irresistible source of conflict and war in the Middle East.

Templar Organization

The Templars' first action was to take fundamental vows to God and the Christian community to assert their existence and achieve their mission. First, they took the three perpetual vows of chastity, religious life, and missionary labor; then they added the crusader's vow of maintaining Christian access to the holy grounds.

To those vows were added the austere rules concerning the chapel, refectory, and dormitory. The Templars also adopted the white habit of the Cistercians—as white as the robes of the Pythagoreans—adding to it a red cross.

The solemn pledge was characteristic of the time and survives in contemporary monasteries and secret societies. All knights, Templars or otherwise, took their vows in public, making their promises all the more binding. The public was an essential part of the action, expected to testify to the holiness of a vow taker's achievement. Knights felt that they could not reach their goals without the intense trust of a public they could not betray.

In the case of the Templars, the vows were part of a system that provided the moral shield needed for the slaying of infidels by Christians who were supposed to be non-violent, a contradiction that made them fundamentally sinful and guilty. Obedience completed the vows. As is stated in their rules of order, the Templars "assiduously accomplish the very noble virtue of obedience"; that is even clearer in a version that says, "Permanently wear the armor of obedience." Obedience was the moral key, the armor of virtual steel that protected a Templar against his own guilt, setting him free to act as a soldier.

Daily Life

We know in detail how the Templars were organized and what they did in daily life because the Pope and the Church elaborated their governing rules (laws) with great care. For the first time, and contrary to the most fundamental Christian teachings, a religious order was created to engage in combat and shed blood. For this, total agreement throughout the Christian community was compulsory. A special council of archbishops, bishops, and abbots was held in Troye in 1128 to define the rules of life and limits to the activity of the Knights Templar. Hugues de Payens represented the knights. Bernard de Clairvaux, a leading authority on religious rules (he founded 70 monasteries in his lifetime), headed the assembly. We have the resulting rule, including the 486 clauses of its later version in Latin and a full translation in Middle French. In an attempt to balance freedom of action and power with a daily life as tightly framed as that of monastery-dwelling monks, the rules clearly dictated that this armed chival-ric body was "to slay the enemies of the Cross without guilt." As we saw above, it was the "armor of obedience" that protected the knights against any qualm about their un-Christian violence.

Interestingly, this paradoxical principle remained unchallenged in Europe by the military until the middle of the twentieth century. It was questioned during the Nuremberg trials, in which the Nazi military chiefs were denied the right to excuse their crimes with the obligation to obey hierarchical orders.

Such was the enthusiasm for the Templars' mission that to ensure their success, they were granted several outstanding privileges. They did not pay the church tax, or tithe (equal to a tenth of the harvest), and were permitted to build and consecrate their own churches and appoint their own priests. They also allowed wine and more meat than normal monks took. Those privileges placed them outside the normal hierarchy and eventually led to the jealousy and enmity of other religious orders, which were strictly taxed and closely supervised by the Pope.

Being created to survive and fight in difficult situations well outside the normal realms of Christianity, the Knights Templar could not have functioned without exceptional freedom and resources. The Church was fighting on two fronts besides Jerusalem and the Middle East: against the Muslims who had been established in southern Spain since the eighth century and against the emergent sect of the Cathars in southern France.

As a result, the system worked almost too well as far as resources were concerned. The Templars received extravagant gifts of every sort, including farms and land, from people who wanted to support their actions. They managed those gifts extremely efficiently, accumulating even more wealth, and multiplied their commanderies throughout France and all of Europe, from Scotland to Italy, Germany, and Poland.

Besides being warriors, the Templars acted as bankers or escrow agents, and that expanded their wealth. This practice started with protecting pilgrims on their journey to Jerusalem, during which the knights protected their belongings as well. Before leaving, a pilgrim would go to the closest Templar commanderie and exchange his money for a guarantee of food, lodging, and protection along the way. Soon people started entrusting the Templars with their money for other occasions, such as long journeys or when they were going to war. They considered the commanderies to be safe: God's law efficiently protected all religious places throughout the Middle Ages. The Templars thus became the first international bankers. They were so competent that they eventually managed fortunes and even the budgets of entire countries, such as the finances of the kingdom of France.

The Templar Template

Internally, the Knights Templar were organized into a hierarchy of assemblies in which every knight could talk, criticize, and vote. A master headed each assembly, and the hierarchy expanded from local chapters in commanderies to regions and countries. The whole order was led by an assembly of masters headed by a grand master, except that the Templars themselves never used the term *grand master*, only *master*.

The proceedings of the assemblies were carefully kept secret to preserve the freedom of expression of the knights. This secrecy ensured a unified image of the order. Viewed from without, they appeared to be and acted as one. The rule further reinforced that secrecy by allowing the Templars to have their own priests, thus allowing them to confess their sins and their secrets exclusively within the community.

The actual knights in the order were only a small part of the whole. Several categories of personnel completed the membership of the organization. The knights wore the Pythagorean dress of white linen, the symbol of purity, with a red cross on the heart. All the other personnel dressed in dark or brown material and were strictly forbidden to impersonate a knight, which was practically enforced by the difference in dress.

Neither a master nor an individual knight could directly enroll a new knight. Only a chapter could receive potential candidates in a ritual ceremony. The recruited knight was asked formally to take the fundamental vows of the order. The chapter then asked whether the candidate was "free"; that was an extremely important question. The order accepted only those who were free from debt, any bond of slavery or service, and any link with another order. A knight had to be able to engage himself totally in the mission of the order. This freedom ensured the complete independence of the Templars. The Freemasons ("free" masons) have this in common with the Knights Templar. Other common traits are that the Knights Templar pledged to help one another and the Freemasons used the same system of guilt management through obedience.

Mounted Pythagoreans

If they had been only soldiers devoted to the safety of pilgrims on their way to the Holy Land, the Templars would have led simple military lives, dwelling in barracks. They would not have built elaborate symbolic commanderies. As monks of war, they would have worshipped anywhere, especially in churches, not in temples.

Three factors helped transmute them from monks of war to Pythagorean bankers. The first was the immense amount of wealth they received as tithes. The others were what today would be called loopholes in their laws. To enable them to make war, the Templars were freed from a portion of their guilt, and since they battled in remote places, they answered to the Pope alone, not to the normal hierarchy of the clergy. Their wealth gave them the means and their freedom gave them the possibility of acting differently from other monastic orders. Created to be monks of war, they became international traders, the golden monks of the thirteenth century, so to speak.

Monks in general already led lives different from those of the general population. In many ways, they led the Pythagorean way of life and thus represented the Pythagorean heritage in the Christian world. They followed elaborate rules that helped them concentrate their thoughts and avoid unnecessary distractions. A large part of their work consisted of copying and transmitting the heritage of the Pythagoreans. They built monasteries and chapels in a style of architecture that also transmitted the geometric heritage of the Pythagoreans.

The Templars, although monks too, albeit with greater freedom and wealth than other monks, faced more provocative challenges than did their secluded fellow monks. They inevitably went further in following the Pythagorean trend. Their practice of mathematics was fed by the need to manage a vast number of warring units over great distances. When they took on the additional task of managing the pilgrims' wealth, their math had to become highly professional. In that area they must have reached a level no Pope or Christian king could grasp.

Solomon's Seal

Like the Pythagoreans, the Templars made use of an aesthetic code that can be found in church remnants and surviving architectural plans. Interestingly, following the Christian pattern of connecting the physical and the spiritual, those aesthetic codes had links to the Old Testament and New Testament

Associated with the Temple of Solomon, there is a powerful symbol: Solomon's seal, a crossed hexagram inscribed within a circle, which is shown above. Having an even number of vertices, it cannot be drawn with a single, continuous line; that makes the hexagram an intermediary between the pentagram and the heptagram. However, Judaists manage to reach seven by counting the center as one more vertex.

The seal often is represented as being made of two triangles that can overlap in several different ways. The two triangles inspire different interpretations, depending on the tradition involved. They may represent man pointing up and woman pointing down, as was put forward by Dan Brown in *The Da Vinci Code*. In the Kabbalist tradition, they are fire pointing up and water pointing down. The Kabbalists also gave new life to the legend of the kings Solomon and David by using this seal as a protective shield against demons. The crossed hexagram did not become a specifically Jewish emblem until the sixteenth century.

The picture on the left shows a carpet page from a book written around 1010 C.E. It displays an interesting integration of two stars—a hexagram and an octagram—both of which have an even number of points. There are two triangles inside two squares inside a circle. The text in the center is a dedication to a priest. The rest of the text consists of quotations from the biblical books of Psalms and Deuteronomy. In addition, the octagram displays dots in its empty spaces in a manner later used in the so-called Templar code.

The Templars had a distinctive and descriptive seal that displayed their cross above two mounted brother knights. MILITIAE XRISTI SIGILLVM (see the picture below) is indeed the seal of Christ's warriors, but this is only one seal among many others. Each master had a seal that served to authenticate his documents when it was pressed into a drop of molten of wax. The seals were purposefully difficult to reproduce and were kept carefully under lock and key.

Like everyone at that time, the Templars could recognize the authenticity of a seal at a glance. Seals varied considerably from one master or commanderie to the next. They denoted places or activities. Some referred to religious themes such as the Cross or the Holy Sepulcher, others to their armed duty, and still others to pagan symbols such as the sun and the moon.

No surviving written document explicitly proves the use of Solomon's seal by the Templars. Nonetheless, the order's formal code of conduct, or rule (see page 82), mentions "the house of Christ and of Solomon's temple" several times. The word *and* underlines the importance of Solomon in the eyes of the founders of the order. The knights are referred to constantly as "brothers of the temple," and the master as "master of the temple."

Interestingly, the order's rule quotes David several times, considering him not only as a prophet but as the deputy of Christ. For example, clause 35 of the rule states: "As Jesus Christ said through the mouth of David, and this is the truth, He obeyed me as soon as he heard me."

Although written documentation linking the Templars and Solomon's seal is lacking, evidence of the connection appears in the plans of the Templars' central commanderie in Paris, which was dismantled in 1805. The church was built across a rotunda where arches (drawn in gray on the diagram) clearly reveal Solomon's seal.

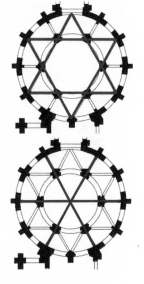

For Christians, the number 3 is extremely meaningful from a symbolic point of view. It represents the Holy Trinity of the Father, the Son, and the Holy Spirit. Sometimes another threesome is added: the life, death, and resurrection of Jesus Christ. Also, the Holy Trinity stands between the multitude of gods in pagan religions and the single god of the Jews. Therefore, Solomon's seal with its intertwined triangles is a natural extension of that symbolism, and nobody could object when the Templars placed it very naturally and in full view in the center of their main church. The rotunda's design displayed the vertices of the seal and, as if to insist on the relationship between the Holy Trinity and the seal, also laid bare the extremities of the three symmetrical axes. Note the characteristic six pillars.

The extant Temple Church in London (see in the diagram at the bottom) has the same design as the temple in Paris, proving that the use of the seal in Templar architecture was intentional. However, six-pillar rotundas were by no means the only architectural style used by the Templars. They did favor rotundas, but many of their buildings employed octagons. They may have reserved the six-pillar structures for special places.

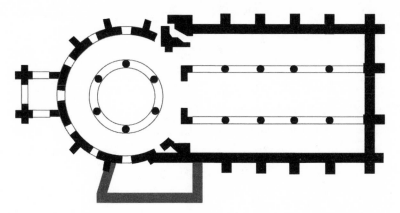

Communication Codes

Much like present-day concerns about using the Internet, when sending a document, the Templars needed to ensure the secrecy of the content and verify the authenticity of the source.

In their attempts to protect the contents, the Knights Templar generally are credited with a practical method of using crosses to produce ciphers. Unfortunately, except for a few traces of strange symbols in their documents, no specific description supports this thesis. We only have the testimony of the Master of Nemours, stating during his trial at the fall of the Templars, that he had taught 400 young knights how to use a cipher.

Indeed, in the course of their banking, which entailed preserving and carrying data over long distances, the Templars must have used a secret system to encipher sensitive information. Moreover, since they were in contact with Muslims who were much more advanced than Christians in cryptography in the twelfth and thirteenth centuries, not only did they need to protect data from them, they might have learned about cryptography from them. During the two centuries of the Templars' existence, they must have varied and evolved their codes. Unfortunately, the exact history of their cryptography is unknown today and will remain so unless new documents are discovered.

The methods ascribed to the Knights Templar are symbolic in that each letter is replaced by a symbol through the use of a systematic scheme. Letters correspond to a logical array of empty or dotted spaces on a geometrical cross. Although the use of a cross befits devout Christians, this is a weak method in light of contemporary knowledge, which allows us to break it by means of the "E backdoor" method (see Chapter 6). However, their method is interesting because it is the earliest example of the use of a "logical system" to organize a substitution code in which each letter is replaced with a symbol. As we'll see in Chapter 6, the main weakness of a symbolic method is that one has to own and travel with a table of the secret symbols; the code becomes useless and dangerous once the table is lost or stolen by one's enemies. A systematic (logical) scheme was an intelligent solution. When they traveled throughout Europe and western Asia, the Templars used a table that left no trace because it did not have to exist. Instead of being written, it was based on a logical principle, so that any member of the order, knowing the principle, could secretly reconstruct the table at will on a board or a piece of parchment.

The elementary nine-square cross encodes the main letters in use in the Middle Ages, where J is I and U is V, as in Roman times. The solution readily comes from reading the three tiers of two crosses (as seen in the diagram on the right), the first without and the second with deliberately positioned dots.

A	B	C
D	E	F
G	H	IJ

L	M	N
O•	P•	•R
S	T	UV

Decode:

The first sentence of the Rule of the Temple, in which the knights are required to renounce their own will and obey the king.

Decode:

Breaking a cross-based code is less simple when you don't know the cross with which it is built. Can you identify and reconstruct the cross used here to code the clause of reception for a new knight?

Decode:

A clause intended to encourage Templars to avoid undue and secret abstinence from food, which would impair a knight's ability to fight. Which cross is used here?

Decode:

What cross is used to code this clause on the Templars' private life? his cross can provide different symbols for all 26 modern letters.

Decode:

This cross codes numbers as well as letters and enciphers the account of a battle. Find the text and the cross.

The Call System

For immediate tactical communication, when they were moving or in combat, the Templars relied on a system of "calls." When the commanding officer issued an order, he chose from among a list of specific calls defined in the Rule of the Temple and cried it out. The call was repeated and spread from knight to knight until the whole troop had heard it and could act on it.

To maintain discipline, Templars were strictly forbidden to act before the corresponding call had been given. When they were on the move, every action was triggered by a precise call: waking up, starting, pausing, stopping for the night, gathering wood, feeding the horses, cooking, and so on. In combat, the calls were even more essential and centered on the all-important banner, or gonfanon, that was managed and carried high by five brothers. A sixth brother had a second gonfanon rolled around his lance in case the first one was destroyed or captured.

The Fall of the Templars

On Friday, October 13, 1307 (a date too heavily loaded with bad omens to have been chosen at random: a Friday, two 13s, and one 7), Philip the Fair, the king of France, launched a vast police action against the Knights Templar. Secretly prepared for months beforehand, it resulted in the imprisonment of all the masters in France. The activities of the brothers came to an abrupt halt.

The reasons for Philip's actions are not as clear as many people believe. Generally, greed and a struggle for power are stated as the king's motivations. In fact, though, the Templars hardly impinged on the king's political or military affairs, and since he had already appropriated most of their wealth in the preceding few years, there was little to seize. Moreover, what remained of the wealth of the order was under the Pope's jurisdiction and eventually was transferred to the Knights Hospitallers, not to the king's treasury.

There are similar doubts in regard to the accusations presented at the Templars' trial, which was devoid of real evidence except confessions extracted under torture and later denied. The Templars were accused of heresy and of adoring a god named Baphomet. For all we know, Baphomet is simply a distortion of Mahomet (Mohammed), a portmanteau word combining the words *blaspheme* and Mahomet cunningly forged by their accusers to disparage the Templars. It suggests that the Templars' enemies resented their contact with Muslims and accused them of adoring the Muslims' prophet. The Pope later absolved the Templars of any accusation of impiety.

Jerusalem Lost

The Knights Templar had outlived their usefulness as Christian warriors. Less than a century after their foundation, they lost Jerusalem. The king of Jerusalem, with their help, was able to maintain his power over the kingdom for the greater part of the twelfth century. He relied on his alliance with Egypt in the south against Syria in the northeast. He also was supported by occasional expeditions of European kings and princes, who came with well needed armed forces.

Unfortunately, the Christian forces badly lacked unity and were disorganized, to say the least. They brought to Palestine not only soldiers but also their old European quarrels and often fought with one another. Some did not respect the all-important alliance with the Egyptians and looted their caravans. Some betrayed other Christian brothers to the Muslims, including the Knights Templar, who were not above playing dirty tricks on the Knights Hospitaller in the midst of a battle, eventually causing their own deaths. Adding to the confusion, a third order, the Knights Teutonic, came from Northern Europe with its own agenda.

All this happened in a typical medieval epic of innumerable acts of outstanding bravery, with the Templars besieging and taking impregnable fortresses and engaging in battles against impossible odds—and eventually losing them: in 1187 Master Gérard de Ridefort attacked 7,000 Mamelukes with little more than 100 knights, only to be captured alone, with all his men having been killed. In twenty-first-century terms, the Holy Land had become the ideal proving ground for bellicose Europeans. Like contemporary enthusiasts of Second Life and World of Warcraft (see Chapter 9), they left their real lands and possessions for a place where they could battle at will, massacre enemies in the form of token avatars, and possibly die with no consequences for their "real" kin and kingdoms in Europe.

The truce with Egypt was finally ruined by the careless and deceitful actions of the Christians but also by the coming of Salah al-Din, a new sultan born in Iraq. He conquered Jerusalem on July 4, 1187, after a battle that was a disastrous defeat for the Christians. In 1226 his successor gave Jerusalem back to the Teutonic Knights and Frederick II, who had crowned himself king of Jerusalem the previous year, for 16 years. Even that didn't last, finally, and the last stronghold on the mainland, Saint John d'Acre, although defended to the last man by the knights of the three orders, Templars, Hospitallers and Teutonic together, was besieged and taken by the Mamelukes in 1291. The title of "king of Jerusalem" remained, but only to be worn offshore thereafter, on the islands of Cyprus, Malta, and Rhodes.

The Templar Heritage

The Templars' greatest achievement was to prove that a brotherhood could survive for two centuries and resist the temptations of power and wealth. No Templar abused his power or enriched himself personally. Unlike religious brotherhoods secluded in monasteries and protected from worldly temptations, the Templars lived in the world, successfully dealing with weapons and money without significantly breaking their vows. Their fall, when they submitted to destruction by the king without resistance, confirms their obedience to the law until the very end.

On a collective level, this makes them a prophetic model for secret societies, heralds of the power of an alliance of strength and purity. They died proving their importance to the living. The symbolism of their teaching is so pertinent and fundamental, it is not surprising that Freemasons, Rosicrucians, and others claim to be their direct descendants.

In a manner that might have inspired Isaac Asimov's *Foundation* saga, in which foundations perpetuate the failing empire "at both ends of the galaxy," the Knights Templar survived and redeveloped through two offshoots with no apparent link to each other at either end of the Christian world: one in Scotland and one on islands close to Asia Minor, the pair of them as far apart as can be. In this way, they were an important factor in the later development of secret societies.

Templar commanderies survived in Scotland, where King Philip the Fair of France had no influence. No longer dependent on a central power, those commanderies eventually gave birth to the lodges of Freemasonry. Though the actual historical descent from Templar to Freemason is controversial, the symbolic heritage is obvious and cannot be denied (see Chapter 5).

In the Middle East, after the loss of Saint John of Acre on the continent, the Knights Hospitallers remained offshore on Rhodes and then in Malta, where they lived in constant dread of the Turks. To support that outpost, they had forts called preceptories all over Europe, much like the commanderies of the Templars. They eventually had to leave Malta in 1798 when Napoleon, then General Bonaparte, took the island on his way to Egypt, before the English took it. However, after a brief sojourn with Orthodox Christians in Saint Petersburg, they survive today under the name the Knights of Malta.

Many people question the actual and continued affiliation of today's knights with the traditional order, yet, as with the Templars and Freemasons, the symbolic heritage cannot be denied.

Le Temple Today

In 1808, a few years after he had taken his crown from the hands of Pope Pius VII and consecrated himself emperor, Napoleon had the walls of the temple destroyed, erasing the last remaining traces of the Templars and Hospitallers from the center of Paris. He also might have wished to erase the place where Louis XVI and Marie-Antoinette had spent their last days before being guillotined to prevent it from becoming a royalist symbol. Ultimately, though, language and symbol have proved stronger than Napoleon's will since the place is still called le Temple.

Above: Le Temple, a public square and marketplace (above rue du Temple, left of rue de Bretagne) in the center of Paris, in an image from Google Earth.

Below: Le Temple: detail of a map drawn by Truschet and Hoyau circa 1552 (called the plan de Bâle because it was found later in Bâle, Switzerland). Note the differing spellings: *tenple* and *tample*.

CHAPTER 4

The Vitruvian Saga

A group of daring artists and architects revolutionized artistic creation in the fifteenth and sixteenth centuries. Inspired by Pythagoras's codebook of aesthetics and by the recently recovered books of Marcus Vitruvius, they came forward and presented themselves as new models of harmony and creativity.

Leonardo da Vinci's Golden Boy

Leonardo da Vinci's Vitruvian man—his *uomo vitruviano*—stands out as the fifteenth-century golden boy. The picture is his best-known drawing and probably the most famous drawing ever. It has been printed in innumerable books and used in countless advertisements to illustrate harmony and geometry in art. Many associate it with the golden mean, a revival of Pythagoras's aesthetic codebook in Renaissance art. Today, with Dan Brown's *The Da Vinci Code*, it has become a symbol of arcane knowledge and hidden powers.

Contrary to popular belief, Leonardo's man is not unique but one among many similar icons. In the Renaissance of the fifteenth and sixteenth centuries, that theme inspired many artists, all of whom referred to a book that had triggered their passion for geometry. After rediscovering the works of the Roman architect Vitruvius, they expressed their own views on art and proposed their own Vitruvian men.

Thus, a series of artists followed a path on which Leonardo represents only one step. We are so blinded by Leonardo's talents that we tend to disregard the works of his fellow creators. Some of them were more intent on refining the Pythagorean code than on creating beauty, but they all worked toward the expression of freedom, toward the creation of a modern man.

Man, Square, and Circle

Vitruvius's books have no illustrations and are generally obscure. However, one paragraph was clear enough to generate the whole Vitruvian style:

> *Similarly, in the members of a temple there ought to be the greatest harmony in the symmetrical relations of the different parts to the general magnitude of the whole. Then again, in the human body the central point is naturally the navel. For if a man can be placed flat on his back, with his hands and feet extended, and a pair of compasses centered at his navel, the fingers and toes of his two hands and feet will touch the circumference of a circle described therefrom. And*

just as the human body yields a circular outline, so too a square figure may be found from it. For if we measure the distance from the soles of the feet to the top of the head, and then apply that measure to the outstretched arms, the breadth will be found to be the same as the height, as in the case of plane surfaces which are completely square. (Marcus Vitruvius, De Architectura, Book III, Chapter 1)

The square-and-circle template began to emerge in Western culture in the twelfth century. It spread slowly at first, often hidden behind a more general interest in geometry. Then it began to stand out, eventually becoming more important than any other geometrical form and undergoing an acceleration in interest in the fifteenth and sixteenth centuries of the Renaissance era. It all but blotted out Pythagoras's pentagram, the geometric center of the Pythagorean world. Only occultists remained concerned with the pentagram, perhaps to emphasize their difference.

A similar interest in geometry had emerged in the Near East in a culture that was also heir to the Greeks and the Romans. However, the Muslim religion forbade representation of the human body, and that led Arab artists to develop different artistic forms. In Muslim art, geometry is all-powerful. The circle and the square play secondary roles, all but buried in mind-boggling networks of fascinating geometrical lines. Rugs and frescoes have virtually no boundaries. Their patterns are poised to replicate themselves endlessly in all directions. Whereas Western art centers on the human body, Muslim art hides man and woman and instead becomes a tool for unlimited conquest of the universe.

In the West, the square-and-circle template created a new world of art. In spite of its extreme simplicity, it appealed to most prominent artists of the early second millennium. For two centuries, mainstream artists explored all possible combinations of the human body and the square and circle. In the twentieth century that practice enjoyed a revival. Mondrian, for one, centered an essential part of his work on the square and the circle (see Chapter 2).

Contrary to their Arab colleagues, Western artists were not concerned with patterns spreading infinitely over the world. They achieved a similar result with what a modern physicist would call radiation technology. The human body is placed in such a strategic situation in the absolute simplicity of the square and circle that it radiates limitless energy over the world and thus appropriates its space. We'll see later in this chapter how a human body empowered by the dynamic combination of the rational square and the irrational circle discovered by the Pythagoreans (see Chapter 2) experiences limitless expansion.

Hildegard von Bingen: Freedom in a Cell

The first known Vitruvian man was envisioned by an extraordinary woman, Hildegard von Bingen, who lived in the twelfth century and literally had visions. As early as age four years, she saw luminous pictures. She was smart enough to keep those visions to herself, knowing that nobody would believe her and that it would only make trouble. Fortunately, she was the tenth child in a wealthy family and it was determined at her birth that she would become a nun. This was the general rule in the Middle Ages; just as the church tax, the tithe, was a tenth of a family's revenues, a tenth of the family's children belonged to the Church.

Hildegard grew up to be a remarkable woman with many talents, becoming a composer, a healer, and a writer. At age 38, she was elected head of a small convent. In the years that followed, in a vision more powerful than those before, she saw God, who ordered her to transcribe her visions. She did that, and her fame became so great and her faith and her intelligence so respected that bishops, kings, and popes came to her for advice.

The manner in which Hildegard received her education had a great influence on her works and possibly on the Vitruvian saga as well. Starting at age eight, she attended school in the cell of a hermit, or anchoress, named Jutta. That woman had vowed to remain in her cell for the rest of her life, and such people were not uncommon in the Middle Ages, choosing lifestyles one step beyond that of living in a convent. To symbolize their choice, they enacted a faux burial mass, entering the cell that was to be their final home in a coffin. That dramatic act showed that they were dead to the world and thereafter would live a life of contemplation.

Jutta made an exception to her contemplative life by sharing her experiences with children. Every day she opened her door to Hildegard and a dozen other girls, who were allowed to witness how a mystic lived in the confinement of a small cell. Joining the hermit in her prayers, they shared her mystic experiences and observed how a woman could remain physically in a cell and expand her mind to reach the extreme limits of the universe.

In spite of her faith, Hildegard later regretted that her education consisted more of prayers than of actual lessons. Her Latin never was good enough to write books by herself, but that may have benefited her. When writing, she needed a scribe to phrase her

thoughts in proper Latin. A Benedictine monk, Volmar, played that role for her. This means that for years Hildegard spoke and exchanged ideas with a monk of the Benedictine order, which was famous for the libraries in its monasteries. This gave her direct access to the knowledge and the philosophy of the Greeks and the Romans, preserved by the Benedictine monks, and allows us to suppose that she read books on Pythagoras and possibly Vitruvius.

In her final visions, Hildegard seems to have combined the influence of the anchoress with that of the Benedictines. In her art she painted characters who communicated with the rest of the world while they stood in round cells. The four winds blow upon them, lines connect them to animals and planets, and a Benedictine scribe watches and records the scene (see the illustration above). In one presentation, the world is turning on itself. In another, the world is inside a man's body that is crowned by the head of God. In both presentations, man is free of clothing and of any tie to others. No crucifixion is ever shown.

Hildegard's Pythagorean inspiration is demonstrated by the similarity of her visions to a bas-relief on a Pythagorean pillar erected in 250 C.E. in Igel, on the Roman road from Trier, Germany, to Rheims, France. The four winds blow on the zodiacal circle where Hildegard placed her Vitruvian instead of the original Herakles triumphally drawn by horses.

Another vision features a woman in blue (see the illustration at the right). Is she Hildegard or her hermit mentor? Although barefoot, she is clothed. The strictly geometric circles around her may represent the purely mystical universe of

the anchoress, with her disregard for mundane interests. The presentation is rather severe for the only known woman in the Vitruvian saga.

In one important detail Hildegard's vision of space is very different from that of later Renaissance Vitruvians. Hildegard's circle is encompassed by a square but does not let the square bind it. The circle breaks away from strict geometry; its line encroaches on the line of the square and all but cancels it. In other words, even if Hildegard followed the idea of the Vitruvian square and circle, she did not feel bound by it. She went beyond its strict geometric code, claiming freedom from the square and circle, a step that even the most creative Renaissance artists would have found it hard to take.

For Hildegard, the square-and-circle presentation meant more than the Pythagorean aesthetic code as she added a mystical dimension. We will see that Renaissance artists ignored that spiritual dimension until the scholar and teacher Cornelius Agrippa (see page 124) reintroduced it through his interest in occultism. Agrippa also would feel the need to reintroduce woman, but only in his literary works.

Villard de Honnecourt

It was a century later when the next Vitruvian man showed his face—still two centuries before the time of Leonardo da Vinci. This man appeared mysteriously in a portfolio

of 33 parchment sheets sewn together and crammed with over 200 drawings. Some of the pages also bear written notes. The book is all that remains and all that we know of its owner, Villard de Honnecourt. We know his name because he mentions it in his writings, asking the reader to pray for his soul.

Browsing through the portfolio is fascinating. One discovers portraits, scenes, animals, automatons, plans of buildings, sculptures, and machines—even a perpetual motion machine. All are drawn with a sure and precise hand, often with humor. Some have called Villard the Gothic Leonardo da Vinci.

Villard's portfolio is one of the only two architectural documents on parchment that have survived from ancient times or even the Middle Ages and the Gothic era. The other document is older—from the ninth century—and happens to be the plan of the abbey of St. Gall, where Vitrivius's books were preserved and rediscovered, later to play an essential role for Renaissance artists and of course the Vitruvians.

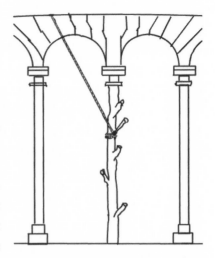

Historians first thought that Villard was an architect and a craftsman. The many plans in the portfolio suggest that he was on the construction sites of at least eight Gothic buildings. Other drawings suggest knowledge of the trade secrets of the mason and carver guilds. For example, he describes the art of cutting stones precisely to build a vault. He even shows the building of a "hanging arch," where two vaults meet and hang without a pillar to support them—a mason's masterpiece, the most daring achievement to which a Gothic architect could aspire. The temporary central pillar is a tree trunk with a rope fastened to it, ready to be pulled out when all the stones are in place (see the illustration above). Although this does not prove that Villard built such an arch, it shows that he was aware of the state of the art.

As was common in the thirteenth century, Villard might have been both an architect and a contractor. He would have conceived plans for buildings and then attended to the management of construction sites, taking care of all the practical details on the spot.

Villard remains an enigma. Nothing in his portfolio proves that he was an architect or a master builder. His written notes on some of the pages give him the right to claim the title, but when he asks future readers to remember him in their prayers, he fails to call himself "Master." Of course, this does not prove anything. On the basis of their analyses of the 250 drawings in the portfolio, historians have written an impressive number of articles and books on "the problem of Villard." Today scholars tend to see him as an artist and a learned dilettante who traveled to observe and take part in the most important events of his time.

Artist and/or architect, Villard was an early and enthusiastic adept of the Pythagorean geometric code. He wrote that "here begins the force of lines for drafting, as the art of geometry teaches." In other words, creation comes from geometry. Geometric lines drive creation. Geometry comes first, the source of all crafts.

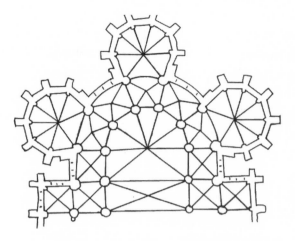

Villard's portfolio shows two different uses of geometry: first as an aesthetic code and then as a craftsman's tool. In the design of a cathedral, the plan may follow geometric patterns: a rectangle for the main building, an octagon for the choir, smaller rectangles for the transept, and so on. If these are all basic geometric figures, they are purely aesthetic choices made by the architect, who wishes to feature only perfect figures. Such choices, however, are by no mean necessary. The architect just as well could have chosen fanciful lines in random directions and at random angles. However, when it came to building the cathedral, he had to obey the laws of perfect geometry if he wanted the stones to stay in place, the vault to bear the weight of the roof, and the walls to remain standing. Perfect plans and random plans thus have the same effect on the stability of the building.

So why take the trouble to design perfectly geometrical plans? Is it nothing but professional pride? Are mason-architects so proud of their knowledge of geometry that they insist on displaying it in every aspect of their work? Villard's portfolio offers a better answer: design geometry and aesthetic geometry depend on each other in that one cannot exist without the other. Geometry in design is a code that architects use to talk to the universe. According to Pythagoras, the universe is built on perfect geometry. If we

build perfect geometrical forms, we are in harmony with the inner structure of the universe, speak the language of the hidden forces of the universe, and draw strength and energy from the same source. This is the compagnon carpenters' ideal goal (see Chapter 5).

Villard's heads, bodies, animals, and scenes are created with precise geometrical figures. He builds heads by using the three elementary figures: the triangle, square, and pentagram.

Both Villard and Leonardo da Vinci are Pythagoreans, but in very different ways. Villard's creations are based on and structured by

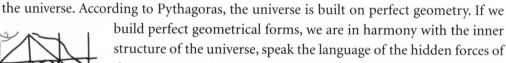

geometry. The geometric lines of the square, triangle, and pentagram are inside the bodies, like bones, as if the lines were drawn first and then flesh was grown on them. On the contrary, as with most other Vitruvians, as we shall see, Leonardo's man inhabits geometry but is not necessarily part of it. Geometric figures lie outside his body. He lives in the inner space, inside the square and circle. He may not be free to leave the square and circle, but within them he is free. Villard's creatures, in contrast, are made of geometric bones but are free to roam the world, bringing their inner geometry with them. Evolution followed both paths, putting bones inside fish and mammals and out-

side crustaceans and other invertebrates. With the advent of modern technology, modern architects can build with either endoskeletons or exoskeletons.

Villard lived two centuries before the revolution in printing brought about by Gutenberg, but like all educated people of that time, he must have read manuscripts. The copying and circulation of manuscripts was an active trade. Books on geometry were translated from Arabic into Latin and even into local languages such as Middle French. Villard may have read copies of those books, along with a copy of Vitruvius's works, in a monastery.

The drawing shown above provides a strange glimpse of the future. Among several other animals, Villard draws an eagle. The geometry reveals that its skeleton is a hidden pentagram. The symbol will assume an important role several centuries later, but this is still two centuries before Columbus landed in America and six centuries before the advent of the pentagram-spangled banner (see Chapter 7).

Another surprise in Villard's work is a drawing (shown at the right) that can only be called *The Perpetual Carvers*. Arranged in a perfectly centered symmetry, four men are carving one another. The composition may be nothing more than a humorous curiosity, an impossible

figure that would not be disowned by someone like Mauritz Escher (see the drawing to the left). That in itself is a surprising feat for a thirteenth-century artist.

However, there is proof that the perpetual carvers are more than a piece of humor. On another folio Villard draws the plans for a perpetual motion engine. Seven weights are arranged around a wheel. As the wheel goes around, each weight falls in turn; its momentum is designed to give the wheel the energy to continue. A note, however, expresses Villard's doubts about its feasibility. This proves that Villard had a

personal interest in both time and physics and had given thought to the problems of time and the possible paradoxes of perpetual motion. His scene relates to the paradox of time forever renewing itself.

On yet another page Villard draws a "wheel of fortune." This was a popular theme in the Middle Ages, but Villard turns it into an exercise in geometry. His characters are geometric puppets. The wheel of time keeps turning and in so doing distributes a fixed catalogue of fortunes to its geometrical characters. Time is nothing but a geometrical figure that reduces its subjects to their geometric skeletons.

This set of drawings suggests at least two interpretations. One is that the perpetual carvers symbolize the eternally surprising birth of freedom. At every instant in time,

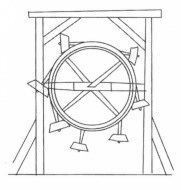

freedom is a possibility if one is carving oneself. Villard and his mutually creating men are forever carving themselves. They are self-carved men, so to speak: the Gothic equivalent of the modern self-made man. They are forever fresh and new in history.

Another interpretation is that the drawings illustrate the Pythagorean theme of the eternal return. Time repeats itself. Given a long enough interval, all things will come to be again and again in a future that is an infinite repetition of itself.

Because he needed it to complete his theory of universal harmony, Pythagoras imported this theme from Egyptian philosophy into Greek thought. The world obeys geometric symmetry in three-dimensional space as well as in the dimension of time.

The two interpretations are not necessarily exclusive; on the contrary, they complement each other. Humankind is part of an eternally recurrent world yet has the hope of carving out freedom from the perpetual wheel of time. We are eternally making ourselves anew.

Whatever Villard's thinking behind the drawings was, the Pythagorean code is present and shows him to be a man of action. Geometry triggers him into action.

The Vitruvian Revival

Vitruvius was all but forgotten in Europe at the beginning of the fifteenth century. Fortunately, Poggio Bracciolini was both a book hunter and an apostolic secretary under several popes and thus had ample opportunity to travel and search monastic libraries throughout Europe. He discovered many Latin manuscripts of books that had been thought to be lost forever.

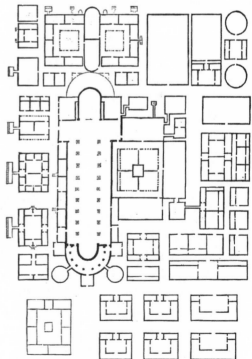

In 1414, Bracciolini went to Switzerland to attend the Council of Constance. Organized by the bishops, who were seeking peace and order in the Church, the council was an event of exceptional importance. When it started, there were three rival popes, one of them an antipope. When it closed, two popes had resigned, a third had been demoted, and a fourth had been elected! The council lasted four years with occasional interruptions of several months, during which Bracciolini explored the libraries in the surrounding area.

In one of those libraries he unearthed a manuscript of Vitruvius's work in the monastery whose ninth-century plan is the oldest known architectural document: the monastery of Saint Gall in Switzerland. He copied the manuscript and sent it to Florence, where it was edited by scholars. Vitruvius's works were available in manuscript form throughout the fifteenth century. They finally were printed, text only, by Sulpitius Veralanus in Rome in 1486, making use of the recent technology of Gutenberg's press. In the meantime, many artists, such as Taccola (see page 112) and Leonardo, would have had an opportunity to read the manuscript or browse through it.

Marcus Vitruvius Pollio was a Roman who lived in the first century B.C.E., a contemporary of Julius Caesar. He was an architect, an engineer, and a craftsman who wrote *The Ten Books on Architecture*, which also dealt with urbanism and mechanical design. His fame is due largely to the fact that his book is the only one on architecture that survived from ancient times through the Middle Ages. Vitruvius never claimed to be an original creator and willingly revealed his sources: the great Greek mathematicians such as Pythagoras, Ctesibius, and Archimedes.

Unfortunately, none of Vitruvius's buildings survived. Other authors mention them, but without enough details to reveal exactly where they stood. Even worse, Vitruvius's book came to us without images. We are left to imagine the plans and designs from his descriptions. Worse yet, his Latin is so obscure and difficult that as Leone Battista Alberti put it, "the Latins thought he wrote in Greek and the Greeks thought he wrote in Latin."

That obscurity enhanced Vitruvius's usefulness as a trigger for innovation. Since his writings were hard to understand, every reader could interpret them in his own way and give free reign to his creativity. As a result, Vituvius's message seeded the world of the Pythagoreans with a variety of original creators, painters, sculptors, and builders, all claiming to follow his precepts. This produced the widely different aspects of the Vitruvian men.

Vitruvius's works, like Greek and Roman culture in general, were preserved and copied through two main channels during the Middle Ages. In Europe, particularly during the ninth century, the "Carolingian Renaissance," this work was done by monks in the "palace scriptorium" of Charlemagne. In the Middle East, the Arabs, who had inherited the Alexandrian libraries, were very active at copying, translating, and preserving ancient books. An "Arabian Renaissance" flourished in the ninth and tenth centuries.

Not all copyists, European or Arab, had complete respect for the original texts. Some people thought it necessary to expand on or explain Vitruvius, occasionally inserting their own views as if Vitruvius had written them. What has reached us is a collective, sometimes misleading work that is nonetheless all the more fecund for the creative reader.

The Case of the Vanishing Mean

A common legend asserts that Vitruvius invented the expression the "golden mean." This story is found in many books and on the Internet. In fact, nothing could be further from the truth. Vitruvius never mentions the golden section anywhere in his book. It appears that he never knew it existed. True, he was a geometry enthusiast and recommended the use of squares and circles in all types of architecture, but he never went beyond squares or mentioned pentagrams. Pentagrams were known to Gothic artists but were all but ignored by Renaissance artists until Cornelius Agrippa apparently rediscovered them through Arabian sources.

As for irrational numbers, the square root of 2—as the diagonal of a square—is the upper limit of Vitruvius's audacity. There is not a single square root of 5 in any of his works and hence no golden mean.

Nonetheless, Vitruvius's editors and translators, all of whom were Renaissance artists, are credited with an intimate knowledge of the golden mean, making daily use of it in their work. In an effort to prove the existence of the golden mean, enthusiasts drew lines across the best works of art. Leonardo Da Vinci, for one, is supposed to have been a golden mean master. However, none of this is true. Leonardo never drew one or wrote about one, and there is no known use of the mean in fifteenth- or sixteenth-century art. The golden mean had been mentioned in geometry books since the time of Euclid, but simply as a mathematical phenomenon that played no specific role in art. It was first mentioned in relation to art in the middle of the nineteenth century (see Chapter 2).

The Square and Circle Template

In spite of the lack of illustrations in Vitruvius's book and the general obscurity of his writings, one paragraph was clear enough to generate the Vitruvian style:

> *Similarly, in the members of a temple there ought to be the greatest harmony in the symmetrical relations of the different parts to the general magnitude of the whole. Then again, in the human body the central point is naturally the navel. For if a man can be placed flat on his back, with his hands and feet extended, and a pair of compasses centered at his navel, the fingers and toes of his two hands and feet will touch the circumference of a circle described therefrom. And just as the human body yields a circular outline, so too a square figure may be*

found from it. For if we measure the distance from the soles of the feet to the top of the head, and then apply that measure to the outstretched arms, the breadth will be found to be the same as the height, as in the case of plane surfaces which are completely square. (Marcus Vitruvius, De Architectura, *Book III, Chapter 1)*

Taccola's Newborn Mason

Mariano di Jacopo (1382–1458), known as Taccola (the Crow), was a talented etcher and carver. He was a technical engineer and the inventor of many machines, such as the vertically axled windmill and water mill, the chain transmission system, and the compound crank with a connecting rod. The last machine was an essential concept for postmedieval technology. He was also one of the first Renaissance architects.

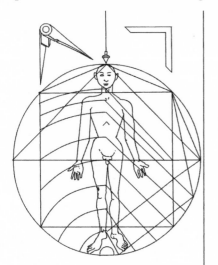

In one of his technical manuscripts, Taccola drew the first known Renaissance Vitruvian man. His character is a craftsman's puppet, geometrically determined by the compass, plumb line, and square. He stands as a template for all the later Vitruvians. There is no fancy irrational line, simply a circle encompassing the body and a square encompassed by the circle. Lines and arcs are generated by the square rule and the compass. Some straight lines are not quite parallel; this may suggest the use of perspective.

Taccola's *De ingeneis* was written before 1450. This suggests that Taccola knew Vitruvius in manuscript form. He might have been the first to transcribe Vitruvius's code into a drawing, expressing the ideas with no other intention than a desire to experiment with the Vitruvian system and see its results. Yet this picture is not a quick draft. The human and geometrical elements are carefully staged to create a harmonic rendering of the geometric universe. Taccola's man is still enmeshed in geometrical lines. He is the first graphic statement of the Renaissance man experiencing his freedom in a new interpretation of the Pythagorean code.

The scene is worth a second look for a different reason. All the sacred Masonic tools are there, such as the square and the compass. Is this a Masonic initiation, strongly influenced by Christianity and closely resembling a baptism? In Christian terms, one might say that a newborn Vitruvian, plunged into a circle-and-square baptismal font and bathed in geometrical lines, is blessed by the compass, square, and plumb line (the thread and lead weight used by a mason to ensure that a wall is vertical).

Is this a traditional Masonic initiation as it was practiced in the Middle Ages? Did the Roman Masonic brotherhoods survive into the fourteenth century? If that is the case, Taccola's drawing is a key document that proves the existence of a well-organized Masonic brotherhood in Italy at a time when Freemasonry was just beginning to emerge in Scotland and England. It lets us imagine the initiation rites. Those brotherhoods may have been active in preserving the Pythagorean and Vitruvian heritage in the Middle Ages.

Taccola's drawing suggests that the first Renaissance Vitruvian was a Freemason.

Francesco di Giorgio Martini

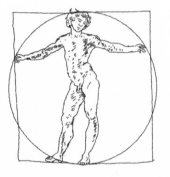

The artist Francesco di Giorgio Martini (1439–1502) created the casual Vitruvians. In his treatise on architecture (*Trattato di architettura, ingegneria e arte militare*), which was written and hand-drawn around 1482, his characters demonstrate total freedom yet are in harmony with the Pythagorean codebook.

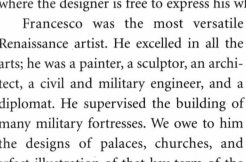

They are bound by the square-and-circle code and never step out of the geometric lines but are free to play inside them and with the elements. The square-and-circle cell is present, but nonchalant postures are welcomed. The Pythagorean universe becomes a playground where the designer is free to express his whims.

Francesco was the most versatile Renaissance artist. He excelled in all the arts; he was a painter, a sculptor, an architect, a civil and military engineer, and a diplomat. He supervised the building of many military fortresses. We owe to him the designs of palaces, churches, and cities. He is the perfect illustration of that key term of the Renaissance: he is a "humanist," always concerned with the presence of humankind in the world. His art, geometry, and architecture work together for the glory of the human body.

At least while drawing his first drafts, Francesco gave his fanciful imagination free reign to create in all directions, although not in vain. He conceived of buildings as clothes happily worn by his Vitruvians. They would try on a tower as a hat. They put on the stone walls of churches and palaces as if they were light satin. The original geometric cell turned into a dress. The aesthetic code became a dress code.

This playful spirit might qualify as childish if Francesco had not been a respected architect who left a legacy of churches, palaces, military art, and paintings. Few can enjoy such freedom of thought while being efficient engineers and builders. Hardly any other Renaissance artist displayed so much joyous spirit.

Leone Battista Alberti

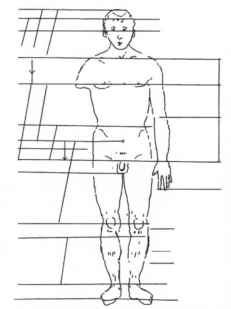

Leone Battista Alberti (1406–1472) was the leading theoretician of his century. He had a talent for building science out of practical knowledge. Although a real craftsman who built churches and palaces, he had a gift for revealing the mathematics behind the practical know-how. He applied his talent to a wide variety of activities. In architecture he developed the theory of harmony, the art of combining symmetry and pleasant proportions. In painting he developed perspective. In cryptography he developed new polyalphabetic methods, or "homophones," as we'll see in Chapter 6, serving as one of the bridges between two aspects of code: aesthetics and cipher. He was also a geographer and, with Paolo dal Pozzo Toscanelli, drew the maps Columbus used when he sailed to America.

Since Alberti was active in the early Renaissance, the first part of the fifteenth century, he became a reference for later artists. His work on proportions was based on Vitruvius's book, but he turned that obscure text into a handy, readable reference. He also spent time studying Roman architecture directly in the ruins of the old city.

Eventually, Alberti became a more frequently used reference than Vitruvius. His *De re aedificatoria* (1452), composed of 10 books like Vitruvius's work, remained the classic treatise on architecture until the eighteenth century. Architects would mention that they had designed a building "according to Alberti" as a guarantee of the aesthetic and structural qualities of their plans.

Alberti's first Vitruvian was reduced to the function of a yardstick. He provided useful measurements for building according to the proportions of a human body. His other Vitruvian, like no other of that generation, was fully dressed. We lack the documents to support this conjecture, but apparently Alberti alone was concerned by dress code as such and the role it should play in the harmony of life in the city. He might have felt that a character's clothing was a sufficient limit to its space. The square and the circle would be added by other creators.

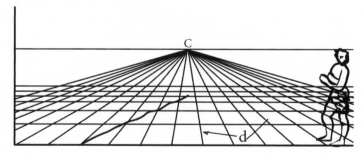

In the illustration above, a character peers at a strange phenomenon: the geometric lines of perspective. In 1457, just as Gutenberg was starting to use his printing technology, in his book *Della Pittura*, Alberti describes how to code three-dimensional space onto a flat surface, giving a third dimension to a canvas or a sheet of paper. This code was so good that even today it fools the human eye into believing that a flat set of lines is a three-dimensional solid. With perspective, Alberti created a new science.

Luca Pacioli's Divine Proportion

Fra Luca Pacioli (1445–1517) was a fine mathematician who was educated at the university in Bologna. One of his legacies is used daily in the modern world: he invented  the double-entry system of bookkeeping, the basic tool of all accountants. His goal was to help poor people manage the little money they had so that they could lead a better life. Apart from this practical invention, he was interested in art and was influenced by the rediscovery of Vitruvius's works. Instead of editing or translating Vitruvius, he wrote his own book about his theories. His *De divina proportione* (*Concerning Divine Proportion*) owes its success mainly to the talent of his graphic artist, Leonardo da Vinci, who contributed his "Vitruvian man" and an impressive series of three-dimensional representations of the Platonic solids.

The attitude of the Vitruvian character displayed in Pacioli's book stood as an aesthetic reference for all the artists of his generation. However, in spite of the fame of those pictures, they are not quite what they seem to be. The reality behind those works is worth exploring in detail.

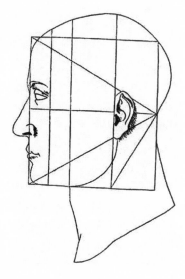

The striking three-dimensional renderings of the Platonic solids (see Chapter 2) by Leonardo seem to show that he had mastered and applied Alberti's science of perspective. It is undeniable that he knew about it. As he wrote in one of his notebooks, "The art of perspective is of such a nature as to make what is flat appear in relief and what is in relief flat." He then went on to explain the theory. In the 1490s, perspective was a fashionable technology. Alberti's first works had been developed further by Piero della Francesca. Thus, it seems logical to consider the solids as Leonardo's application of the new science. However, this is probably misleading: Leonardo was interested in perspective, but more as an artist than as a practicing geometer. There is no proof that he actually applied perspective. Although he wrote extensively on the theory, he left no diagram showing his use of the horizon lines and vanishing points. On the contrary, historical documents reveal that he had the solids made of wood by a joiner. He probably drew them as models, as he would have drawn a face or an insect. We still have the records of the city of Florence later buying the wooden models for a public exhibition.

De divina proportione was published in Venice in 1509. Along with the solids, it featured Leonardo's square-and-circle Vitruvian man, which had been drawn several years

earlier in his notebooks. It would be more accurate, however, to call the character the "active man." He is drawn in perpetual motion, alternately indicating the square or the circle with his hands and alternately standing on the circle or on the square. In doing this, he expresses two ideas: first, he shows that he inhabits Vitruvius's geometric code, demonstrating that the square and the circle are his rightful environment. Second, he manifests Leonardo's interest in the quadrature of the circle.

Squaring the circle is an old problem that resisted the efforts of Pythagoras and Euclid, who looked for a "pure" solution. It consists in finding a square that has the same area as a particular circle. A pure solution would produce the square with the help of the rule and the compass only. That is impossible, but only modern geometry can prove this, hence the failure and frustration of traditional geometers. However, any schoolchild knows the "impure" solution: the area of the square is the square of the radius multiplied by pi. The impossibility of the pure solution comes from the fact that pi is not a rational number.

Leonardo da Vinci mentioned the quadrature of the circle several times in his notebooks. For example, he wrote in 1475: "Archimedes gave the quadrature of a polygonal figure, but not that of the circle. Hence Archimedes never squared any figure with curved sides." In 1504 Leonardo apparently contradicted himself: "This was first done by Archimedes of Syracuse, who by multiplying the second diameter of a circle by half its circumference produced a rectangular quadrilateral figure equal to the circle." In fact,

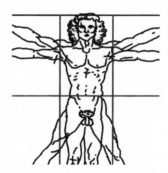

one note refers to the actual computation of the area of the circle, which is indeed half the circumference multiplied by half the diameter. The other note refers to the age-old impossible pure solution.

Leonardo made abundant references to proportions, but they were always simple ratios. Nowhere did he mention an irrational number, let alone the golden mean. For instance, one footnote says, "The cubit is one fourth of the height of a man and is equal to the greatest width of the shoulders. From the joint of one shoulder to the other is two faces and is equal to the distance from the top of the breast to the navel."

Elsewhere he described "Vitruvius' scheme of proportions." This certainly would have given him an opportunity to mention the golden mean, yet instead he wrote: "Vitruvius, the architect, says in his work on architecture that the measurements of the human body are distributed by Nature as follows: that is that 4 fingers make 1 palm, and 4 palms make 1 foot, 6 palms make 1 cubit; 4 cubits make a man's height. And 4 cubits make one pace and 24 palms make a man; and these measures he used in his buildings." This plainly contradicts other authors, who see the golden mean in the proportions of the fingers, the palm, the foot, and the cubit (see page 50).

Decode:

Leonardo da Vinci enciphered some pages of his notebooks to preserve the confidentiality of his notes.

I cannot forbear to mention among these precepts a new device for study which although it may seem but trivial and almost ludicrous, is nevertheless extremely useful in arousing the mind to various inventions. And this is, when you look at a wall spotted with stains, or with a mixture of stones, if you have to devise some scene, you may discover a resemblance to various landscapes, beautified with mountains, rivers, rocks, trees, plains, wide valleys and hills in varied arrangement; or again you may see battles and figures in action; or strange faces and costumes, and an endless variety of objects, which you could reduce to complete and well drawn forms. And these appear on such walls confusedly, like the sound of bells in whose jangle you may find any name or word you choose to imagine.

Decode:

You probably solved the preceding cipher in a few seconds either because you already had heard of Leonardo da Vinci's secret scheme or guessed its method. Leonardo could have imagined similar methods, such as this one, which codes an unexpected joke by the master:

It was asked of a painter why, since he made such dead things, which were but dead figures, serujif lutitu-ably and his children by night, and his pictures by day, that he made his children by night.

When golden mean fundamentalists claim its presence in Leonardo's Vitruvian man, they are obliged to disregard the proportion lines provided by the artist. They draw a horizontal line through the navel, whereas Leonardo draws one over the pelvis; draw vertical lines outside Leonardo's vertical lines; and so forth. Why this disregard for the lines Leonardo himself put into his picture?

Giovanni Giocondo

Fra Giovanni Giocondo (c. 1445–c. 1525), a Franciscan friar, was the editor and publisher of the first illustrated translation of Vitruvius, which was published in Venice in 1511. Like Vitruvius, he was an architect and an engineer; he was responsible for the drainage system of Venice's lagoons. Like Leonardo, he was court architect to a king of France and helped bring Renaissance art to that country. In Paris, he built the bridge across the Seine to Notre-Dame Cathedral, which is still standing.

Giocondo's edition of Vitruvius features images of Vitruvian men. Somewhat less elegant and daring than Leonardo's, they are displayed one in a square and one in a circle. Instead of juxtaposing the two geometric figures in an allusion to mathematical research, Giocondo remains as straightforward as possible and develops the difference between the figures. The straight lines of the square offer only a barren cell for its personage. The softer curves of the circle provide a flowered cell with a happier inhabitant, less formally crucified, although his head is tilted slightly as in many other crucifixion scenes (see the illustration to the left).

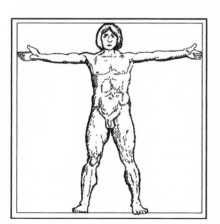

Here, contrary to Leonardo's presentation, both cells are firmly enclosed within heavy frames. Even the flowers remain inside the (Eden-like?) square encompassing the circle. The meaning is clear: total freedom, but only within the cell. Is this due to the fact that Giocondo was a Franciscan monk? He does not attempt to escape from formal geometry, whereas Leonardo draws his code in light lines and has his active character step on it as a springboard—a golden Icarus, ready to fly to new adventures.

Giocondo makes no attempt to show more details of the Vitruvian code beyond the circle and the square. The symbols are clear enough; there is no need to exhibit proportions.

Cesare Cesariano

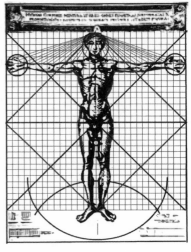

Cesare Cesariano published the most abundantly illustrated translation of Vitruvius in 1521. He displays two Vitruvian men, both tied up in a swarm of geometrical lines (see the illustrations to the right and below).

One is pinned like a butterfly between two webs. A checkerboard background ensures that the space beneath him is closed. A foreground of wide rhombi stands as a fence, keeping him from jumping away from geometry. His hands and head are haloed in circles, with perspective lines receding toward a vanishing point above his head.

Perspective is mentioned but not used. Other than the man's body, there is no cube or other solid to demonstrate three-dimensional space. The body is outlined in graceful

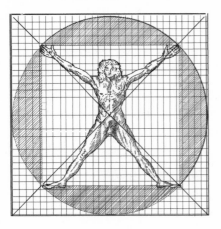

shapes, softly rounded like polished marble, in contrast to the lifelike muscles of the Leonardo da Vinci figure.

The receding lines also can be seen in reverse, radiating from the top of the head. In this case, the circle around the head reinforces the halo and emphasizes the saintly nature of the Vitruvian man. Two other arcs enclose a magic space around the figure's feet.

Cesariano literally quarters his second Vitruvian man on a square-and-circle figure. However, the geometry is less ambitious than Leonardo's. The square is no longer the fancy circle-squaring puzzle of Leonardo. It is only the largest square that can be drawn inside the circle, the square encompassed within a circle—an easy problem that any school child can solve.

Francesco Giorgi

In Francesco Giorgi's *De harmonia mundi totius* (*Concerning Universal Harmony*), which was published in Venice in 1525, there appears the simplest Vitruvian man of all. The character is naked inside a bare circle. He is, however, in an original posture that gives him five points of contact—head, hands, and feet—with the surrounding circle in such a way that the picture becomes a subtle display of the pentagram without actually drawing it. Those who know will see it as the first official sighting of the pentagram since Villard de Honnecourt.

Giorgi (1466–1540) was a friend of Heinrich Cornelius Agrippa, with whom he worked at developing a Christian Kabbala. This move toward occultism led Giorgi and Agrippa away from the purely aesthetic use of the Pythagorean code and toward the realm of the mystical.

Giorgi's official business in England was to help Henry VIII with his divorce. The Catholic king placed great hopes in the help of an Italian friar with his problems with the Pope. There are those, however, who see Giorgi as a secret agent of Venice who was sent to foreign countries, especially England. He has been called "the Cabalist Friar of Venice." His mission would have been to spread the intellectual poison of occultism among the scientific circles of London. The antiscientific irrationalism of magic was to be used to undermine scientific progress in England. An early example of psychological warfare?

Geofroy Tory

Geofroy Tory (1480–1533), a typographer and creator of fonts, was the most accomplished Parisian printer of the Renaissance. He pioneered Gutenberg's technology in the French language and added accents, apostrophes, and cedillas to the fonts. He worked at designing new roman capitals that would be outside the Gothic tradition and not look like handwriting. To do that, he needed the presence of the Vitruvians, whom he summoned like aesthetic demons to his print shop. Willingly or not, they were obliged to stand inside his letters, sometimes in uncomfortable positions. They were necessary witnesses to the quality of his work; their presence guaranteed that he was following the aesthetic codebook to the letter, so to speak. Without them, he could not have imposed the new look of his fonts on his readers. Yet we may wonder why Tory showed so little respect for his models' freedom. Was he stating that the Vitruvian codebook had become an aesthetic tyrant?

It is worth noting that a disciple of Tory's, Claude Garamond, is still famous. In 1545 he was asked by King Francis I to design a new font that would befit the development of the Renaissance arts in his kingdom. He produced the Garamond, the font in which this paragraph was set. The font was so well designed and readable that it has survived with little change.

Decode:

Browse through this book and note the different fonts that have been used, some of them very different from Garamond. Unless you are a professional, you will not be able to name them, but you certainly can count them. How many different fonts were used to code this book?

Font design is an art. Before computers, it was very much like sculpture. For each letter, the artist had to sculpt a die in steel that looked exactly like that letter. Then the die was used to make a mold or matrix in which the mobile type was molded in lead for employment in print shops. Lead type wore out quickly and had to be replaced. The matrices wore out too, although more slowly. The dies were preserved carefully and used as rarely as possible. Some of the original ones are kept in museums.

Font design and usage is a code within a code. The first step involves language, which is a means of coding thought. Writing a text in a specific language entails using a specific language code that readers can decode easily to get at the meaning of the text. That is followed by the making of the book and the publishing of the text. Among other issues, such as the paper format, paper quality, the layout of pages, the types of titles, and the cover, there is an essential choice: the fonts that will be used to display the text. Although few people notice it consciously, the fonts that encode a text are all-important for a book's look and feel.

Jean Goujon

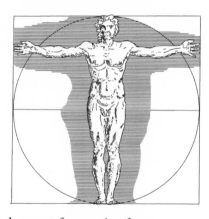

Jean Goujon is famous for his bas-reliefs, sculptures, and architectural designs. He was born in 1510, and an unconfirmed legend states that he was murdered in Paris in 1572 on Saint Bartholomew's Day, during the mass slaying of Protestants by the Catholics. If this is true, it would make him a martyr of the Renaissance period.

Goujon's talent as a sculptor is evident in his illustrations of the French translation of Vitruvius. His Vitruvian man (see the illustration below) is clearly a pure geometer: He is entirely naked except for a pair of compasses in his right hand. His left hand rests on a rectangular block that seems to indicate a concern for perspective. In fact, real perspective is disregarded in the picture as a whole, where its display is perfunctory. The boards above and below the character have different—and geometrically false—horizon lines and vanishing points.

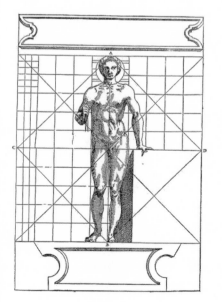

More interesting is the presentation of the character. The geometric web is centered on him, with the center point on his manhood. It is composed almost entirely of squares and diagonals, with the exception of rectangles that could be approximations of golden rectangles. A more remarkable feature is the circle around the head.

This Vitruvian man does not stand in a pseudo-crucifixion pose, but nonetheless religion is present with the saintly halo around his head. Goujon offers us a geometer-evangelist caught naked in the web of his geometrical codebook, armed with his compass and radiating faith in divine proportions, ready to encompass the world in his perfect lines.

Heinrich Cornelius Agrippa

Heinrich Cornelius Agrippa von Nettesheim (1486–1535) led his Vitruvians into sulfurous lands. Unlike the earlier creators, he was not a painter, architect, or engineer. Earthly matters did not concern him. To earn a living, or try to, he practiced medicine, law, astrology, alchemy, and teaching. He was an extremely erudite scholar. Very early on he decided to speak nothing but Latin. He then extended his mastery of languages to Arabic, Hebrew, and several others.

Under the influence of the Kabbalists and a mysterious Arabian book called *The Picatrix*, Agrippa devoted his life to the study and teaching of magic. His main book was *De occulta philosophia* (*Of Occult Philosophy*), written in 1510 but not published until 1533. It dealt with magic, occultism, and astrology.

Let us examine how Agrippa opened a new world in which an old Pythagorean figure made a comeback.

Agrippa made the pentagram, which only was suggested by his friend Francesco Giorgi, completely obvious in two presentations. With the pentagram, as well as the numbers and astrological symbols, Agrippa stood at a crossroads between the pure Pythagorean aesthetic of the Renaissance architects and artists and occultism, a trend that would grow apart from the mainstream of art. On that

road, the human body, the circle, the square, and the geometric lines were still present but new symbols added a different sense. Building and painting were no longer on the agenda. The new goal dealt with communication with other worlds inhabited by mysterious entities such as angels and demons.

The pentagram represents a star, as it does, for example, on the U.S. flag. Agrippa's first Vitruvian man (see the illustrations to the right) spreads his arms and

legs to inhabit the star. On the outer ring, the symbols of the planets relate him to astrology. The second man spreads his arms to reach out to—and hold—the stars. This man has a halo around his head that seems to give him a saintly nature and may make him too pure to mix with magic symbols.

The art of numerology is central for Kabbalists. To introduce a world governed by numbers, Agrippa places the third Vitruvian man in a new posture, standing in front of numbers and geometric figures. The vertical extension of his arms is new in the Vitruvian world. He is acting as a pillar, providing the measure of the numbered world. He also holds the top of the square, keeping it open for numbers.

The next Vitruvian man demonstrates humankind's submission to astrology. The 12 astrological symbols close the square around him. He is quartered on the straight diagonals determined by the astrological theme.

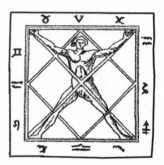

The fifth Vitruvian man is below the eye of the seer. He stands between the offer of knowledge by the serpent of Eden and the threat of the sword.

With Agrippa died our last hope of seeing a Vitruvian woman. He did not draw any, and in all his Vitruvians, the male attributes are obvious enough so as to leave no room for doubt. Yet Agrippa is the only Renaissance creator who wholly redeemed himself in that area. He actively defended the rights of women by writing a "declamation on the female sex," a book titled *Declamation on the Nobility and Preeminence of the Female Sex*.

For Agrippa, more important than this world were other worlds and mysterious entities. To communicate with them, he researched new languages and alphabets. He designed "divine letters" to communicate with the sun, the moon, and the planets. He also had a general-purpose "celestial" alphabet that looked like zodiacal lines joining stars. His "magic" alphabet is displayed below in a set of 26 symbols, with the addition of several modern letters to accommodate modern English.

We will explore Agrippa's alphabets further in Chapter 10.

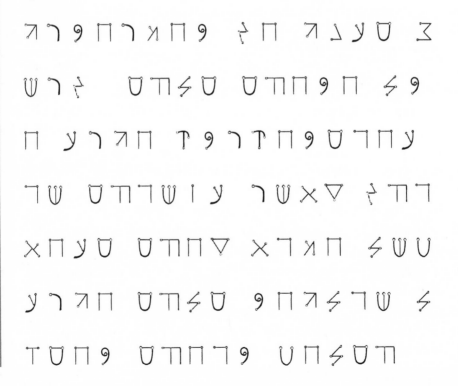

Decode:

This sentence from Agrippa's *Of Occult Philosophy* is written in the celestial alphabet.

John Dee's Dead End

In an ultimate appearance, late in the sixteenth century in the kingdom of England, a distant part of Europe from a Renaissance point of view, the Vitruvian symbol all but hid the square, the circle, and the Vitruvian man himself. Pentagrams and polygrams of every dimension became all-powerful, occupying all possible space. Magic symbols and references blackened the background. This "Seal of God" (see the illustration to the right) indeed seals off the last adventures of the Vitruvians. John Dee, like Cornelius Agrippa and Francesco Giorgi, is more engaged in magic than in aesthetics, producing a magical slide rule rather than a work of art.

In this dark side of the Vitruvian universe, the human body is no longer a hero, free at the center of the world. The situation is reversed: the human body is dwarfed by the predominant forces of darkness, subject to the influence of stars and demons.

John Dee (1527–1608) enjoyed great fame during his life and was an important councillor of Queen Elizabeth I. As a true mathematician and scientist, he tried to synthesize science and magic. As the queen's official cartographer, he drew the maps that made the British navy successful on all the seas. Similarly, he hoped to successfully charter the unknown. He went so far as to try to code magic, structuring it in a theory of axioms, logical deductions, and theorems as the Greeks had done with mathematics. Yet the part of his work he devoted to magic proved to be a dead end that brought no lasting result. The two could not meet, and hard science eventually beat hard magic.

A Celled Creativity

Vitruvian men are a paradox. In their move forward, where they display their freedom from the Dark Ages, they also go backward, surrendering their new freedom to the even more restraining rules of geometry. On the one hand, they seek liberty from traditional constraints; on the other hand, they pay total respect to the most severe codebook of all: geometric figures and laws.

The contradiction is obvious in the posture of most Vitruvian men. With both arms extended to follow geometric lines, those drawings remind us of crucifixions.

They are crucified on the altar of geometry. The cross is only suggested, with no need for nails and wooden beams. Most smile, enjoying their sacrifice. They voluntarily follow the rites of the Pythagorean gospel, speaking the words of Pythagoras and Euclid and Vitruvius.

These crucifixions cannot be a coincidence. All these artists knew what they were doing. In the course of their normal trade, they had drawn and painted countless crucifixion scenes on canvases and on the walls of churches and convents. There is no freedom in Renaissance productions, simply a change of codebooks, a change toward purer codes and more strictly logical rules.

The Vitruvian men stand naked in their webs, born again in a new world. None of them seem to suffer even in situations of physical duress. Are the geometrical lines coded webs or coded cribs? They seem poised to generate new worlds.

CHAPTER 5
Freemasons from Guilt to Free

Four centuries ago, in the New World as well as in Europe, thinking freely was a dangerous practice. The trials of the Inquisition and witch hunts were ongoing threats. Fire and the stake awaited those who did not conform to the Church's system of thought. However, relying on the model of the Templars and the tools of the craft brotherhoods, the Freemasons emerged and survived.

Yes, you read *guilt* where you expected *guild* in the title of this chapter. We usually think of medieval guilds as the ancestors of the Masonic brotherhoods. The pun is intended here to stress two important points I wish to make. First, the Masonic lodges were originated by craftsmen and workers, not by their bosses: the merchants and the workshop owners. Second, *guilt* is a keyword in understanding the inner workings of a Freemason brotherhood.

Compagnon Brotherhoods

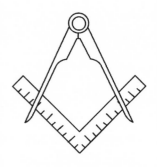

The most ancient brotherhoods that are still in existence are the craft brotherhoods of masons and carpenters. They are living links to the past: to Minoans, Egyptians, and possibly even older peoples.

We have testimony that throughout the Middle Ages most builders of important places—churches, castles, cathedrals, and town houses—belonged to craft brotherhoods. Those builders still are referred to by the French word *compagnons*: those who cut bread together. Much better than the term *brother*, which refers to closed communities, the word *compagnon* presents a picture of fellow craftsmen working together toward a common goal in a worldly environment. Compagnons are called *Gesallen* in Germany and *journeymen* in Great Britain. In the United States, the Washington Journeymen Stonecutters ceremonially laid the cornerstone of the Capitol in 1792.

Craft brotherhoods have been in existence for millennia and have served several purposes. As schools, they transmitted knowledge of the trade and educated the young. As trade unions, they strove to protect their members from the conflicting interests of clients and employers. They took care of the general welfare of members and their families. Finally, they ensured the quality of the members' work by insisting that good craftsmanship should always be accompanied by high moral standards. Thanks to these brotherhoods, buildings were erected using state-of-the-art technology and the workers who put them up were paid fairly and lived in the best possible conditions.

The picture was never perfect, of course. Brotherhoods occasionally fought among themselves: history records bloody battles between organizations competing over territory or religion. Yet the quality of the workmanship was always high; the compagnons had the greatest respect for their work.

Compagnon brotherhoods should not be confused with guilds. In the Middle Ages, guilds were created by merchants who formed trade associations to protect themselves against competition. Then craft guilds began to include shop owners, also to fight against competition.

Those guilds were concerned more with increasing the profits from their activities than with improving the quality of their production or the welfare of their employees. Enjoying an important economic power, they inevitably grew to have political power, coming into conflict with strong governments. They eventually became chambers of commerce and underwent revolutionary change: modern economic laws let them promote their activities but strictly prohibited them from fighting the competition. Brotherhoods of compagnons, in contrast, from the Middle Ages to now, concern craftsmen, people who are close to matter, who do their basic work with the ideal of producing masterpieces or at least high-quality works and are relatively unaffected by fluctuations in government and the economy.

Yet, as can be expected, depending on eras and countries, there was not always a clear-cut distinction between the brotherhoods and the guilds. The best examples of organizations that straddled the boundaries are the British livery companies, also called worshipful companies, which were associations of tradesmen and craftsmen. Among the 107 that still exist in London, only a few, such as the Scriveners, are still operative while others are charitable foundations. The oldest worshipful company is the Carpenters' Company, which dates back to at least 1271. Here we are concerned with its much younger sister, the Carpenter's Company of Philadelphia, founded in 1724, whose meeting place, Carpenters' Hall, played an important role in the American Revolution (see Chapter 7).

The Knights' Compagnons

It seems that compagnon masons and carpenters were literally the Templars' "companions." They lived with them and built their chapels and commanderies and traveled with them to build their boats and the other machines of war. Later, when the Templars were merged with the Hospitallers, they became the Hospitallers' companions too.

If only for practical reasons, the compagnons shared most of the knowledge and symbolism of the knights. They were the ones who built the chapels, probably drew up their plans, and sculpted their symbols in stone. It is easy to imagine them living in symbiosis with the knights. The knights were the masters, the visible picture of the

organization; the compagnons provided the tools. Note that as a clue to their common culture the compagnons always made references to the temple and to Solomon. They continue to do so, as in the song, reproduced later in this chapter, which is still sung by Compagnons. Legend has it that when Philip the Fair overthrew the order of the Templars, the compagnons rebelled. Bands of compagnons, armed with the tools of their trade, desperately tried to storm the king's soldiers to free their imprisoned masters. Why the compagnons and not the Templars' own troops? Legend says that all over the country the compagnons laid down their tools and deserted the cathedral sites in a general strike. Indeed, in the fourteenth century the great enthusiasm that had fed the construction of cathedrals began to slow down, but as Marie Delcols and Jean-Luc Caradeau note in *L'ordre du temple* (*The Order of the Templar*), this can be explained by a general decline in the European economy.

The picture above is a fifteenth-century miniature illustration that depicts a ceremony that took place in 1480 in the fortified harbor of the island of Rhodes, which was held at that time by the Knights Hospitallers. The grand master of the order is formally receiving the compagnon masters, who are displaying their tools. In the background, compagnons are seen at work in various capacities building forts and ships.

From Rabbit to Master

The education of an apprentice, today as in centuries past, is both practical and symbolic and is accomplished during an initiatory journey. For several years, the young craftsman, called, oddly, a "rabbit," travels from workshop to workshop and from site to site run by the masters of his brotherhood. *Journeyman*, the English equivalent of "compagnon," clearly evokes the initiatory journey of compagnonship.

Brotherhoods have networks of inns operated by "inn mothers" who accommodate both traveling apprentices and local or traveling compagnons. A special etiquette assures that the inn is more than an ordinary restaurant. A compagnon is not waited on but must fetch his food himself. When he sits at the table, he must not leave a space between himself and the next compagnon. Conversation must avoid such topics as politics, religion, or even shop matters. The inn is a place to relax, exchange ideas, and share friendship, definitely not an extension of the workplace.

Each point on the journey teaches the apprentice some complementary piece of knowledge, some kind of know-how, or a secret of the trade. After a day at work, he goes to school in the evening to enhance his general education and learn the theory of his trade.

In the typical logic of traditional networks, during the trip an apprentice not only gathers information but also transmits it. He learns while acting as a link between local communities.

The apprentice's initiatory journey is a pilgrimage of skill and knowledge and climaxes when he returns to his starting point. If his education has been successful, he is made a compagnon through symbolic rites. His former identity "dies," and he is born again as a compagnon. Some brotherhoods actually place the apprentice in a mock tomb from which he arises into a new life. He is baptized and receives a new name that refers to his skills and moral qualities. He pledges to obey the masters and help his brother compagnons. He receives his "colors," a set of colored ribbons that he attaches to his hat when traveling to identify him and his brotherhood. He is given an elaborately decorated cane (see the illustration above) that will help him on his trip toward perfection. He is introduced to certain secrets of the brotherhood, including covert signals that will enable him to recognize other companions under any circumstances, should he so need.

The Born-Again Craftsman

The similarity of this ceremony of rebirth and baptism to Christian rituals caused the compagnons to have trouble with the Church. In the eighteenth century, Rome decided that the compagnons had created a sect and were mocking Christian rites. The Church was mistaken. Most compagnons were good Christians who wanted to honor their craft by putting into practice the rites of death and rebirth they had learned in church. They were condemned by Rome nonetheless and had to go into hiding. In the nineteenth century, after revolutions had changed the cultural landscape in Europe and America, they resurfaced. They borrowed symbolic references from the Freemasons, who had grown considerably in that period.

After his rebirth, the life of a compagnon is directed toward the production of a "masterpiece," a display of all his talents and expertise, and the attainment of the level of master through new rites and ceremonies. Working on a masterpiece is the craftsman's equivalent of the crucible-poking alchemist working toward his ultimate, if unattainable, goal of making gold. The work is meant to act on the very worker, lifting him into a superior state of being. As with alchemy, in which genuine mastery involves not the occasional crumbs of gold in the crucible but the actual transmutation of the alchemist into a superior being, the real masterpiece is the human being.

Logically enough within that line of thought, the compagnons sanctify their tools. The instruments that transmute ordinary material into a masterwork are considered essential agents in the transformation of both ordinary matter and the compagnon into a master. In the process, tool and craftsman play equally important roles. Traditionally, the tool carries so much mythic power that it equals the talent of the human hand. Together, hand and tool, an inseparable couple, are all-powerful in the creation of perfection. More important, beyond the production of objects, each agent acts on the other, the hand as part of the tool and the tool as part of the hand: the hand perfects the tool, and the tool perfects the hand and the man.

The compass and the square (the tool, not the geometric figure) naturally became the emblems and insignia of the masons' and carpenters' brotherhoods. They are so fundamental that they appear among the symbols of other brotherhoods, such as those

of bakers and confectioners, who have no practical use for them. They are especially obvious on roofs, where a master carpenter signs his work with a coded weather vane.

The picture on this page shows a personal symbol belonging to the author. While writing this book, I realized the meaning of the zinc weather vane on top of my own roof, right above my desk actually. Though I lack the necessary documents to put an exact name on him, I know that an ancestor of mine built this house, and he left a signature more precious than a name.

This weather vane proves that he was a brotherhood mason and/or carpenter. As on many other rooftops throughout the world, the fundamental mystery of the myth that guided his life stands there, moving freely in the wind. Note the trumpet or bullhorn. Long after the mason's death, the little angel continues to shout the signature of a brotherhood in all directions. Are these winds the same as the mystic winds on the Igel monument and in Hildegard's visions (see Chapter 4)?

Codes and Secrets

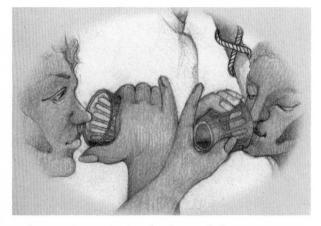

As for written codes, we need not expect to find any in the brotherhoods' paper archives: there are none. The compagnons have always been practical artisans who express themselves in their craft with little to say or write beyond that. In addition, they have been persecuted in so many ways that they know better than to leave documents lying around. According to legend, they met (and still meet) each year with all the papers they had used over the previous 12 months, burned the papers in a huge fire, mixed the ashes with wine, and drank it. For that reason, the present account of the compagnons should be considered timeless. It still stands, yet it's nearly impossible to trace it back to an exact beginning in the past.

The absence of an archive does not mean that no archive exists. It seems that there were archives that preserved the history and the secrets of the brotherhoods, and they probably were transmitted orally. These archives and their protection were essential when the brotherhood was threatened by government and by other brotherhoods. To maintain the purity of the organization and perhaps to keep essential secrets, the archives have been preserved and maintained. Indeed, when one starts asking a compagnon questions, there always comes a point at which he refuses to answer and politely ends the session.

This compagnon song reproduced below evokes certain "sublime secrets" transmitted from King Solomon. A song like this tends to confirm the existence of links between the Templars and the compagnons, referring to the same symbolic past.

THE TEMPLE OF SOLOMON

Verse 1:

Under Solomon we built a temple
Where the worker earned renown,
But that good king to make them wiser
Arranged them in three grades:
Apprentices, compagnons, master.
All worked toward this beautiful union.

Chorus:

Rather die martyrs and real apostles
And carry the secret into the grave.
(Repeat)

Verse 2:

Beneath this Lebanon where the worker
Toils with great courage,
Apprentices cut cedars,
Compagnons came to work them,
And we raised a splendid portico
To the three: wisdom, strength, and
beauty.

Verse 3:

The king of Tyre sent the architect
To direct these illustrious works.
But the great man always full of zeal,
Drew new plans for the workers.

One evening he disappeared into the
shadows.
Our compagnons went out to search
for him.
Beneath a heap of rubble they saw
An acacia that led to his discovery.

Verse 4:

He who wrote these stanzas, brothers,
Is a child of great King Solomon,
Initiated into the sublime mysteries.
He was a Burgundian compagnon,
He swore to love, cherish his brothers,
He is faithful of heart toward humanity.

Masons' Marks

Masons' marks were recorded in the Middle Ages in Europe but might have been in use for thousands of years before that time. Not all of them are literally masons' marks. Some were chiseled onto every stone in a quarry to identify the cutters and determine their salary—so much money for each finished stone—when the stones were sent to the building site. Others were the personal seals of artisans, also used for computing salaries. Such symbols were sets of simple geometric lines, carved rapidly but with enough precision to avoid errors. Still others were assembly notes specifying how the stones were to be set. Such marks can be seen in Scotland in Melrose Abbey, Glasgow Cathedral, Rosslyn Chapel, and Dunkeld Cathedral, as well as in many other landmarks throughout the world.

1127 Dunkeld Cathedral

1200 Glasgow Cathedral

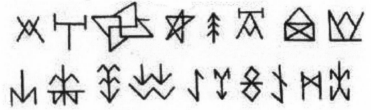

1400 Melrose Abby

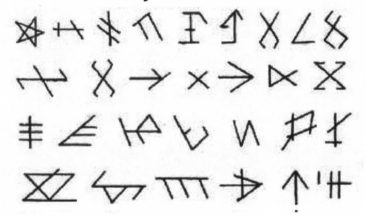

1446 Rosslyn Chapel

The marks on the stones of the Minoan palaces in Crete, which were built around 1650 B.C.E., probably played the same role and were created with the same technique—simple lines, rapidly carved—yet with a markedly different style from those of the European Middle Ages. Minoan masons' marks tended to be less abstract and more representative of nature (tree roots and branches, as in Chinese ideograms), tools (such as the trident), stars, and human silhouettes (with raised arms). Below are some of the more significant marks collected by Insup and Martin Taylor and displayed on their Internet site mmtaylor.net/.

The Carpenter's Alphabet

For similar reasons, compagnon carpenters carved their own marks on the wooden beams they cut and assembled. A close look at the framework of old buildings often reveals the original marks; however, the carpenters had additional reasons for leaving those markings. To reduce transport as much as possible, timbers were delivered to a construction site and beams were cut on the spot. The carpenters cut discrete personal marks that were meant to be hidden when the beams were assembled. More obvious marks, often visible today, were cut to indicate how and where the beams should be placed. A compagnon who cut beams on the ground would assemble them to check the structure and then disassemble the whole, adding clear signs before sending them up to the heights of a cathedral so that fellow compagnons several hundred feet above would know exactly how to place the building elements.

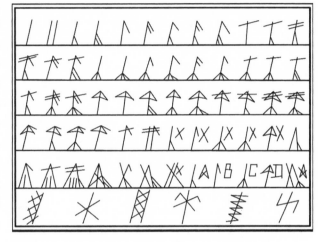

To do this, carpenters had a specific "carpenter's alphabet." Although it looks like a runic alphabet, much like Tolkien's alphabet discussed in Chapter 10, in reality it is a description of all the possible ways of putting beams together. The "alphabet" on the right is on exhibition at the Musée du Compagnonnage in Tours, France.

To complement the alphabet with numbers, carpenters derived a specific set of digits from roman numerals.

Another type of alphabet used by both masons and carpenters invokes the heritage of King Solomon. It's called a Solomon clock because the assembly symbols are arranged in a circle around a central cross. It is a portable reminder of the main signs of the craft and how to cut and assemble stone or wood. It is also the title of a novel by Raoul Vergez *La pendule à Salomon* (*Solomon's Clock*), Juliard, Paris 1970 on the lives of the brotherhood members.

The carpenters' choice of the word *alphabet* to name the symbols of their trade was not innocent. They believe that through language they literally can communicate with objects. By speaking to wood in the right language, they symbolically talk a piece of wood into accomplishing the project they have in mind. They might have called this language the alphabet of wood, as it is meant to be the language that wood understands.

Masons and carpenters were particularly proud of their ability to work in three dimensions, whether in carving or in building elaborate stone structures or amazing frameworks. The basic education of a new compagnon started with learning a new language, the art of tracing, which taught an apprentice a no-nonsense, intuitive three-dimensional geometry. By learning a language of practical formulas, the apprentice became an expert builder despite having hardly any knowledge of mathematical theory.

This education resulted in an intimate knowledge of space, as the compagnons directly "spoke" to the stone and wood with which they built the framework and complex structures of Gothic arches that still stand, sometimes after having survived several wars. They still practice their half-secret three-dimensional technology nowadays with continued success. Many modern architects would never dream of undertaking the erection of complex structures without their aid. When Gustave Eiffel built his tower, for example, among the hundreds of workers on the site, there were a few dozen compagnons holding key jobs.

Beam Talk

However wary they were of keeping written records, as noted lovers of codes and secrets, compagnon builders must have had many more subtle tools available for communication. For example, there is the manner in which they constructed their buildings. Have we looked closely enough at all the details that were left to compagnons once they were handed the architect's plans?

Look at the building on the right, which is near Notre-Dame in Paris. The geometry of the timbering on some of the walls diverges from the necessities of mechanical logic. Beyond the basic geometrical framework that holds together the structure of the building, some beams are oriented at quaint angles in inexplicable places.

Why would the builders use such bizarre arrangements of beams? Were the carpenters so clumsy that they couldn't cut and assemble their beams in accordance with regular geometry as is done today? Or were the brotherhood carpenters and masons adding a hidden blueprint, seizing the opportunity to do something other than simply build a house? Were they burying a message in the layout of the beams?

Until the sixteenth century or so, the brotherhoods were still powerful and well organized; the structure of beams on walls and facades was complex and contained enough apparent chaos to embed a concealed meaning. Later, when the compagnons were less powerful and were controlled by the government, facades became simpler, with a symmetrical geometry that could convey no meaning. It was as if the walls no longer were allowed to speak, as if they had been forced into silence. Yet as we'll see, the compagnons may have invented other ways to express themselves.

Although we have no documents to support it, let's suppose that compagnon builders purposely assembled their timber to display a message. Taking a close look at their buildings, we can imagine the kinds of codes craftsmen would have used. Walls were made of elementary cells: rectangles and triangles. For lack of any other clue, let's choose the rectangle as the basic cell and consider that lines and triangles are meaningful elements within rectangles. This principle is then enough to allow us to suppose an alphabet. Below is an alphabet of 24 rectangles with the letter combinations I and J and U and V counted as one letter apiece. Blank rectangles and windows are unavoidable voids.

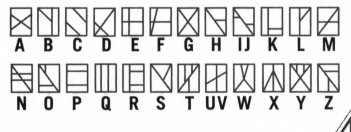

Decode:

Suppose a fundamental credo is encoded in the façade to the right with the beam-talk alphabet discussed above. What is the well-known sentence?

Decode:

A mason signed the house shown below with a more worldly message.

Tile Talk

Masons who used walls as a support for coded messages might also have used another type of "facade alphabet," as suggested in the picture on page 143. Here the elementary beam cells are regularly placed and express nothing in particular. The areas between them, however, regardless of shape, contain various patterns of tiles. The meaning of the cells is not defined by their triangular or polygonal shape but by their content, the arrangement of the tiles within them. In the picture, a mason has taken pains to place the tiles in very precise patterns. Each pattern could correspond to a letter. On the following page is a sample alphabet using tile patterns similar to those the compagnons could have used to communicate hidden messages.

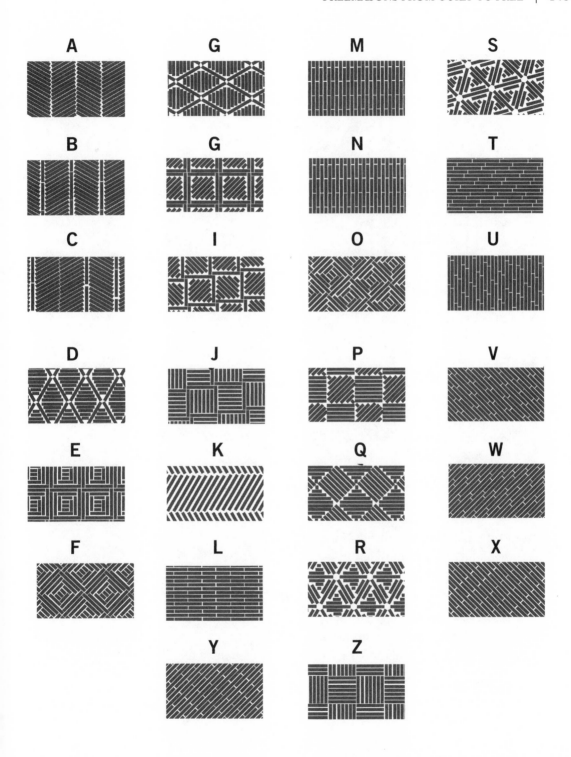

Decode:

Decode this proverb of King Solomon.

Stone Talk

A third technology available to masons to make their walls speak were the stones themselves. Certain walls display a varied surface in their stonework, as in the picture below.

The Freemasons

Neither free nor masons, the Freemasons are a paradox. Indeed, the average Freemason never lays a stone in his life and is required, as his first traditional rite of entry, to pledge absolute obedience to his lodge, formally leaving his freedom, so to speak, at the door.

The keys to understanding this paradox lie in the symbolic history of the movement. Modern Freemasonry formally appeared in 1717 with the foundation of the First Grand Lodge of London. Masonic lodges existed well before that date; the oldest known lodge on record is the Edinburgh Lodge Number 1, which was founded on July 30, 1599. We know of the lodges through their books of rules, which are referred to as constitutions or charges. During the seventeenth century they received a growing number of members, not masons by trade but people who shared the moral ideals of the craft brotherhoods and intended to live by them. In 1717, the Freemasons of the Grand Lodge clearly resolved that their lodge was "speculative" rather than "operative." The term *operative* refers to craft brotherhoods that actually dealt with mortar and stone, whereas *speculative* refers to assemblies that dealt with purely intellectual matters.

The new form of Freemasonry appeared in Philadelphia, at roughly the same time as the First Grand Lodge of London. Daniel Coxe was the first grand master of the

Provincial Grand Lodge. He was followed by most of the prominent Americans of that time. When the government of the newly founded United States built the Capitol at the end of the century, the cornerstone was laid by the "speculative brother" George Washington in a joint ceremony with the operative Lodge of the Stonecutters of America on September 18, 1793. By that time Freemasonry was flourishing in France as well, and Washington wore a formal Masonic apron that had been conferred on him by the Marquis de Lafayette.

The Freethinker's War

Freemasonry used operative masonry as a stepping stone to the gradual creation of its own movement. Deliberate or not, that turned out to be an effective strategy for dealing with persecution by Christian Church.

Speculative Freemasons emerged as freethinkers, the intellectual equivalents of the Vitruvian men: those Renaissance artists who freed themselves from the weight of religious traditional art. Predictably, they armed themselves symbolically with the compass and the square, the tools necessary for drawing the circle and square of the Vitruvian revolution. Stonemasons' brotherhoods were the ideal places to put such tools to work, if only virtually. Yet to exist, they still needed to overcome handicaps, both internal and external.

The biggest obstacle to free thought and action seldom is mentioned yet is paramount: guilt, the fear of going against one's conscience and morals and, even worse, against the customs and moral codes of society at large. Moreover, society generally enforces its moral code by means of ostracism and even physical punishment.

Conscience and morals are ambiguous concepts. In normal circumstances they maintain a stable and viable society, yet they are a serious obstacle to change and evolution and a serious handicap in extreme situations in which society is faced with unexpected circumstances such as wars and revolutions.

The meaning of the word *free* has evolved through time. Until the nineteenth century it had ambiguous social implications. To be free meant that your mind was uninhibited but also that you were neither a bondsman belonging to a landlord nor a slave belonging to a master. Today an apprentice mason still pledges his freedom, which is not only his legal freedom from a landlord but also freedom of thought from a possibly conflicting religion or another secret society.

Obedience as a Weapon

To counter this guilt and be able to sustain a bloody non-Christian fight against the "infidels," the Christian Templars resorted to a psychological tool: absolute obedience within a community dedicated to battle (see Chapter 3). Obedience, sanctified by the Church, armed them against their personal guilt, whereas the Templar community preserved and institutionalized their exceptional status in the larger Christian community.

Masonic lodges employed the same tools. Like the Templars, their members pledged absolute obedience to their own communities devoted to free thought. A Masonic organization still is called an obedience. In this context, the word *obedience* does not mean giving up one's freedom but relying on the strength of the community and its dedication to freedom of thought.

Historically, the link between Knights Templars and the Freemasons is controversial. Nothing links Templars and Masons except circumstantial evidence. Masonic lodges did develop early in Scotland, where the last Templars survived after the fall of the order in 1307. They share a common reference to King Solomon and the temple, but this seems to come more from the heritage of the craft brotherhoods. Their common moral rule based on the practice of obedience is another inconclusive clue.

A Symbolic Laboratory

The heritage of the craft brotherhoods provided a useful set of symbols for anchoring the intellectual dealings of the Freemasons in daily reality. The basic reference to stone and masonry acts as a strong reminder of the need to be logical and practical. It stands as the cornerstone, so to speak, of their continuing success compared with the rapid decline of competing movements such as the Rosicrucians and the Illuminati.

Being the virtual masons of a future world, the Freemasons bear the tools of the real trade. They display square and compass and wear mason's aprons in ceremony, and their language is based on references to building. If need be, the Supreme Being becomes the Great Architect of the Universe. Borrowing the symbols of the brotherhoods of stonemasons, the Freemasons drew on the symbolic power of a thousand-year-old tradition. They continued and extended the work of King Solomon, building his mythic temple. In the four centuries since the emergence of the Freemasons, symbols have passed back and forth between the craft brotherhoods of the compagnons and the Masonic lodges. Solomon became a common mythological ancestor, the ideal mason and architect who built the legendary temple of absolute wisdom.

As a result of this treasure of knowledge and wisdom, organized free thinking proved successful and productive in general. In most Western countries Masonic lodges acted as political laboratories. Governments not necessarily dominated by Freemasons, as in the early United States, made abundant use of the work of the lodges and passed laws elaborated there to develop democracy and a better society.

Blatant Secrecy

The Freemasons succeeded in pulling off an impossible social feat: conspicuous secrecy. They were able to do that because of the convenient ambiguity of their language of symbols. A symbol is the opposite of a clear written statement. It's potentially meaningful but depends on the interpretation of the person reading it. It's a clue, loaded with invaluable references for the initiate and opaque or, at best, indefinite for the ignorant. A Mason can safely parade in public wearing an apron covered in symbols and be the only one who knows their meaning.

The flexibility of symbols is demonstrated by the letter G in the Freemason's emblem: the compass and square. For some time Freemasons publicly avowed that its meaning was "God," thus encouraging good relations with the Church. When it was pointed out that in many languages the word *God* does not begin with the letter G and yet this still featured in local Masonic symbolism and blazonry, they suggested that it stood for "geometry."

The resulting situation is a balance between total openness, which would hamper a freethinking community's creativity, and absolute obscurity, which would be unacceptable to the general public.

This semisecrecy is also a tribute to the original guilt of freethinkers. Like Christians plagued by original sin and banished from Eden for eating the fruit of the Tree of Knowledge, Freemasons are plagued with guilt and banished from the light of day for eating their own fruit of knowledge. From a symbolic point of view, one could say that as long as they bear this original guilt, the Masons will remain in their twilight zone, never quite benefiting from the full light of day enjoyed by the rest of society.

Proxy Powers

More important, the blatant secrecy of the Freemasons is a direct response to the tragic error of their ancient brothers, the Pythagoreans. In Greece, the Pythagoreans chose a political strategy that proved to be a disaster. Wrongly confusing philosophy and power, they ran the state by themselves, and that led to rebellions and the Metaponte catastrophe, in which they were all but wiped out of history. With that failure in mind, the Freemasons resolved never to exercise power except by proxy.

The political masterpiece of the Freemasons that served as a template for their future actions was their role in the American War of Independence. Freemasons such as George Washington, Benjamin Franklin, and Thomas Jefferson triggered the action, fought the war, founded the new state, and then ran it as briefly as possible before returning to the blatant secrecy of their lodges.

The Language of the Apron

Every Freemason owns a traditional stonemason's apron richly embroidered with symbols.

George Washington's is the most famous. Besides being Masonic, it has historical significance because it was a gift from a French Mason bringing the aid of his country to the War of Independence. Madame de Lafayette is credited with the embroidery.

The symbols on the apron provide an extensive tour of Freemasonry. Normal descriptions count 43 visible symbols, but we may suppose that initiates see many more. Among the ones anyone can see are the following:

- A beehive at the top to evoke industry
- The all-seeing watchful eye that evokes God or the Great Architect, a convenient way of paying symbolic homage to all faiths at once
- The colors red, white, and blue surrounding the apron, representing courage, purity, and fidelity—and possibly the common colors of the French and American flags
- The rainbow evoking the ninth architectural arch under Solomon's Temple, supported by the pillars of wisdom and strength
- The front pillars symbolizing those of Enoch, erected in fear that the principles of the arts and sciences might be lost
- The dove carrying Noah's message that the flood was over
- Jacob's ladder evoking ascension in the degrees of knowledge
- The plumb line, trowel, square, and compass, which, along with the apron itself, are the symbolic tools of the speculative masons, symbolically equivalent to the working tools of operative masons
- The five-pointed star, which signals a direct link to the Pythagoreans. The checkered mosaic pavement reflecting the floor of Solomon's Temple and symbolizing the way good and evil are interwoven in human life
- There are more symbols that are less meaningful for a noninitiate and hidden symbols that only an initiate can see and understand.

Death and Resurrection

The books and Internet sites that show Washington's apron are silent about the main symbol right in the foreground. At the bottom of the apron, situated on the natural path leading to the temple, there is a coffin. This symbol of death is emphasized by the presence of a skull and crossbones on the lid. Why do official commentaries ignore its real meaning and dismiss it with a few innocuous words as "a symbol of death"?

The real reason why a graphic image of death physically lies there can be found earlier in this chapter in our discussion of the rites of the compagnons. The rites of entry into and progress within a Masonic lodge are not essentially different from those of the compagnons. There are three steps apprentice, fellow (practically a synonym of *compagnon*), and master, along with an infinite variety of rites, depending on the lodge, obedience, and country. In campagnon initiations, death must be passed through before one can enter the temple. An apprentice must die symbolically die before he can become a brother. Likewise, being a Freemason means living a new life beyond that of the normal and everyday and, hopefully even beyond the original guilt of knowledge.

Religious Christians strongly resent this parallel with Christ's Passion and have opposed it wherever and whenever they could. The rite is too similar to Christ's death and resurrection. A Christian's symbolic birth takes place in the baptismal rite, and there is no need to undergo any other baptism. Masonic baptism is considered a pagan rite that contradicts and potentially cancels out Christian baptism.

Whether to show fealty to that most significant of numerals in Christian symbolism or for more obscure reasons, a common symbol in the writings of Freemasons is composed of three points: the extremities of an equilateral triangle. This symbol is so powerful that it can mean anything and even replace important words, enhancing their meaning. For instance the word *Freemason* can be written "F . . . M . . ." The semiobscurity of Masonic protocol thus is transferred to written documents. The compagnon brotherhoods adopted that symbolism as well. The three points also are said to refer to the past, when early lodges were governed by triads of masters.

The mythic experience of death and resurrection appeals so strongly to some Freemasons that an important trend of thought among them says that Freemasonry owes its power to a resurrection of the Templars. This represents the entire Freemason movement as a single body: the resurrected Templars. Should we consider Masons as reborn Templars seeking to redeem themselves both from their onslaught on so-called infidels and from their failure to liberate the Holy Land?

It should be noted that the death-life myth in our society is not limited to Freemasonry. It has been known for some time but became public knowledge in 2006 that many prominent personalities, some of them as unlike each other as John Kerry and George Bush, belong to an elite Yale University secret society called the Skull and Bones. Members are called Bonesmen and remain absolutely silent about their membership. The rules of the society are unknown, and the society is more shrouded in obscurity and mystery than Freemasonry ever was. The only clue is the title that relates to death. The next section discusses the death-life myth from a different angle.

The Mythic Journey

To understand the persistence and usefulness of secret societies, especially the Freemasons, we need to explore a specific activity of the human mind that has played a constant role throughout history in all civilizations and forms a major link among many parts of this book. The "mythic journey" is essential for our sanity and as a spiritual, emotional, political, and technical tool. When practiced assiduously and with the right focus, it provides clues about the solutions to problems. This mythic journey relates closely to code. We'll see how we can benefit from immersing ourselves in a coded universe.

Practically speaking, the mythic journey consists in temporarily quitting our usual, mundane environment to spend some time in another, mythic place: a different setting, real or imagined, with a different mindset. To the logical no-nonsense mind, the mythic journey seems like a way to avoid a problem or go in the wrong direction, yet it addresses challenging issues more efficiently than does any other approach.

The journey can be fantasized or physical. A typical example of a physical journey is a pilgrimage. Someone feels uneasy, may have committed a "sin," or faces an important moral issue in terms of his or her religious beliefs. That person can go on a pilgrimage, leaving normal business and daily life behind for weeks or months and visiting a sanctuary in a remote place. Along the way the pilgrim prays, exchanges thoughts with other pilgrims, sees different regions, and lives surrounded by and as part of a different way of approaching life. He or she looks forward to a personal change upon reaching the destination. Then the pilgrim returns to his or her previous life, secure in the knowledge that the sin has been redeemed. He or she has a fresh outlook and renewed mental energy.

The mythic journey also can be more collective and condensed. In a traditional religion, believers gather to relive a fundamental myth together. They take time out of their daily routine to visit a sacred temple and take part in a ritual that symbolizes the timeless history of that myth.

The historian of religion Mircea Eliade, who theorized about the matter in *Myths, Dreams, and Mysteries*, cites the ancient Germanic peoples and their annual communal ritual reliving Ragnarök—the "Fate of the Gods" in Norse mythology—as one example. In this myth, the host of demons confronts all the gods in a vast battle, and the demons win. The world returns to a state of chaos and comes to an end, only to be born again, fresh and renewed. In consonance with this myth, each believer underwent a personal battle between his or her own demons and gods; lived through the defeat of the gods, personal chaos, and death; and eventually was regenerated as a newly born person.

Another example of the mythic journey as a personal inner experience involves the Senoi of the rain forests of Malaysia, who practiced a form of "lucid dreaming" in which they would be totally conscious during dreams. This practice is found in many civilizations and does not imply waking up during a dream. The Senoi made it a way of life. Hunter-gatherers, they did not need to work too hard and routinely devoted their mornings to sharing the dreams of the previous night. They considered the time spent in dreams as being at least as important as their waking lives, whose only real value was that they provided an opportunity to share their dreams. They trained themselves to fearlessly confront the inimical entities—people or animals—they met in dreams and try to befriend one another.

Explorers who studied the Senoi in the 1930s testified that they were the happiest and most socially balanced people they had ever seen. They were an extreme case in which mythic time truly balanced the importance of historical time, but they lost their unique culture when World War II forced them into a deeper involvement in historical time.

Games are also mythic journeys. We tend to consider games as meaningless pastimes, though this is belied by the scenarios and art of most contemporary games. A well-known computer game is aptly named Myth.

Whether we play chess or poker or spend some time in the virtual universe of World of Warcraft, we leave mundane historical time to live in a different time line, adopting different moral codes in a differently coded universe. The "rules of the game" are in fact a well-balanced code staging its scenario, creating the characters, establishing their code of conduct, and setting up suspense about the outcome: who's going to win and how? All the players have the same psychological experience: they all become immersed in the time line of the game and completely forget normal mundane time.

We revisit adventure games from another point of view in Chapter 9, but whether on maplike boards, computer screens, or networks, an excursion into game universes has all the aspects of a mythic journey. The players spend time in outlandish environments, away from their usual time-frame and with different sets of logic and references.

We have little knowledge about the games played in the days of Pythagoras, but all traditional games, including the most abstract, such as chess and checkers, are examples of mythic journeys. Though perhaps lacking a genuine religious and ritual dimension, games generally involve the same psychological traits. Essentially, as one interpretation of the term *pastime* implies, they are a passage into parallel times and different universe codes, and the human mind obviously enjoys and benefits from journeys into codes outside its own.

This view is supported by Christianity's constant battle against gaming. That battle started when Bishop Cyprian of Carthage preached against games, especially dice games, in the third century. In the Middle-Ages, monastic rules expressly forbade game playing. When Savonarola launched his religious coup in Florence in 1494, one of his first moves was to gather all game boards and gaming materials and burn them. What we seem to be looking at here is a competition between mythic journeys.

The initiatory journey of the apprentice compagnon described earlier in this chapter is a typical mythic journey, a veritable round trip through the world of his craft. It is crowned by another journey: a condensed virtual voyage through the symbols of the brotherhood, the death rites of the apprentice, and the rebirth of the apprentice as a senior craftsman.

Of course, death is the most prestigious and meaningful journey. For Pythagoreans and in some Eastern religions, a soul goes through death to come back in a different body, possibly an animal's. Although few travelers ever came back to tell the tale, hosts of initiates in a wide variety of brotherhoods of all kinds have undergone and still undergo the ceremony of death. When undertaken with profound commitment and the right cultural and emotional preparation, the passage through death and to resurrection is an efficient way to step into a new mindset, move into a new life.

Another, more mundane practice is used by group leaders of creativity and idea research workshops, a discipline that bloomed in the second half of the twentieth century. Those group leaders introduced "parallel world" technology, which consists in transposing a problem to a different universe and then coming back with clues to resolve the problem. When they workshopped in groups, their first priority was to meet somewhere quiet, in a different environment far from day-to-day business concerns and with limited access to the outside. If they were working, for example, on developing a new braking system for an electric car, to intensify the parallel world effect, the group leader would disregard all logic and make a suggestion such as "Let's imagine we're Stone Age people solving this problem. What would we come up with?" or "Let's impersonate ant engineers in an ant nest and solve the problem with our tools." Separated from its usual environment, the human mind is freed from countless constraints limiting its productivity and readily accesses another, parallel mode of thinking in a move similar to what Edward de Bono has called "lateral thinking." Proving efficient on thousands of occasions, this is now a routine tool for research and development.

The most outlandish mythic journey of all introduces an altogether different universe. It is from Pythagoras and involves sojourning in a world whose code has little to do with ours: the world of mathematics. That universe is so strange that hardly any science-fiction stories takes place there, with the notable exception of Edwin Abbott Abbott's novel *Flatland: A Romance of Many Dimensions*. Numbers have no equivalent in our world and the pure figures of geometry are only remotely related to our physical objects, yet we are trained to make short journeys into arithmetic or geometry to solve a variety of problems. We have learned to go mentally into mathematics, select the numbers and geometric figures that fit a problem, deal with them mathematically, and come back to the real world with a solution.

All this gives us a key to understanding secret societies, whether Pythagorean or Masonic. A secret society is organized to provide the ideal environment for implementing a mythic journey and promoting parallel thinking. Initiates meet in secluded places such as lodges and underground temples where the parallel world effect is reinforced by an environment made up of symbols. The coded rules the members have vowed to obey place them in a universe with different codes. In following the code of conduct, members behave among themselves in a way that sets them apart from the society outside. The stage is deliberately engineered to turn their meetings into mythic journeys, liberating them from the cultural constraints of the outside world and enabling the full power of their creativity. With such a backup, they are likely to come up with clues to new and often radical ideas. This explains why the Freemasons have conceived innovative political projects that would have been impossible with ordinary thinking and its usual channels and methods (see Chapter 7).

CHAPTER 6

Homophones and Vigenère

Homophones are words that sound alike no matter how different they look. They are one of the greatest inventions in the history of ciphers. Homophones closed the E backdoor and opened the door to modern cryptography.

The E Backdoor

Roger Bacon, Geoffrey Chaucer, and their European contemporaries in the late Middle Ages (that is, the thirteenth and fourteenth centuries) were unaware of a critical weakness in their ciphers. They thought that the use of a cipher alphabet in which each letter in a text was replaced with a mysterious symbol was the ultimate technology for protecting their secrets. Indeed, ciphered text appears completely unreadable to an innocent eye that sees nothing beyond quaint symbols.

However, such ciphers are much less unbreakable than they look because of some particularities of languages that were ignored at that time. In Latin, Middle English, Middle French, and all the other European languages, including their present-day variants, words are not made of random collections of letters. Some letters are used more than others. For instance, if one computes the frequencies of the 26 letters in any English text that has 1,000 letters, the letter E will stand out, and one is likely to come up with roughly 125 E's, 97 T's, 82 A's, 77 I's, and practically no Q's or Z's (see the table on page 160, which shows the percentages). Hence, in an English text in which each letter is replaced by a symbol, the symbol for E will stand out statistically and reveal the text's meaning. Like English, every language has a characteristic distribution of its letters. E stands out in most Western languages; thus, following contemporary computer jargon, we can coin the expression "their E backdoor."

IN ENGLISH

Most frequent letters	e t a o i n s h r d l u
Most frequent first letters	t a s o i c p b s h m
Most frequent last letters	e t s d n r y o f l a g
Most frequent bigrams	th er on an re he in ed nd ha at
Most frequent trigrams	the and tha ent ion tio for nde
Most frequent doubles	ss ee tt ff ll mm oo
Most frequent letters that follow E	r d s n a c t m e p w o
Most frequent 2-letter words	of to in it is be as at so we he
Most frequent 3-letter words	the and for are but not you all
Most frequent 4-letter words	that with have this will your from they

Frequency characteristics also extend to pairs or sets of letters, such as sets of two letters (one following another in a text), or bigrams, and sets of three letters, or trigrams. Among the possible combinations of two letters, some occur often and others never occur (see the table on page 158).

Using these statistics as a tool, a codebreaker can break down a code into sections that are easier to translate and sections that are obscure (the statistics are not always precise). Then, step by step, using intuition, codebreaking methods, and trial and error, if the text is long enough, the codebreaker can translate it.

The Europeans realized these statistical weaknesses in the fifteenth century but can't be credited for it. They discovered them when they started to explore Arabian science. Cryptography had been in active use in Arabian culture for centuries. The best example of an early use of cryptography is the fifth-century *Kama Sutra*, in which the forty-fifth of the 64 arts recommended for women is cryptography. Several centuries later, as early as the ninth century, the Arabian linguist Al-Kindi computed letter statistics in his language. He also wrote the earliest known book on codebreaking, *A Manuscript on Deciphering Cryptographic Messages*, which was copied and slowly found its way to Rome and Florence mainly through Andalusia in southern Spain, where Christians, Moslems, and Jews more or less peacefully shared a common civilization.

It's hard to believe that for more than four centuries no one in Western Europe knew of Al-Kindi's work. Of course, the Knights Templar, who desperately needed a good cipher and were in contact with Muslims, might have known about and used his book but kept it to themselves.

It was the Italian Renaissance architect Leone Battista Alberti who first analyzed the problem fully and organized systematic techniques for cracking ciphers his contemporaries thought invulnerable. He was interested in cryptography as well as art, architecture, and mathematics because these were activities in which impressive progress was being made every day in fifteenth-century Italy. Following Simeone de Crema (see page 160), who had used the system earlier, Alberti advocated the replacement of each letter with several possible symbols. If E is replaced at random by different symbols, its frequency stops showing up. This hides the statistical weakness of alphabetical languages and literally closes the E backdoor. The rate of recurrence of the letter E is hidden behind its various representations.

This homophone technology is called polyalphabetic because it uses multiple alphabets.

E	12.41
T	9.69
A	8.20
I	7.68
N	7.64
O	7.14
S	7.06
R	6.68
L	4.48
D	3.63
H	3.50
C	3.44
U	2.87
M	2.81
F	2.35
P	2.03
Y	1.89
G	1.81
W	1.35
V	1.24
B	1.06
K	0.39
X	0.21
J	0.19
Q	0.09
Z	0.05

The table on the this page is a list of the frequency percentages of the 26 letters computed in a survey of contemporary English. Only the order of the most frequently used letters is significant. The exact percentages will vary from one document to another, depending on the text chosen for analysis, and so, apart from E, you cannot depend on statistics alone for the identification of all letters. Statistics tell us roughly what zone of frequencies a letter lies in, and that helps narrow the possibilities.

In the other Western languages, E stands out ahead in German and French. In Spanish and Italian, it is challenged by the other vowels. In terms of frequency, E is harder to distinguish from A in Spanish and from A and I in Italian, as you can see in the table below.

The following hints are useful for deciphering an English code:

- U always follows Q except in foreign words such as *Iraqi* and *qat*
- H is the most frequently used letter before a vowel.
- N is the most frequently used letter after a vowel.
- ED, ES, and ER are the most frequently used word endings.
- The average word is 5.5 letters long.
- If a word begins and ends with the same letter, look for S, T, or D.

The cipher gallery in Chapter 10 will give you an opportunity to practice these codebreaking techniques in a wide variety of graphic alphabets.

THE MOST FREQUENTLY APPEARING LETTERS IN WESTERN LANGUAGES

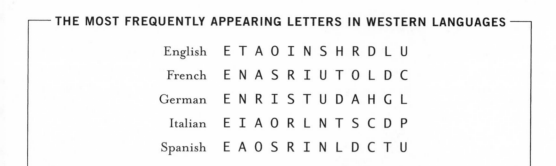

English   E T A O I N S H R D L U
French   E N A S R I U T O L D C
German   E N R I S T U D A H G L
Italian   E I A O R L N T S C D P
Spanish   E A O S R I N L D C T U

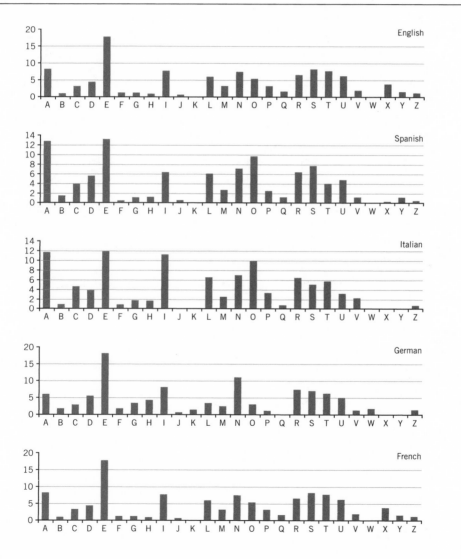

Decode:

Use the E backdoor technique on this text by Leone Battista Alberti from his book *On Painting*. It uses the symbols from a 1540 homophone table that is shown in the Solutions section so that you can later compare the efficiency of homophones compared with simple substitution. To help you in this first exercise, the spaces have been preserved.

ᑲ∩Ⅹ⋏ᴣⅩ⋏Ꮎ⫞ᑲ⋏ᴣ∩Ⅹ⋏⑁∩ᒍⲬᎾⅩ⋏ᴣ♄ᑲᴥᴣᴣⲬ⋏ᴥⅩ⫞ᴥ

⋏ᴥᴣ ᑲ⋏ᛁ♄ ꓕ∩ᵻⴅᴥ ∩ⴱᴥᴣ⋏ᴣ ꓕᴣ⋏ ᑲᴥᴣᴥᴣ⋏ᴣ ∩ᴥ

ᴘᵻ∩ᏟᴇⴱᴇᴅᴇⴅᴣⴱᴰᴣᴅᴰᴑᴇᴣꓕᴥᴣᴥᴣᴇᴣᴥᏨ♄

ᴣⵌᴣ⫞ᴥ∩⫞⑁ᴣᴣꓕ∩ᛁꓕᴥᴣᴥ∩ᛁⅩᴇᴣ ᴣᴇᴣ⋏ ∩♄ᴣᴣᴑ∩⋏♄

⑁ᴣ⋏ᴣᴇⴱⅩⴱⴅ⋏ⴅ ᴣⵌᴣ♄ ∩ᴣᴣ ᴣᴣⵌᑲᴇ⋏ⵝᴣⴅⅩⅩᴣⵌᴇᴣᴣ∩ⴅ

ᑲᛁᴣ∩⑁ᴇᴣᴣ ∩⋏ⴅⅩⅩᴣⵌᴇᴣᴣ∩ᴣ∩ⴅᴑⅩᴣ∩ᴣⅩᑲ⋏ ♄ᑲᴣ ᴣⵌᴣ

♄ⴱⴅᴇᛁ∩ⴼ⋏Ⅹ⋏ⵌᴥ∩Ꮯ⋏ⵌᴥ⑁ᴣᴣ♄ᴇ∩ⴅ♄ᴣ ᑲ♄ ∩ꓕ∩⋏⋏ⵌᴥⅩ⑁∩ᛁᴣⵌ∩ᴅ♄

ⴅᴣ∩ⴅ ⴅᴣᴣᴣ∩Ⅹ⋏ᛁ♄ ⅠⅩᴇᴣᴥ ∩ ᛁᑲ⋏Ꮎ ᛁⅩ♄ᴣ ᴣⵌᴑⴱᴇⵌ

ᑲ∩Ⅹ⋏ᴣⅩ⋏Ꮎⵌᴑᴣᴣⵌⵌ⋏⋏♇ᴣⵌ∩ᴣᑲ∩Ⅹ⋏ᴣⅩ⋏Ꮎⵌⵌ∩ᑲᴣⴅ

ᴣⵌᴣ ᏴⴱⴅⵌⅩⵌ⑁Ⅹᴣᴣᴣ∩ⴅᑲᴣᴣⴅⴼ♄ᴣⵌᴣ ⋏∩ᴣⵌᑲ⋏⑁ Ⅹᴣⵌᴣᴣ-

ᴣ∩Ⅹ⋏ᛁ♄⋏∩⑁ᴣⵌᴣⵝᴣᴇᴇᴣ∩ᴣᴣⵌᴣᎾⅩ♄ᴣᴣᑲᴑᑲᴣᴣ∩ᛁⵌ♄ᑲᴣ

ᑲ∩Ⅹ⋏ᴣⅩ⋏ᎾⅩⵌᴑᑲⵌᴣᴇⵌᴣᴣ♄ᴇᛁᴣᑲᴣⵌ∩ᴣ ᑲⅩᴣᴣ♄Ⅹ⋏ⵌⅩ⫞ⵌ

ⴅᑲⅩ⋏ⵌᴇⵌᴣ ᴣᑲᴣⵌᴣ Ᏼⴱⴅⵌ∩ ⋏ⴅⵝᴣᴣᑲⵌᑲᴇᴣⵌᑲᴇⵌⵌ ♄ᴇⅠⅠᑲ♄

ᴣⵝⅠⅩᎾⅩᑲ⋏

Decode:

This text on painting by Alberti describes how he introduces geometry into a picture. The symbols from a 1552 homophone table are randomized to produce a different symbolic index. Spaces have been deleted and letters have been grouped in fives as in the regular professional presentation that helps prevent transmission errors.

Cipher Adulthood and Homophones

It's never too late to be smart. When Europeans finally realized how simple it was to crack symbolic substitution through the E backdoor, they followed the lead of Simeone de Crema and Battista Alberti and armed themselves with the new technology of homophones.

Simeone de Crema

The earliest known document that made use of homophones was written by Simeone de Crema in Mantua in 1401. He coded the alphabet by inverting the order of the letters and then exchanged a few in the middle of the alphabet to avoid the presentation of M on its own. Practically speaking, a single letter on its own is of no use to a codebreaker who doesn't know anything about the code, but creating a completely different coding for the alphabet must have seemed important. Finally, the table offered homophones: three optional symbols each for the vowels A, E, O, and U.

The author disregarded or was unaware of the fact that C, D, I, L, N, P, R, S, and T appear more frequently in Italian than U does and might merit homophones as well. However, de Crema's code, which is shown below, must have been good enough to defeat most traditional codebreakers.

Note that the large number of symbols—many more than the normal 23 letters of the fifteenth-century alphabet—unveiled the new technology, for in older cryptography each letter was coded by only one symbol. This may have inspired de Crema to use digits as extra symbols so that a potential codebreaker would mistake them for actual numbers.

Decode:

This statement about the city of Mantua is coded in four different ways with the Simeone de Crema homophone table.

It's worth noting that the last of the alternative symbols for O is literally out of character in that it uses a different graphic style. This symbol is a right angle with a dot, as in the Templars' code. The year 1401 was less than a century after the dissolution of their order. The exact date of the importation of homophones into Western Europe is not known, and de Crema may very well not have been the first to use them. The Templars might have imported and used homophones well before him. They had been in contact with the Arabs, and their need for a good coding system might have necessitated their interaction with Arabs to use homophones.

Breaking Homophones

François Viète (1540–1603) had a great mind and might have been a great mathematician if he had lived in a quieter century and not been such a good codebreaker. He was one of the founders of modern algebra but was so useful to his king, Henri IV, and was called on so frequently to read secret diplomatic messages that he never had enough time to do fundamental research. Nonetheless, although he hardly published during his lifetime, the University of Nantes has given his name to one of its research centers.

Viète left a short untitled treatise, written a few weeks before his death, on his codebreaking methods. He was both logical and pragmatic, using both his knowledge of language and all the practical data he could garner from spies, intelligence, the news, and his analysis of the messages as they were written on paper.

Homophones would have been uncrackable if they had been used by perfect people in a perfect world. Fortunately for codebreakers, security of transmission in the sixteenth and seventeenth centuries was the same as it is in the twenty-first century: nonexistent. Just as Morse code over wire and radio was intercepted and all our phone calls and e-mails are intercepted, all mail between kings, embassies, and generals at that time was intercepted and copied before it reached its destination. Every state had a not-so-secret "dark chamber" where the job was done overnight, with copies handed to the codebreakers, a situation not unlike today's, when all e-mail is intercepted and put in data banks, making snail mail far more confidential.

In addition, important messages often were sent several times to deal with the physical insecurity of couriers crossing Europe and continued to be sent until the sender was certain they had arrived. This multiplication of identical content in different messages greatly aided Viète in defeating homophones. The sender, with no photocopying machine, did not have a copy of previous messages, and so each time he coded a message, he used new homophones that were chosen at random. Viète got precious clues by comparing the variants.

Another powerful method that was used to break all sorts of codes was to look for probable words. In every situation, words not yet included in the codebook (if there is one) come up and are included in a message, possibly several times. Those words could include the name of a place the army had just reached or the name of a newly mentioned person. Using such a word and the pattern of its letters (for example, LONDON = abcdbc), the codebreaker went through the message, applying the trial-and-error method.

Numbers as applied to people, money, or dates were looked for to yield precious clues.

Another weakness was formal headers, which were compulsory at the beginning of messages to kings or popes. Worse still, copies often began "This is a copy of…"

Only when all these practical techniques had been applied did Viète recommend the use of statistics and specific linguistic tools. Languages add to the imperfection of our world. As we've seen with statistics, they do not make use of all of their letters with the same frequency; on the contrary, they expose themselves through all kinds of patterns. Codebreakers should spend a long time analyzing and recording all the patterns they notice and then form hypotheses and try them until the code is cracked.

Coders were weakened by two forms of etiquette. One was the etiquette of language: spelling and grammar. The real content of a text is comprehensible even if words are misspelled, L's or E's are not doubled, and an occasional article is left out, yet coders still attempted to transmit messages as faithfully as possible, thus leaving clues that undermined their work. Worse, social etiquette forced them to introduce polite formulas and hierarchic titles when addressing important persons. That trend, which was catastrophic half a millennium ago, still holds. Several codes were broken during World War II because of clues provided by etiquette.

Viète's talent almost got him into deep trouble when he quickly broke the code of Philip II of Spain and then boasted about it. The king was so proud of his 500-symbol personal code that he became irritated. He formally accused Viète of sorcery and brought the matter before the Inquisition. Luckily for Viète, the Pope made so much use of codebreaking that he rejected the accusation.

Michele Steno

Another acknowledged document on the development of homophones is a page written in 1411 by Michele Steno, then doge of Venice, which displays a table of symbols (it is shown in the Solutions section). This is no surprise. Venice was intensely active diplomatically and commercially and thus had need for good codes.

All five vowels were provided with homophones, although with a smaller choice than in de Crema's table, but the technology was improved by the introduction of two new devices. One is a set of null letters that the coder can insert at will in the message to make the task of a codebreaker working with statistics harder. The second is a code list of symbols for recurrent words that the sender no longer needs to replace letter by letter, further misguiding the codebreaker. A specific symbol for the Pope suggests that he was referred to in the vast majority of messages.

Before you look at Steno's table in Chapter 11, here is an opportunity to practice breaking homophone codes in the same way as a codebreaker of that time who often was provided with several versions of the same message by his intelligence agencies. Steno's table is applied to the same text three times, producing three different-looking messages.

Decode:

Leonardo da Vinci's notes on a "method of proving that the earth is a star" (*Notebooks*, page 867).

$$;f\,\text{X}\zeta\,\Xi\delta\iota\Upsilon\,f\,\ast\,d\,\Xi7d\zeta_3\varphi2\delta e'\ast2\text{X}k2\delta'f\ast\div\Xi'\mathbb{H}'\mathbb{X}5\delta;'$$

$$2\delta\text{H}3h\div7\bot3d\div\xi\mathbb{Q}f\Theta\,\Xi;\delta1\zeta h3\Xi\zeta2c\Theta\bot\bot33\div\delta'2\iota2\text{X}2\iota\Theta$$

$$\div\gamma\text{H}'\text{X}\diamondsuit\div2\Xi\delta1d\zeta\Xi'45\bot\gamma\delta5\text{X}\div7b\bot\ast b\omega4\zeta\ast\delta'\Theta\div1\div\mathbb{X}'$$

2ζ1÷Υd '4Ƨδƒ'*ζ13αΞƒζ☊δ'*ΞδhΘdζ;Ξb♧ζ3ξx÷

1δ*b3÷δ'**3*1÷bγΘΥΥδ'1δxƒƌ'2δH3÷7⊥3÷ξα♤εδ'

*hΞδ1ζΞƧ*ζ*ζ2Θ⊥⊥3x÷δ'2Ξδ1ζiΞ1dΞ3αδΞd2*☊

Ξƒδ4φ2δ'Θδδ'i3ΞδH α3÷7⊥xb÷ξΘ99*1ζΞδ♧φ*Θ÷

27dδ*÷Ξ34d÷Θξζ*ΘδΘiΞδ' g2γx1c☊2δ2ζ♤ƌ'*c

φ4γ3♤ƌ'2ƒΞδαΘζδd'*ζ*ƒ4ζ*δd'*bΞδ1ζφ*x÷ξ⊥⊥g

ζgξ*ζδ'Θe÷δ'*c*Θζδc'δc'3Ξ☊♤hδxe4÷c2gƒƒ*i

7δ*Υx÷ƒΘα÷xα÷Ξδ1÷δH4Hd⊥ΥΦ*Θζ193ΥΥ♤HφⅠx

÷dξe4ƒƌ'*ΞxΞ24ƒdδα'2ΞδΘζδ'd2÷9ζi♤2δ'1dδδ

'*αΞƧζƒΘ7*4ƒδ'k2i1dxdζƧ'*ζ2xdδ⊥x2Ξ74d÷δ3ξ

Ƨ♤ƧΞδ4ƒxζ2d1÷eγδ'i*ΞHζƒd17d24ƒƌ'2ƒd3ζ*αH'*

kζ2ix δ2÷cΥkΞ1ζ*kδ'♤Ξ2hx÷δ♤Ƨ'x7'δ'2Ξ♤⊥1ζζΘ3

Ξ92÷2δζΘδα2⊥c÷Υδζ1;÷hΞ☊xδδ'23☊Θξg2Ξk♤ƌ'

2'*ΘHc2÷ƒ⊥αxkφk4Υd3*Ξ⊥1ζξ*Ƨα'*÷δ'*xζ3Ξe

Decode:

Here is the second version.

f x k ζ Ξ δγ2 Ξ7ζx φg✱kδ '✱c2x2δ; '✱÷dΞ'k4H'φδ'✱δ5

k3÷7⊥3÷ξ4fΘcΞδΘζ3Ξζ✱1⊥⊥⊥33÷δ'✱b✱x2Θ÷gγhH

'3 4÷e✱ΞδΘζΞ'451dγδhHx÷7⊥✱ω4ζ2δ';Θ÷1÷4δ'

2ζΘ÷γ'4Hhδh'2gζd13Ξfζ4ωα δ'✱ΞδΘζΞ ζ3ξ3÷1δ

f2e3÷dδi'e22xα2α1÷γkΘγγδ'1δxfδ 'd✱;δ5;x÷7⊥xα

÷ξφfδ'✱ΞδfΘζ;Ξ52ζ✱iζ2h1⊥⊥g33÷δ'c2fΞδd1ζΞ

Θ Ξg3δiΞ✱✱ωΞδφ2δ'1δδ'xΞδdH3;÷7⊥x÷;ξ199✱Θ

ζΞδ4φe2Θ÷✱7δ2÷Ξ3dφ÷1Ξξkζ✱1δf1Ξδc'k2dγ3Θ

ω✱δe2ζα φδf'd2φφ3h4fδ'✱ΞδkΘζδ'2ζ✱df ζ2δ'✱

ΞδΘζφe✱x÷ξf⊥1ζξ2hζδ'b1c÷αδ'i✱2hΘζδ'δ'xΞω4

gδ3φ÷✱$f$$f$27δ✱γ3÷1÷$k3k$÷Ξδ1÷$k$δ$b$H H⊥$b$γφ✱1ζΘ

f93γγ4d5;φ⊥x÷bξhφ$f$$i$δ'✱Ξ3Ξ✱$d4f$δ'✱$e$Ξδ1$d$ζδ'✱

÷9ζ45g2fδ'd1δδ'✱dΞHζfΘ7f✱φδ'2Θ3ζe5'2ζi23δ

⊥x✱Ξ74÷δd3cξH45Ξδφx ζ✱cΘ÷γδ'i2;Ξb5ζfΘ72d4

$d$$f$αδα'✱$c$$f$3ζ2$f$5'✱ζ23δ2÷γΞΘ$i$ζ✱δ'4Ξ$g$23÷δ H$c$'3

k7'δ;'c2Ξφ1ζζcΘxΞ92÷2δζ;1δc2g1÷γδζ1;÷Ξhω3h

δδd'd23dωΘξ✱Ξφfδ'✱d'b2ΘHα✱÷⊥kxφ4γbx2Ξ

⊥g1fζξ✱dHb'✱d÷αδ'✱3dζd3Ξf2Θ÷γΞωΘ⊥⊥H'2÷

Decode:

Here is the third one.

$f\,3\zeta\Xi\delta\gamma*\Xi7\zeta3\varphi k*\delta'2b2h32\delta'2k\div\Xi'\langle H'45\delta'2\delta5 3b\div7$

$;\bot x\div\xi\varphi f\,1b\Xi\delta c\Theta d\zeta k3\Xi a\zeta*f\,\Theta\bot k\bot x3\div\delta'*2d\times*1\div\gamma5$

$'x\Leftrightarrow\div*\Xi\delta1 d\zeta\Xi'45\bot\gamma g\delta d5\times e\div7c\bot*\omega\,\delta\zeta*\delta'1\div\Theta\div\omega$

$\delta'*\zeta d1\div\gamma'\langle H\delta'*\zeta\Theta3 d\,\Xi cf4\omega\delta' k2\Xi\delta\Theta\zeta\Xi\,\delta3\xi x\div d1\delta$

$h*3\div\delta d'*23k2\Theta\div\gamma1\Upsilon k\gamma\delta'\Theta\delta x f\,a\delta'*\delta H3\div7e\bot i x\div\xi4$

$h f\delta'*\Xi\delta1\zeta\Xi5*\zeta*\zeta c2\Theta\bot\bot3k3\div\delta'2\Xi b\delta\Theta d\zeta\Xi h1\Xi3\delta\Xi$

$k22\omega\Xi\delta\langle\varphi g*\delta'1\delta\delta'x\Xi\delta H3\div f71\bot3\div\xi1992\Theta a\zeta\Xi\delta f\,\langle e$

$\varphi21\div*7\delta*\div\Xi x4\div1\Xi\xi\zeta d2k\Theta\delta\Theta\Xi\delta d'2\gamma31\omega*e\delta2\zeta c4$

$f\,\delta'*\varphi4\gamma b x4 f\,\delta d'a*\Xi g\delta e1 f\zeta\delta'2\zeta*f\langle\zeta h2\delta'*\Xi\delta1\zeta$

$\varphi*3g\div h\xi\bot\Theta\zeta h\xi a*b\zeta k\delta'1\div\delta'*21\zeta\delta'\delta'x\Xi\omega f\,4\delta x\Leftrightarrow\div$

$2ff\,27a\delta*\gamma x\div1\div x\div f\,\Xi g\delta1\div\delta Hd45\bot\Upsilon\varphi k2\Theta\zeta e1 69 x\gamma\Upsilon$

$d\,\langle H\varphi\bot d x\div\xi\varphi\delta'2g\Xi3\Xi2\varphi\delta'2\Xi\delta1;\zeta\delta f'2\div9e\zeta45b2\delta'$

$\Theta\delta\delta'*d\Xi5h\zeta f\,1724 f\delta'21 x\zeta He'2\zeta i23\delta132b\Xi i74\div\delta x a$

$\xi5 d\,\langle H;\Xi\delta\langle g fx\zeta*\Theta\div\Upsilon i\delta'*k\Xi5\zeta;f\Theta7*\langle d f\delta'*f3\zeta2H'*$

$\zeta*x\delta*\div a\Upsilon\Xi1\zeta2\delta'\langle\Xi2x\div c\delta\langle e Hi'3 d7'a\delta'*\Xi d\,\langle e\bot\bot d\zeta$

$h\zeta1 h x\Xi9 b2\div*\delta d\zeta\Theta\delta2 i\Theta\div b\gamma\delta\zeta1\div k\Xi\omega3 a\delta\delta g'*x\omega b$

$1\xi2\Xi\varphi\delta'*'2\Theta Hf\,2\div\bot3\varphi4\Upsilon x2\Xi d\bot\Theta\zeta\xi*H'2c\div e\delta'*3\zeta$

$3\Xi21 c\div\Upsilon d\Xi\omega d\bot\bot\bot a5 h'2\div h\delta'*x d\Theta;\zeta d*4\div\delta'*\omega2\zeta$

$x\gamma x\Theta\div$

Giambattista Palatino

The table of homophones shown below was devised in 1540 by Giambattista Palatino, who expressed his talent in the art of handwriting (and example is given after the exercise below). His production was so fine that he was called "the calligraphers' calligrapher." Like Leonardo da Vinci, he practiced left-handed mirror writing. For our purposes here, he extended his art to the invention of tables of homophones.

A	B	C	D	E	F	G	H	I
▽	∩	I	X	U	٩	ƀ	₽	ƀ
ɗ						ƀ		

K	L	M	N	O	P	Q	R	S
╫	⊥	૧	Ɔ	٩	Ħ	Ħ	℮	X
				I				

T	U	X	Y	Z				
ƀ	ʮ	ɗ	Ɔ	♃				
	✦							

Palatino must have trusted his abundant set of 12 null letters more than the homophones, though: The vowels have only one alternative symbol each. Unfortunately, we do not know if the high quality of his ciphers deterred codebreakers.

Decode:

Leonardo da Vinci on secret inventions and Archimedes.

ƀ٩ɗƆ♃7ɗƆII✦ⅼXₚɗ✦ Xƀ XII✦℮Xƀ₽ ✦ƀ♃IXƀHI✦℮X I٩ƀ₽

IɗƆƆIƆƀƆɗⅼⅬƀƀX✦ɗ℮ƀI✦ X٩I℮7 Xɗ ƆXₚɗ✦ ƀƀ✦Ɔ X✦I₽ɗ XI℮ƀ

ƀI ƀ₽ ℮I7ɗƆX ✦ƀƀ₽✦₽ɗƀℯɗHƀXƀƀ♃ ✦I✦⊥X ƀ₽Ɔₚɗ✦ IIƆ╫℮X

The Duke of Montmorency

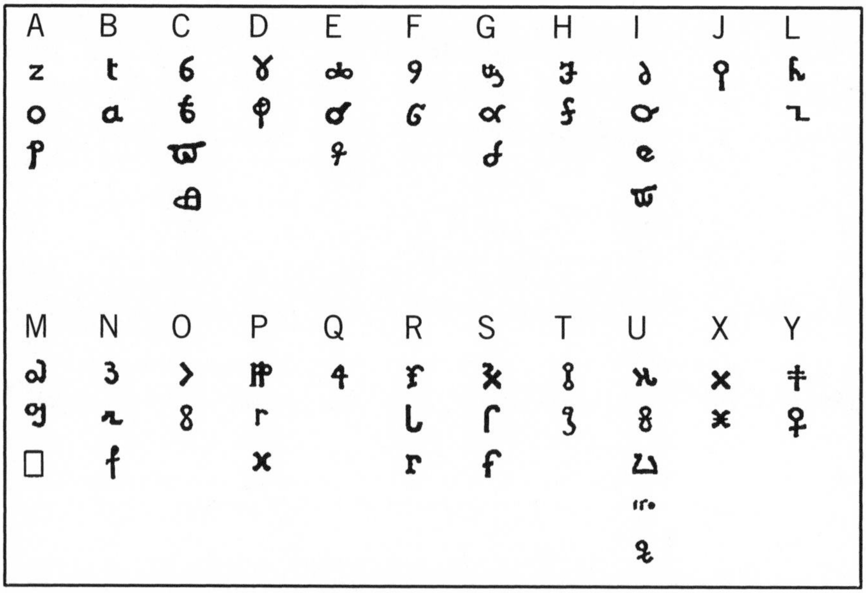
A B C D E F G H I J L
M N O P Q R S T U X Y

The homophone table above was used by the Duke of Montmorency in his correspondence with the Duke of Northumberland during the Dudley conspiracy in the middle of the sixteenth century. It is far more developed than the preceding tables. Most letters, even relatively rare ones such as B, have variants.

The table also features an outstanding innovation that went almost unnoticed until it played an essential role in the twentieth-century computer industry and the Internet. This table includes an early, perhaps the first, appearance within a text of markups as we now know them. They were to become essential language tools, first as GENCODE and SGML (Standard Generalized Markup Language) in programs for print shops, then in word processors, and then in that cornerstone of the Internet through Sir Tim Berners-Lee's HTML (HyperText Markup Language) and the various other languages that now use the suffix ML: the ever-growing varieties of Markup Languages.

Just as "<a>" means "here starts a link" and "</a>" means "here ends a link" in HTML, \ or] in the Montmorency code means "here starts a special segment of the text," and] or _ means "here ends the special segment of the text." In 1552, what they really meant was "here begins the actual message; disregard everything before" and "here ends the message; disregard everything that follows."

| Message begins: **25** or **33** | Message ends: **33** or **23** |

With some planned ambiguity, the figure 33 was included at the beginning and end, probably to cause confusion in the codebreaker's (but not in the receiver's) mind. Misinterpretation was easy to prevent, however, if the message was coded correctly. The decoder looked first for the markup symbol for "start" and then for the other, possibly identical symbol meaning "end."

With this technology, letters and symbols begin to take on more meaning. Depending on the markups bracketing them, they can be null or meaningful. Letters and symbols also can be markups, and that lets them become active, changing and formatting whole portions of text. It's no wonder that this technology appeared in the sixteenth century, when Western mathematicians were rediscovering algebra and the use of abstract symbols to represent known and unknown quantities. Markup technology is the same sort of step toward an abstract treatment of language. However, no further work seems to have been done in developing the use of markup languages in cryptography at that time.

The table also features nine nulls and a vocabulary of small words, as shown below.

| ño | 6 | ſc | mon | 61 | ✳ | pre | tt | T |

con	and	et	war	do	done	me		the
qz	tu	et	m	ꝰʒ	♉	ⳑ		Ⱳ

peace	that	who	who	if	you	us
m̃	23	⟨	ſ	⊘	4	#

Decode:

A definition in Wikipedia of the old print shop use of markup, a printer's procedure that may date back to Gutenberg.

Henri II of France

Henri II of France used the code table below, which was created in 1558, to correspond with Philibert Babou de la Bourdaisière, his ambassador in Rome. It features yet another new tool in its attempt to hide double letters, a weak point in many languages. Every common double letter is represented by a single specific symbol.

ee	ff	ll	mm	nn	pp	rr	ss

The table also contains two short codebooks or vocabularies: one for frequently used proper names and the other for common words and frequently appearing groups of letters:

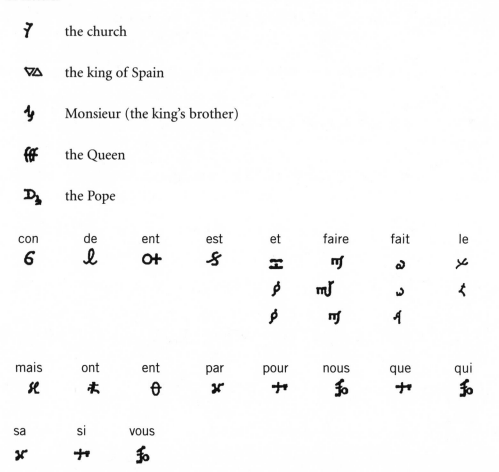

the church

the king of Spain

Monsieur (the king's brother)

the Queen

the Pope

con	de	ent	est	et	faire	fait	le

mais	ont	ent	par	pour	nous	que	qui

sa	si	vous

The author shows a greater awareness of statistics and makes more logical use of letter frequency than did his predecessors. Homophone variants are not restricted to vowels. Frequently used consonants such as R, S, and T have several symbols each. Common words and groups of letters are provided with homophone variants too, and the nine null letters shown below complete the table.

There are no markup signs.

In the main table shown below, I and S have the most homophones, twice as many as E, which is by far the most frequently appearing letter in French.

A	B	C	D	E	F	G	H	I	J
ʈ	ɑ	ʋ	∂	✗	☉	ʄ	+	℻	ℓ
⊶	ſ	m	u	A	ⷈ	ʃ	ҕ	ꞯ	ʒ
n				M				♭	
								Ɠ	
								n	

M	N	O	P	Q	R	S	T	U	X
⑂	⋊	⑀	⑁	℣	⟨	2	ℛ	9	Ɠ
#	℡	ꝙ	∞	S	✚	9	Ɜ	♣	Ϛ
		ʋ			✗	ȶ	Ɛ	✳	
		∂			↯	⑂		C	
				▣					

Decode:

Machiavelli, whose works inspired many princes and kings, among them Henri II, writes on "what fortune effects in human affairs."

Mary Stuart's Terminal Code

Mary Stuart was an emblematic victim of bad cryptography. Mary became the rightful queen of Scotland when she was six days old and was officially crowned Mary I at the age of six months, hence the name Mary I, Queen of Scots. Brought to France from Scotland by Henri II's navy at the age of five and former wife of Henri II's son, who died before he could reign, she was a potential contender for the throne of England that went to Elizabeth I. Being a devout Catholic in a Protestant country, she had little chance of being accepted. Nevertheless she sailed back to Scotland. During the ensuing adventures that are described in several historical novels and films, she trusted herself to a bad coder and lost her head because of his weak system. In 1586, 185 years after Simeone de Crema, her code contained no homophones. It was a simple substitution alphabet that was protected only by four null symbols and a vocabulary of 35 symbols for frequently used words. Moreover, as only one of its kind, it featured a naive gimmick: a symbol placed before letters to signal that they should be doubled, the typically pointless creation of someone with no real experience as a codebreaker. Inevitably, her code was cracked and turned against her. In a ploy later borrowed by Sir Arthur Conan Doyle in "The Adventure of the Dancing Men" (see Chapter 10), a false message was sent to her, leading her to betray herself through a return message that revealed her goal as well as her associates and gave Elisabeth I a legal reason to condemn her.

Decode:

In one of her controversial "casket letters," this is the paragraph that betrays Mary's wish to murder her husband—if the letter is authentic.

Mary's final code may remain forever undeciphered. Richard Wingfield, a witness to her execution at Fotheringay castle on February 8, 1587, relates that "her lips stirred up and down almost a quarter of an hour after her head was cut off." Alas, there was no lip reader present to interpret her last statements.

From Polybius to Guillotin

Mary Stuart's fate closely resembles that of Marie Antoinette. The Austrian arch-duchess who was married to Louis XVI of France played unrestrainedly with ciphers until one of them helped bring about her death. In a message to friends in Austria, she called on them to attack France and put an end to the revolutionary republic. The code was broken, and she was imprisoned in le Temple and convicted of high treason. Later she died under Doctor Guillotin's beheading machine.

Marie Antoinette used the Polybius 5 × 5 grid (see Chapter 1) but enriched it with two inventions. The first was the use of null symbols: Because the grid uses only the digits 1 to 5 (see the illustration at the top of page 184), all the other digits were used as null figures that coders could insert between useful numbers.

The second invention weakened the system by making it vulnerable to all omissions of digits in the transcription of the code. To improve the system, its inventors,

	1	2	3	4	5
1	K	I	N	G	A
2	B	C	D	E	F
3	H	J	L	M	O
4	P	Q	R	S	T
5	U	V	W	X	Y

Talon and Mirabeau, first normally translated all letters into couples of digits, then wrote down all the first digits of the couples and then all the digits that came second. If a digit was lost, there was no way for the receiver to retrieve the correct couple.

Marie Antoinette's security would have been better if she had been able to use an improvement of the Polybius grid that seems to have been invented in the nineteenth century. In this advanced version, the sender and the receiver agree on a code word that individualizes the grid. The code word is written at the start of the grid, ignoring repeated letters if there are any, and then the grid is filled in with the rest of the alphabet. On the grid above, the code word is *KING*.

Practically speaking, this grid method is nothing more than an automatic substitution code in which pairs of digits take the place of symbols. As in all one-to-one substitution, it leaves the E backdoor wide open.

Decode:

A few words from Marie Antoinette's last letter.

```
2 2 8 1 5 0 1      1 7 9 1 1 3 4    1 3 6 1 9 3    1 1 1 4 8 8 3

1 1 1 9 0 4 2      4 7 3 1 2 6 5  2 5 5 9 4 8 4  5 4 7 5 5 0 4

3 9 5 4 6 5 5      4 7 5 1 5 7 3
```

Decode:

Part of a letter that helped convict Marie Antoinette; it was sent to her secret Swedish friend Fersen. She names Mercy-Argenteau, the Austrian ambassador, to whom she had betrayed the plans of the French generals. Find the grid and the code.

```
31 15 35 44 14 41 23 31 41 25 15 35 14 44 44 14 41 25 14 43

45 12 23 14 35 14 43 22 55 31 11 15 52 14 51 43 25 14 23 11 31

35 35 12 44 45 14 35 13 11 15 45 31 22 15 34 34 55 45 12 31 41

44 31 44 45 45 11 15 45 53 12 43 23 44 21 14 44 15 31 23 15 41

23 15 22 45 31 12 41 45 15 33 14 41 15 45 34 12 41 25 34 15 44
```

45 53 11 31 22 11 53 31 34 34 35 15 33 14 44 12 35 14 31 35 13

43 14 44 44 31 12 41 11 14 43 14 45 31 35 14 31 44 43 51 41 41

31 41 25 44 11 12 43 45 31 45 31 44 31 35 13 12 44 44 31 21 34

14 45 12 53 15 31 45 35 51 22 11 34 12 41 25 14 43 31 15 35 44

14 41 23 31 41 25 45 11 14 21 34 15 41 33 44 31 25 41 14 23 13

15 13 14 43 44 53 11 31 22 11 55 12 51 43 14 42 51 14 44 45 14

23 15 23 31 14 51 53 11 14 41 44 11 15 34 34 53 14 35 14 14 45

15 25 15 31 41 31 41 13 14 15 22 14

Henri IV of France

Henri IV's homophone table, which is shown below, must have been devised by François Viète, who was the official cryptographer, codebreaker, and mathematician to the king. This no-nonsense code is sober and efficient, as befits an author who knows all the tricks and their limits. Most consonants have variants, according to their actual frequency. The vocabulary contains only three words.

The table also features one markup sign: **⚬**

This is enough to signal all the beginnings and ends of null portions, as opposed to the message sections of the Montmorency table.

The code list is a tiny set of three words: par = **Ꮯ** , that = **ᴑ** , you = **ꝺ**

Decode:

Two extracts from J. J .O'Connor and E. F. Robertson's biography of François Viète, mentioning his invention of a technique we now take for granted.

Over time, as codebreakers became more efficient, table designers tried to improve security with longer lists of coded words, as in the codebook below, which was used by Union General Joseph Hooker's code clerk during the American Civil War.

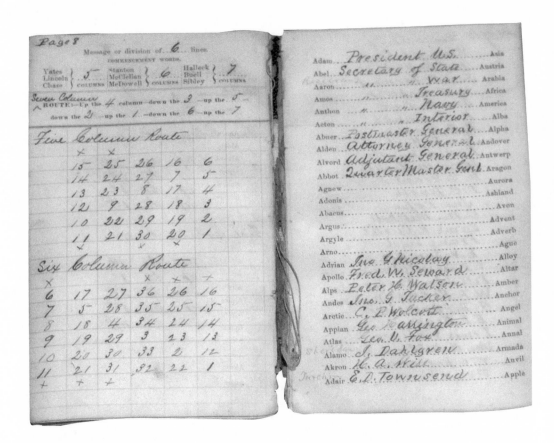

Unbreakable!

Homophone tables wore out rapidly and needed to be replaced fairly often. The technology made the E backdoor harder to penetrate but left a different door open for thieves to steal the code table. Coders, transmitters, and receivers were all vulnerable links in the security chain. Their tables were so complex that all those people had to keep them with them and travel with them, making themselves a target for spies and thieves. Furthermore, sooner or later enemy codebreakers would gather enough intelligence and clues to create their own perfect copies of a table.

Alberti's Wheels Within Wheels

Very early on researchers started to seek out better systems. Their goal was to beat the E backdoor by multiplying cipher alphabets in some other way. In the middle of the fifteenth century, around 1446, Leone Battista Alberti came up with a solution that was the first step toward modern cryptography.

The illustration to the right shows two disks bearing alphabets. The outer disk is fixed and displays the uppercase letters A to Z and the figures 1 to 4. The inner disk is mobile and displays 24 lowercase letters in random order, uses u for v, and has no w. A letter on the outer ring, for instance, A, is chosen as the index letter. The coder and the receiver both have identical wheels and know the index letter.

The coder chooses a random position on the inner disk and specifies it at the start of the message by writing that lowercase letter beneath the uppercase letter A. Each uppercase letter then is coded with the lowercase letter beneath it.

At several points later in the message, wherever he or she chooses, the coder introduces a number from 1 to 4 into the original message, writes its lowercase letter code into the code, and then turns the inner disk till that lowercase letter comes under A. The coder then continues coding the message with the new correspondences.

By using the first letter, the decoder knows how to position the inner disk. Later, when the decoder comes across a letter corresponding to a number, he or she knows where to move the inner disk.

Decode:

Use Alberti's wheel within a wheel to learn how he expresses his taste for mathematics applied to artwork (excuse for the absence of H's in Alberti's wheels).

cxysf	xpuzd	codon	doynk	bconc
sdncs	fbczf	xedos	fpcsf	yxoii
zjjbf	nzuty	itgnz	ubuxb	cgipp
gsbzg	cizto	yztbf	tnunf	boubm

opxyi	ctgcb	rafry	jdcqf	gmmrn
imrnj	hznip	fjdhj	pbizg	qprjd
njdcp	ifzpi	hnjyi	rdazg	mieeb
eucmq	qpdgd	fczcd	mfdmz	abdxc
mqdix	acqzf			

This coding method is very safe. The more often the coder turns the inner wheel, the safer it is. The chief weaknesses are material: physical possession of the wheels and knowledge of the index letter.

The Belaso Breakthrough

For all its good qualities, Alberti's wheel was not adopted by many cryptographers in his era. That might have been due to the poor quality of networks linking professional scientists at that time.

In 1553, Giovan Batista Belaso published a method that solved all problems involving simplicity of use and confidentiality. Regrettably, again because of lack of communication in the scientific community, Belaso was not recognized for his invention during his lifetime. For centuries, all the fame went to Blaise de Vigenère, whose name is still linked to the technology, whereas Belaso remains largely unknown. Because his authorship has been proved and to give Belaso his due, we'll skip Vigenère's name from now on. He did make Belaso's system famous by publishing it during the reign of Henri III in France but should return to his correct place in the annals of cryptography.

Belaso went further than Alberti, adding a considerable improvement. Instead of switching among 4 alphabets when a signal number was introduced two or three times into a message, he switched among 26 different alphabets at every letter in the message.

He made new use of a table invented by Johannes Trithemius, a square array of as many lines as there are letters in the alphabet: Today this would be a square of 26 by 26 letters. He decided that each row of the table would be in a different alphabet, as in Caesar's code. A secret keyword determined which alphabet was to be used for each letter.

In practical terms, this means that the keyword was written repeatedly beneath the message. For example, if the message is "Elizabeth considers marrying Henri" (in fact, a marriage between Elizabeth I and Henri III was considered) and the keyword is *heir*, we get:

	A	B	C	D	E	F	G	H	I	J	K	L	M	N	O	P	Q	R	S	T	U	V	W	X	Y	Z
A	A	B	C	D	E	F	G	H	I	J	K	L	M	N	O	P	Q	R	S	T	U	V	W	X	Y	Z
B	B	C	D	E	F	G	H	I	J	K	L	M	N	O	P	Q	R	S	T	U	V	W	X	Y	Z	A
C	C	D	E	F	G	H	I	J	K	L	M	N	O	P	Q	R	S	T	U	V	W	X	Y	Z	A	B
D	D	E	F	G	H	I	J	K	L	M	N	O	P	Q	R	S	T	U	V	W	X	Y	Z	A	B	C
E	E	F	G	H	I	J	K	L	M	N	O	P	Q	R	S	T	U	V	W	X	Y	Z	A	B	C	D
F	F	G	H	I	J	K	L	M	N	O	P	Q	R	S	T	U	V	W	X	Y	Z	A	B	C	D	E
G	G	H	I	J	K	L	M	N	O	P	Q	R	S	T	U	V	W	X	Y	Z	A	B	C	D	E	F
H	H	I	J	K	L	M	N	O	P	Q	R	S	T	U	V	W	X	Y	Z	A	B	C	D	E	F	G
I	I	J	K	L	M	N	O	P	Q	R	S	T	U	V	W	X	Y	Z	A	B	C	D	E	F	G	H
J	J	K	L	M	N	O	P	Q	R	S	T	U	V	W	X	Y	Z	A	B	C	D	E	F	G	H	I
K	K	L	M	N	O	P	Q	R	S	T	U	V	W	X	Y	Z	A	B	C	D	E	F	G	H	I	J
L	L	M	N	O	P	Q	R	S	T	U	V	W	X	Y	Z	A	B	C	D	E	F	G	H	I	J	K
M	M	N	O	P	Q	R	S	T	U	V	W	X	Y	Z	A	B	C	D	E	F	G	H	I	J	K	L
N	N	O	P	Q	R	S	T	U	V	W	X	Y	Z	A	B	C	D	E	F	G	H	I	J	K	L	M
O	O	P	Q	R	S	T	U	V	W	X	Y	Z	A	B	C	D	E	F	G	H	I	J	K	L	M	N
P	P	Q	R	S	T	U	V	W	X	Y	Z	A	B	C	D	E	F	G	H	I	J	K	L	M	N	O
Q	Q	R	S	T	U	V	W	X	Y	Z	A	B	C	D	E	F	G	H	I	J	K	L	M	N	O	P
R	R	S	T	U	V	W	X	Y	Z	A	B	C	D	E	F	G	H	I	J	K	L	M	N	O	P	Q
S	S	T	U	V	W	X	Y	Z	A	B	C	D	E	F	G	H	I	J	K	L	M	N	O	P	Q	R
T	T	U	V	W	X	Y	Z	A	B	C	D	E	F	G	H	I	J	K	L	M	N	O	P	Q	R	S
U	U	V	W	X	Y	Z	A	B	C	D	E	F	G	H	I	J	K	L	M	N	O	P	Q	R	S	T
V	V	W	X	Y	Z	A	B	C	D	E	F	G	H	I	J	K	L	M	N	O	P	Q	R	S	T	U
W	W	X	Y	Z	A	B	C	D	E	F	G	H	I	J	K	L	M	N	O	P	Q	R	S	T	U	V
X	X	Y	Z	A	B	C	D	E	F	G	H	I	J	K	L	M	N	O	P	Q	R	S	T	U	V	W
Y	Y	Z	A	B	C	D	E	F	G	H	I	J	K	L	M	N	O	P	Q	R	S	T	U	V	W	X
Z	Z	A	B	C	D	E	F	G	H	I	J	K	L	M	N	O	P	Q	R	S	T	U	V	W	X	Y

E L I Z A B E T H C O N S I D E R S M A R R Y I N G H E N R I

H E I R H E I R H E I R H E I R H E I R H E I R H E I R H E I

L P Q Q H F M K O G W E Z M L V Y W U R Y V G Z U K P V U V Q

The coder would look up the substitute for each letter in the rows of the key. This one yields the following:

LPQJH FMKOG WEZML VYWUR YVGZU KPVUV Q

An omission of any letter scrambles the system, sliding the letters of the keyword out of place. This makes it even more important that the code be written in groups of five letters.

Another source of error stems from the use of the table. When coding long messages, a coder may mistake alignments and confuse rows or columns. The best way to prevent that is to use Alberti's disks without the index numbers. Both rings bear the letters of the alphabet in the correct order. For every letter in the message, the coder places the key letter beneath A and reads the coded letter that is under the original letter. When the Confederates used this system as their field cipher during the American Civil War, all their military units had brass cipher disks. Belaso's system is so powerful that stealing the disks did

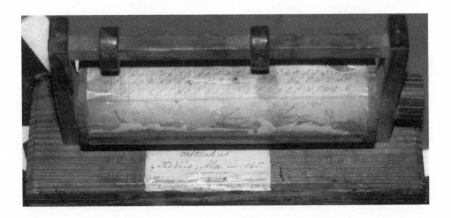

not stop the rightful recipient from reading the messages, for he could draw the grid on paper, and did not help the codebreaker, who didn't possess the key.

Decode:

Test your understanding of the Belaso system by reading Abraham Lincoln's statement in 1861, at the beginning of the American Civil War. Appropriately, the keyword is *WAR*.

EHRRE	EKPLN	PFOEU	ERVYT	CUOIE
NUERV	YTCUT	FENKA	RWARV	SIKDT
YAIEO	TZPUK	EOEKF	JHAMA	RPENK
DEJPA	KASND	EIAIK	AXZOT	JEBVH
IVREZ	DAMAN	FHANB	UCNIX	DTKKD
FOORJ	DZDAM	ANFEN	THIEW	TZKNK
KDFOO				

Note that although this system had been published during the reign of Henri III, that king's successor, Henri IV, still used traditional homophones, as was discussed earlier. Nonetheless, the system was adopted during the seventeenth century and was considered the absolute best for the next two centuries.

Cracked! The Babbage-Kasiski Breakthrough

As late as 1868, Lewis Carroll, working as the mathematician Charles Dodgson rather than the author of *Alice in Wonderland*, published a paper in which he declared Belaso's system "unbreakable." However, his fellow countryman Charles Babbage already had broken it while playing at codebreaking with a friend in 1853, and Friedrich Kasiski cracked it independently later. Babbage, who was more interested in inventing computing machines, didn't bother to publish the results of what he considered a pastime. Kasiski, a Prussian officer, published his solution in Berlin in 1863.

The weakness Babbage and Kasiski exploited in the Belaso system is algebraic. It stems from the logical combination of the systematic repetition of the keyword and statistical occurrences of groupings of letters in language. If a text is long enough, the components of the language inevitably repeat themselves and identical groupings of message letters fall above identical groups of key letters. As a result, identical groups of code letters will occur. If the code breaker notices those groups in the code, he or she will assume that they come from repetitions of the key and that their distance must be a multiple of key length.

For instance, this quote from George Bernard Shaw is coded with the keyword *DOG*.

IOFTENQUOTEMYSELFITGIVESSPICETOMYCONVERSAT**IO**N

DOGDOGDOGDOGDOGDOGDOGDOGDOGDOGDOGDOGDOGDOG**DO**G

LCLWSTTIUWSSBGKOTOWUOYSYVDOFSZRAEFCTYSXVOZ**LC**T

IO appears twice above DO, each time giving the code LC. The distance between the two LCs is 42, a multiple of 3, the length of the word *DOG*.

There are three other repeated bigrams:

WS at 3 and 9 = 6 spaces
YS at 21 and 36 = 15 spaces
CT at 34 and 43 = 9 spaces

All four of these spans happen to be divisible by 3, but most situations are far more complex : some identical bigrams can be produced by chance coincidence rather than repetitions of key and code. Since the picture is not so clear, a codebreaker will have to try several possibilities. Here, the codebreaker would start with a three-letter key.

Once the length of the key is known, the cipher becomes less of a mystery. In this case that means that the letters can be regrouped into three sets, each one a Caesar cipher: those coded by the first letter of the key, those coded by the second, and those coded by the third. In each set, a frequency analysis suggests that the most frequently appearing letter is a substitute for E, thus suggesting the key letter that has yielded E.

Some trial and error still is needed to crack the code.

Decode:

Use the Kasiski-Babbage method as a help to break this coded fateful quote from Robert E. Lee in May 1861.

ATCMJ	SAYMV	SQIGM	DWWMVV	XOLFZ
LVYPH	JKCES	DOMMH	LZYTZ	LTINY
QSUKZ	FCLMO	WFHIV	DWNBJ	AOHLD
AZFGV	LOJIY	WQCTA	WHBXK	WHYKT
ABUMP	GBUGK	HZOVR	GTNAL	KCOMO
SBXLV	MHBXY	FDIEP	LWWBH	FGXHU
GHUIW	JSWBH	LSNAL	FIGUL	JGLXZ
GILVL	KOHWW	SHCXU	LDYKZ	WJYKH
FQYHM	LVYGV	JHBUV	LVMBK	WGZHY
YSNMO	SHQXH	JSUES	SAYKP	UOHLP
XCLXZ	WSNAH	LCOKJ	GIHMY	QKCES
HOMLA	ZFINN	ZONXY	JWVEL	GFXXH
DOHXJ	WGMTY	QSRIP	SHCHU	HSLAH
HGZHY	GILGH	LWIGH	DGCGZ	

CHAPTER 7

Washington 108°

Matrix of a newborn nation, the capital town of Washington, D.C., was purposely designed with the creative help of a mythic "child" to have all the ingredients of a place of myth.

The following account of the history of Washington, D.C., is unconventional. Traditional historical points are hardly mentioned, if not totally omitted, and unexpected items are developed beyond the usual extent, if not unearthed from oblivion or disregard. That treatment follows the logic of a book devoted to the history of code and its multiple emergences through symbols, languages, and art forms. Just as an economist would base a history of that subject on commerce and money flows or a historian of religion would deal with the spread of faiths, a historian of code must follow all the threads relevant to this field, however awry from usual history books. Military history is mentioned in this chapter only to supply the needed background, with no attempt at coverage of all events. The underlying links among many points in this chapter are more often poetic than logical, but poetry is what makes people go to war.

Pentagram City

Washington is one of the rare cities where drivers can make 108° turns. The 108° angle is the conspicuous feature that reveals the underlying presence of pentagons and pentagrams in a design. Geometrically, along with its 36° companion, that angle determines both geometric figures. It presided over the creation of the capital city at the very start of the Union, long before pentagonal buildings or even the city was conceived of.

The history of the pentagram in America has several sources: the Masonic culture of most of the Founding Fathers, the life of a strange architect, and a revolution in the design of gardens. True, there was a pentagram embroidered on the apron presented to George Washington by the Marquis de Lafayette (see Chapter 5), but it was one among many Masonic symbols and did not stand out. The geometric five-pointed figure would need support by deeper forces to gain so central a place in the psyche of the newly founded nation.

Guardian Angles

We must play on words in breaking coded symbols, for that is how the human mind uses language to imagine and create. The ambiguities and fortuitous proximities of words are the wealth of a vocabulary. Wordplay and rhymes are the fuel of poetry and myth.

For example, the inversion of L and E is a clue that reveals the hidden closeness of the words *angel* and *angle*. Suddenly the imagination exclaims, "Oh, of course! What better image of the two wings of an angel than the sides of an angle? An angle is a stylized angel! Look how the 108–36 angel flies!" This symbolic animation of the flying angles parallels Leonardo's flying Vitruvian man (see Chapter 4).

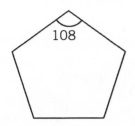

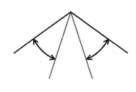

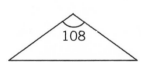

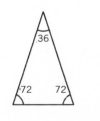

The angled angel that symbolically guarded the birth of the Union was all the more potent in that it was the angle of the pentagram that had watched over the Pythagoreans symbolically two millennia earlier. Most of the Founding Fathers were educated well enough to know that the pentagram was Pythagoras's seal. Consciously or not, they felt that the new nation needed such a seal to verify its existence. Two centuries later, when the nation decided to erect a building devoted to its armed protection, the obvious design for it was a pentagon.

The 108° isosceles triangle sometimes is called the "luminous delta," the 36° one with 72° angles at the base, or the "sublime triangle" (see Chapter 2).

Why limit the playing and rhyming on our way to symbolic truth? As you'll see, symbols are the game. What more poetically correct bird than an eagle to rhyme and fly with angels and angles?

The Pentagon symbolically signals to the entire world the power and determination of the United States. A rarely mentioned fact is that it follows up on the symbolism of Fort McHenry, a highly significant stronghold that defended Baltimore against the British Navy on September 13 and 14, 1814, and thus reestablished the country's independence.

Fort McHenry was first built in 1776 on the Whetstone Peninsula, commanding the entrance to Baltimore's harbor, an earthen, star-shaped building. It did not play an active role during the Revolutionary War except

as a deterrent. It later was turned into a masonry building by the French engineer Jean Foncin from 1799 to 1802 with money raised by James McHenry, who served as secretary of war under George Washington. The victory in 1814 was celebrated by Francis Scott Key's poem "The Defense of Fort McHenry," which was declared the national anthem of the United States in 1931.

The Pentagram-Spangled Banners

The symbolic number 5 appeared early in the symbols of the War of Independence. The flag was its natural birthplace. In 1776, the flag of Washington's head-quarters at Valley Forge, which had been cut and sewn by Betsy Ross in her upholstery shop in Philadelphia, did not feature pentagrams. The 13 states of the

Union were represented as hexagrams, but the symbolism of 5 was present: the stars were displayed in a quincunx, a pattern of entwined five-pointed star elements that appeared on the apron offered to Washington by Lafayette (see Chapter 5).

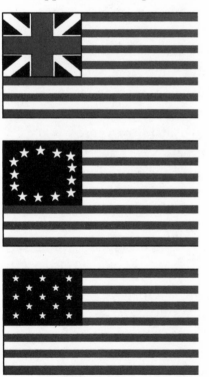

After the Declaration of Independence on July 4, 1776, the 13 stripes of the founding states appeared, but a period of confusion began. Either the 13 stripes enclosed the Union Jack of the British Empire or the 13 stars were laid out in a circle, a design later adopted by the European Community.

On June 14, 1777, Congress unified the design. It defined the first official flag of the United States as having 13 alternating red and white stripes and the Valley Forge arrangement of 13 stars. It was on that occasion that the stars became pentagrams, and they have remained so ever since.

The exact origin of the pentagram on the flag has yet to be discovered by historians. It could have originated with Congressman Francis Hopkinson, who is credited with the design of the first official flag, but his favorite Masonic symbol was the hexagram, and he marked the books in his library with a bookplate bearing three six-pointed stars. It might have come from Betsy Ross. One website relates that when George Washington and Robert Morris came to visit her to order the Valley Forge flag, Betsy, "a standout with the scissors, demonstrated how to cut a five-pointed star in a single snip." The hexagram remained on the first flag, possibly because Washington and Morris were carrying specific orders from the Continental Congress, but they might have been impressed sufficiently by Ross's stunt to suggest the pentagram for later flags. Besides, from a practical point of view, the single-snip trick makes the pentagram easier and quicker to cut than the hexagram. The pentagram might have been suggested, along with his suggestion of the American eagle, by Pierre Charles L'Enfant (see below). Finally, the quincunx on Washington's Masonic apron is made up of pentagram stars.

In fact, as is often the case with important historical events, the choice of the pentagram was overdetermined. All three origins and possibly others as well must have come together to promote the pentagram and signal the Pythagorean presence in the symbolism of the Union.

Later, as new states joined the Union, Congress realized that adding a stripe for each one would make the flag too long or the stripes too narrow. It was decided that after July 4, 1818, the flag never would have more than 13 stripes to symbolize the founding states but that a star would be added for each new state. Curiously, the European Community has chosen pentagrams to represent member states on its flag, oriented one point up, like the American stars.

The design of a flag has an importance that is both symbolic and practical. Symbolically, it is a reminder of a country's history or values, and practically, it is a signal in times of war to differentiate friends from enemies. When the American Civil War broke out, both sides remained sentimentally attached to the colors and pentagrams and kept them on their banners. From March 1861 to May 1863, the first Confederate flag was the Stars and Bars, a circle of seven stars and three horizontal red and white bars, similar to the Stars and Stripes of the Union forces. At the First Battle of Bull Run on July 21, 1861, the similarity of the flags, which were difficult to distinguish at a distance, brought much battlefield confusion; that confusion eventually led to the design and adoption of the Battle Flag or Southern Cross by the Confederates.

Pierre Charles L'Enfant

Because of his role in the conception of Washington, D.C., and in American history in general, Pierre Charles L'Enfant needs to be discussed in some detail. If you have never heard of him or only have noticed L'Enfant Plaza as a Washington subway station, expect a surprise: no epic poet inventing a myth, however inspired, would dare write a story as romantic and full of symbols as the life of Pierre L'Enfant.

Army Engineer and Artist

Pierre L'Enfant was born in France in 1754 and, since his father was a court painter, grew up in artistic surroundings. Yet he was educated as an architect and engineer and became a lieutenant in the French colonial army. In 1777, he boarded the ship *Le Comte de Vergennes* of the pseudo-commercial Hortalez and Co. line, which in fact was used to bring men and military supplies to America. He landed one month before Lafayette did on La Victoire and joined the Revolutionary Army. Like Lafayette, he was a volunteer who paid his own expenses. The American scene at that time was a melting pot of paradoxes, making it one of the most creative periods in history. In short, the British were fighting against the independence of the American states even though they strongly believed in freedom and democracy, and the French came to fight the British even though everything British was fashionable in France, where the king attended plays by Shakespeare and the French philosophers' ideal of liberty came mostly from British Freemason lodges. To make matters even more confusing, George Washington in his early military career had fought the French under the British flag in the French and Indian War. In the first half of the seventeenth century, the French owned a territory called Louisiane that covered 15 current American states, from the mouth of the Mississippi up to Canada, and there were disputes over the border with the British colonies. Those disputes were resolved in 1803 when Napoleon sold Louisiane to the United States. Its southern part became the state of Louisiana in 1812.

King Louis XVI sent a fleet commanded by Admiral d'Estaing and his best general, Rochambeau, to help develop an American republic; ironically, that form of government eventually would lead to the end of the French monarchy and his own death. Indeed, the Indian chiefs, who had been on good terms with the French, expressed their surprise when they met Rochambeau and wondered whether the king of France was in his right mind in siding with a republic.

In the 1770s, there were crowds of young Frenchmen enthusiastic about the war for freedom and willing to battle more for an ideal than against a specific enemy.

L'Enfant took part in several battles. He was wounded at Savannah, was busy recovering in Charleston when the enemy arrived, took part in that battle, and was taken prisoner and then exchanged. He was promoted to major of the engineers in 1783 by George Washington, who could not speak French and often referred to him in letters as "Lanfang."

L'Enfant spent the next few years close to Washington, developing a deep friendship with him. He made himself useful and was appreciated for his knowledge of the arts of fortification and the organization of military discipline. He was always ready to offer his artistic talents, drawing pencil portraits of Washington and his brother officers. This led to his becoming the "designer ordinary" of Valley Forge. He was involved in any project concerning art, whether it involved a decoration, a jewel, a fortress, a procession, a building, or the staging of a feast. He was as important to the army's morale as Baron von Steuben was to its efficiency. A former Prussian general, Steuben organized a very efficient training program that allowed the American soldiers to emerge from the harsh 1778 winter in excellent order.

1783

Eagle of the Cincinnati

With the War of Independence over, in 1783 L'Enfant went back to France to see his father. He had been entrusted with a symbolic mission by the recently created Society of the Cincinnati.

That society had been formed to honor officers who had served in the Revolutionary Army and help those who were in need. All army officers, including those who had died in service, were eligible. Living officers who elected to join contributed a month's salary to the society's funds.

More importantly, the society was seen as a permanent link between the past and the future. In another American paradox, the men who had fought the hereditary power of kings and established a democracy now felt the need for a form of hereditary transmission similar to that in royal families. The oldest son of each generation of future Cincinnati families would be eligible to become a member and take part in the transmission of the ideal when his father died.

The content of that transmission, however, was of a very different nature. The Latin word *Cincinnati* is the plural form of *Cincinnatus*, which refers to Lucius Quintus Cincinnatus, a Roman farmer of the fifth century B.C.E. Cincinnatus had been called on to save the Roman republic, had triumphed, and then had declined all honors and gone back to his farm. Cincinnatus was to serve as a civic example in contrast to that of the military, which often triumphed only to hang on to power and take over the leadership of the nation.

Although it was never stated openly, General Henry Knox, who was considered the society's originator, and his fellow officers George Washington and Baron von Steuben, among others, must have feared that the military would seize power in the newly freed states. America needed farmers, not warlords. To set an example, Washington resigned his commission as commander in chief as soon as the peace treaty had been signed. He did that primarily to advertise the fact that the republic and the ideal of democracy were above personal interest and that free elections would take the place of military power. The English poet Lord Byron called Washington the "Cincinnatus of the West." In introducing the George Washington Papers, the Library of Congress Internet site states: "His willing resignation of his military powers and his return to private life are considered striking because democratic republics are thought to be especially vulnerable to military dictatorship."

In December 1783 Washington was elected the first President General of the Society of the Cincinnati and remained in that office until his death in 1799.

Power is a dangerous addiction. The hereditary honor of membership in the society could serve as a channel for military officers to set themselves up as hereditary rulers.

Washington was well versed in history. He knew his Caesar, and his intuition allowed him to forestall experiences like that of Napoleon, who served his republic but later overthrew it and became an emperor.

Membership in the Society of the Cincinnati was not limited to Americans: Pierre L'Enfant was commissioned to start a French chapter. The officers of the French service met at the houses of Lafayette and Rochambeau. They elected Admiral d'Estaing president and persuaded the king to accept the presence of the Cincinnati as a foreign society on French soil.

L'Enfant was expected to order the eagle insignia the members if the Cincinnati would wear from a good jeweler in Paris. This was the first appearance of the eagle as the emblem of America. L'Enfant had suggested it when the Cincinnati was created: "The Bald Eagle, which is particular to that continent and distinguished from those of other climes by its white head and tail, appears to me to deserve attention." The eagle was adopted by the General Society of the Cincinnati on June 19, 1783; the European eagle had been the Roman Empire's emblem and thus reinforced the link to Cincinnatus.

One day short of a year later, Congress voted the eagle the official seal of the United States. Here again, as in the notebook of Villard de Honnecourt (see Chapter 4), the pentagram and the eagle are symbolically united.

There is no record of L'Enfant mentioning Villard, but he certainly knew Villard's drawings, which had been rediscovered and published in 1666 and 1696 by André Félibien des Avaux, a court historian of Louis XIV and secretary to the Royal Academy of Architecture. As a court painter, L'Enfant's father must have known the book and shown its unusual pictures to his artist son. L'Enfant also would have had an opportunity to see those pictures while studying architecture at the academy. Both eagles are in the same posture, facing the viewer with wings spread and head in profile.

Villard's eagle looks east, whereas that of L'Enfant looks west. On the American flag as on Villard's eagle, the star pentagrams are one point up.

The eagle was by no means a new symbol on the American continent. A few thousand miles below Washington, D.C., and a few centuries before the American Revolution, the Aztecs honored the eagle as their emblematic bird. The Mendoza Codex (see the illustration above), a book written and drawn by Aztec scribes in the middle of the sixteenth century for Antonio de Mendoza, the viceroy of New Spain, shortly after the conquest by Spain, features an eagle perched on a nopal, an edible cactus, at the center of the cover. The diagonal cross under the eagle might have inspired the Confederate Southern diagonal cross bearing pentagram stars.

To this day, the Mexican flag has an eagle on a nopal at its center.

En Grand

The high honors conferred on L'Enfant and his warm reception in Paris contributed to a personal trait that was to be both his strength and his weakness: he started to see everything more and more *en grand*. Once in his hands, all projects became ambitious undertakings that nothing could rival. That suited the Americans, who thought highly of their future, but was beyond the limited resources of a new nation. L'Enfant spent far more than was expected on his mission in Paris. The Society of the Cincinnati agreed to increase the budget, but the first shadow of doubt about L'Enfant's managerial abilities had appeared.

On his return to America, L'Enfant became an architect and engineer in New York, where the congressional session took place, and became prosperous. He took an active part in two public events that marked the first years of the young nation.

A Grand Federal Procession was planned for July 1788 in Philadelphia by Francis Hopkinson, a poet, judge, and signer of the Declaration of Independence. It celebrated the adoption of the Constitution by the nine required states but also was intended to persuade the remaining states, particularly New York, to vote for it as well so as to strengthen the Union. Craft brotherhoods were the main actors in the show. Forty-four organizations displaying the tools of their trades were represented, as were farmers and followers of all the intellectual pursuits. The trades rivaled in impressive show, with blacksmiths, for instance, actually beating swords into plowshares on a real forge.

The symbolism of the procession featured the Grand Federal Edifice, which was created by the Carpenters' Society of Philadelphia and was carried on a carriage drawn by white horses. Its conception was based entirely on the symbolic number of the 13 states of the Union. Thirteen Corinthian columns, 10 of them complete and the other 3 unfinished for the states whose vote for the Constitution was still pending, supported a dome, and their pedestals bore the initials of the 13 states.

The parade ended in a grand banquet, with the crowd feasting on roasted bullocks. The president and many members of Congress sat under an elegant dome devised by L'Enfant and surmounted by the figure of Fame proclaiming the new era with a trumpet.

L'Enfant had been commissioned to remodel New York's city hall on the corner of Broad and Wall streets into the first Capitol of the United States. New York had been the temporary capital of the Union since the Congress had left Philadelphia, but there was no certainty that it would remain so. Other state capitals were competing for the honor, and New York placed great hopes in L'Enfant's ability to produce a building that would make the city the permanent federal capital.

Everything was set for L'Enfant to visualize the project en grand, and he rose to the occasion. He spent twice what was planned but delivered a building that won everyone's admiration. Inside, the decoration was enhanced by splendid American marble. The symbolic numeral 13, promoted by Francis Hopkinson, was displayed abundantly, particularly in the form of a monumental eagle holding 13 arrows in the talons of its left foot.

Regrettably, in 1812, well after the government had left New York in 1789 for Philadelphia and then moved to Washington, D.C., the building was pulled down. There is no trace of the "truly august" eagle displayed on the front, the marble chimneys of the senate chamber, the pilaster capitals "of a fanciful kind, and the magnificent frieze divided into 13 metopes to symbolize the 13 states.

George Washington was inaugurated as the first president of the Union there on April 30, 1789. The ceremony took place on the second-floor balcony. All that remains of the building and its ornaments is the central section of the balcony railing where Washington must have leaned. That piece of wrought iron with its molded rail on top is now on exhibit at the New-York Historical Society Museum (see the illustration above and to the left). A troubling point is that the design is not exactly symmetrical. Did L'Enfant purposely refuse to compete in perfection with the Great Architect and, like craftsmen in the Middle Ages, add small imperfections to a masterpiece to avoid the sin of pride? Should we look for a hidden code even though we have only a small part of the design? Another notable point is the band of ovals on which the whole structure is resting. Was L'Enfant the first to import ovals into the graphic logic of the Union?

Design of the Capital

When he heard that the federal capital would not be in any existing city but would be built on an empty spot, L'Enfant wrote a letter to Washington on September 11, 1789, offering his services as the architect of that city. In his somewhat eccentric English, he presented a clear view of the situation and its future: "No nation, perhaps, has ever before had the opportunity offered them of deliberately deciding on the spot where their capital city should be fixed... And, although the means now within the power of the country are not such as to pursue the design to any great extent, it will be obvious that the plan should be drawn on such a scale as to leave room for that aggrandizement and embellishment which the increase of the wealth of the nation will permit it to pursue at any period, however remote. Viewing the matter in this light, I am fully sensible of the extent of the undertaking."

L'Enfant was wrong, of course. Capitals had been designed and built in empty places to emphasize the creation or renewal of nations many times before. Kyoto, for example, was built on such a site in 794 to replace Nara Heijo-kyo, which had been built on an empty site in 710. Both capitals followed the model of Chinese capitals, which were built on empty sites, but L'Enfant was right that it was the first time a free democracy had designed its own capital.

With his accomplishments and devotion to the nation, L'Enfant deserved the commission, and Washington gave his approval. Despite his knowledge that L'Enfant's talent was wild and difficult to manage, he didn't hesitate to entrust him with the project and wrote to David Stuart on November 20, 1791: "Since my first knowledge of the gentleman's abilities in the line of his profession, I have received him not only as a scientific man, but one who has added considerable taste to professional knowledge; and that, for such employment as he is now engaged in, for prosecuting public works and carrying them into effect, he was better qualified than any one who had come within my knowledge in this country."

The Capital Statement

L'Enfant was aware of the implications of the creation of a capital for the life of its nation. A capital is the manifest expression of a nation: it states what the nation is and what it's not. In other words, symbolically, it's a central code, a matrix that generates the nation. It is not a passive reference for people to look up when they need data. On the contrary, the capital code is an active matrix, powerfully generating the daily life and development of the state in the minds of its citizens.

One example clearly shows that L'Enfant understood the symbolic power of urban design. It would have been convenient in the late eighteenth century to have the president live in the Capitol so that he could be informed of and attend meetings of the assembly whenever that was necessary. In a telephoneless era when information could be transmitted only on foot or horseback or through clumsy optical signals, placing the president far from the Congress, with a park and a mall between his residence and the Capitol, was a problem; an optical telegraph could not be installed easily. However, L'Enfant planned to keep a distance between the White House and the Capitol, and George Washington supported his plan. This was the embodiment of an essential idea of eighteenth-century philosophers: the separation of powers, a central aspect of modern republics. That placed government in a matrix in which Congress and the presidency worked together yet independently, meeting as prescribed by the Constitution.

When he worked on the Federal Hall in New York, L'Enfant had to make the most of a place imposed on him in a commercial surrounding. In Washington, D.C., where he could design the place and its environment, he expressed another principle. In an obvious display of transparency, he placed the government on a hill in a park, away from the bustling commercial neighborhoods but in full public view at the crossroads of wide avenues. That design presented the government as a public entity.

The "Desert" Revolution

To understand what was going on in the minds of the founders of Washington, D.C., including Washington, Jefferson, Franklin, and L'Enfant, we need to explore a quiet revolution that was taking place in certain gardens in Europe. A detour through symbolic gardens would be irrelevant in a conventional history book but is fundamental here to make a connection between two places on different continents. One place is today the center of the world, whereas the other is all but ruined and hidden in vegetation. However, the link between the two is clear: same period, same cultural environment, and decisive people visiting or creating both places. Moreover, these "deserts" are an important step in the aesthetic of parks and gardens. Let's look at the drama step by step.

Revolutionary Theme Parks

L'Enfant had promised to make the capital city "a garden of Eden." Nothing could have been more appropriate, for in the eighteenth century a small revolution was under way in gardens everywhere. After the superb geometry of the parks of royal palaces such as Versailles in the previous century, architects were designing theme parks in which symbols were embodied in buildings called follies or fabrics.

The purpose of the new gardens differed from that of the gardens before them. The earlier parks had imposed the powerful logic of human design on nature. Garden designers forced plants and topography into implacable planes, lines, and symmetries, revealing their real goal of reminding one and all of the artful yet implacable power of the king over his nation. Louis XIV built Versailles to demonstrate that he and his government were an outstanding work of art. He was an art lover, a promoter of creations, and an excellent dancer who frequently took part in premieres of ballets on the stage, but he conceived of art as a code for his absolute power. His artists created freely and beautifully but within strictly coded limits, building specific structures for plays, language, poetry, and so on.

In contrast, the designers of the new gardens were conducting a dialogue with nature rather than imposing their will on it. One of their basic themes was that human design should blend with nature and that nature could dominate human creation. Some follies were built as artificial ruins, partially buried in vegetation, showcase victims of nature and time. In the Park Monceau, at that time a private park outside Paris, the columns of a ruined Greek temple were grouped around a forgotten shrine drowned in a pond. A related theme was that of the humble place of the present time in the limitless perspective of eternity, symbolized, for instance, by the cave of the first man. Another was the reminder that Western civilization was only one among many; this could be represented, for example, by a Chinese house.

Because they generally featured follies such as pyramids, the hallmark of the desert sands of the Nile valley, those gardens were called deserts. Western culture was busy rediscovering Egypt and its enigmatic past, and Egyptian hieroglyphs, which would not be deciphered until the next century, retained their mystery. The world of the pharaohs was a powerful stimulant to the imagination, suggesting ancient and lost knowledge. The name desert also was a mock criticism of their situation: the vast green desert of the countryside, far from all towns.

Le Désert de Retz

The most famous and the first desert was the one started by François Racine de Monville in 1774 and completed in 1799, two years after his death. The garden revolution had passed through Monville's mind before he had embodied it in his garden and other parks.

Monville had wealth that could sustain his passion for that most expensive of all arts, architecture, and began his exploration with Etienne-Louis Boullée, who built two residences for him in Paris. Boullée was a visionary creator. His work was the essence of classicism, pushing the power of pure geometry so far that he seemed a veritable utopian, planning and building the future.

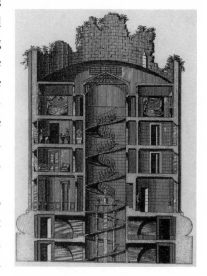

In 1774, Monville was well known in Parisian society as a dancer and a harp and flute player. However, he decided to break with Paris and his love of classicism by creating his own universe in the small village of Retz well to the west of the capital. For 10 years he continued to acquire land that would be landscaped and populated with philosophical follies. His creation was such a success that the most famous people of the period, from Benjamin Franklin to Marie Antoinette and Gustav III of Sweden, came to visit his inspired desert.

Unfortunately but perhaps intentionally, Monville left no writings, and we have no idea how his mind worked. What made him go through the major change of code from Boullée's dictatorship of the geometric mass to an ecological conception of the symbiosis of humans and nature? During his time in Paris he had lived surrounded by the absolute perfection of Boullée's structures; on moving to Retz, he used a broken column to symbolize the imperfect and forever unfinished work of humankind.

After a brief and unsuccessful experiment with a local designer, Monville decided to become his own architect. The "shattered column" (see the illustrations on page 211, middle left and bottom right) was the master folly of his desert. Designed as his residence, it was a vast column ending in ruins above the fourth floor. Like a destroyed Boullée volume, the planned devastation makes it look as if Monville were coding in stone the coming revolution that would destroy the absolute power of the monarchy and the noble class to which he belonged (it was members of that class, enthusiastic bearers of the advanced ideas of the Enlightenment, who actually triggered the revolution).

Monville made it his home: a cozy, fancy, Titanic bubble floating on the flow of freedom that would be its destruction. A spiral staircase at the cylinder's center led to rooms, some of them oval, on the first two stories. The third story looked out on the desert through its oval windows.

The desert finally included 17 follies, among them a Chinese pavilion, the Column House, a pyramid-shaped icehouse, a Temple of Repose, a Temple of Pan, a Tartar tent, an open-air theater, a botanical garden with plants from all over the world, hothouses, and herb and vegetable gardens.

The main gate into the desert was designed to represent an initiatory entrance into a different world. Visitors approached it through the forest and were invited to discover it as a cave half hidden in the woods. Passing through a rock tunnel, they emerged into a new universe.

The Oval Code: The Drach Findings

It is to Michel Drach, a researcher devoted to numerology, that we owe an in-depth study of the desert from the geometrical and numerological points of view. In his book The Retz Desert Seen from a Particular Angle, Drach demonstrated the abundant presence of the 108° angle in all types of alignment. He found the following:

Fifteen instances of 108° angles
Two sublime triangles
One luminous delta
Two Pythagorean 3–4–5 right triangles

Drach indicates that 108 symbolism is older than the eighteenth century. Applying his 108 yardstick to two bas-reliefs in the Temple of Luxor in Egypt (see the illustration on the previous page), he comes up with no fewer than eight examples, far more than coincidence would allow. In two instances, the 108° angle deliberately orients and sustains the creation tool of the god Min, who symbolized fertility and power.

The number 108 is also essential in Taoist and Buddhist symbolism. At the time of Buddha and Pythagoras, Hindu mathematicians divided the circle into 360 degrees. That number was coherent with their year, which had 12 months of 30 days each (with corrections every four years); 12 months, or planetary houses, times 9 planets yields 108. This explains the number's widespread symbolic occurrence: Buddhist malas (rosaries) have 108 beads, Japanese Buddhists ring a large bell 108 times at the begin-

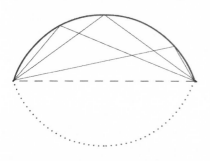

ning of the year, there are 108 exceptional failings of the vows of a Buddhist nun, there are 108 Buddhist saints who decided to forgo their sainthood and be reincarnated on Earth to serve suffering humanity, and many Buddhist temples have 108 steps. The remarkable equivalence of this number with the number of degrees in the angle of the pentagon makes both the number and the geometric figure all the more symbolically important.

Drach's breakthrough idea was the notion that the angle of 108° can be seen as more than an angle. He used the classical property of peripheral angles linking angles to arcs. An "arc capable" is the set of all the points from which a segment is seen from a certain angle. With this property, an arc corresponds to each angle and thus to an oval, made up of twice the arc. With this addition, the same symbol can show up in any of three incarnations: as an angle, a number, or an oval.

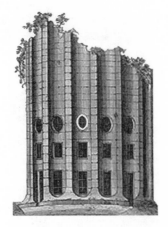

It should be noted that an oval of this nature is not an ellipse. It is made up of two arcs of a circle and creates backward curvilinear angles at both extremities that have to be artificially rounded, or opened, as we'll see on a major site. An ellipse, on the contrary, is a continuous curve that has no angles. Geometrically, an ellipse has two centers. The farther apart the centers, the flatter the ellipse. When centers fuse, the ellipse becomes a circle.

Drach simply mentions the 108° oval, but as though leaving it to later researchers to take advantage of the tool, he does not apply it to specific instances.

With a display of 108° in the park's plan, one would expect to find the 108° oval shape in Monville's architecture as well, but none of the three oval rooms in the tower have that shape. Perhaps for reasons of comfort, Monville flattened out and rounded the shape. Fortunately, one need only raise one's eyes and look at the windows. The 16 third-floor windows indeed adopt the symbolic shape, and so Monville's choice of oval windows becomes meaningful. With their built-in pentagrams, the 16 windows are Pythagorean eyes looking out on the world.

Visitors and Evangelists

Monville's numerous visitors were amazed at the philosophical wonderland they entered. Some went on to build their own deserts, adapting his principles to their own taste.

In 1784, Gustavus III, the king of Sweden, enjoyed Monville's hospitality so much that he remained at the desert for six weeks. Back in Stockholm, he added follies to his Haga Park north of the capital. To help with the project, Monville sent him drawings and maps that are now in the Nationalmuseum in Stockholm and are the only remaining architectural documents relating to the desert, the originals having been lost during the French Revolution.

L'Enfant was in France that year. We have no specific evidence, but it's difficult to imagine that he did not visit the desert.

Queen Marie Antoinette was particularly interested in the desert's contact with nature: its botanical garden, hothouse, and farm. It inspired her creation of the Queen's Hamlet, the mock farm in Versailles. Yet the queen's park displayed no specific symbolism beyond her fateful disregard of politics.

Another noble visitor was Philippe d'Orléans, cousin of the king and father of the later king Louis-Philippe. Philippe was grand master of the Grand Orient de France, the first French Freemasonic obedience, and became a close friend of Monville. This strongly suggests that Monville was a Mason too, although there is no proof. Philippe built his own desert in his park, which was called the Monceau plain and is now the Parc Monceau in Paris's eighth arrondissement. Among other follies still standing, there are a pyramid, several tombs, and the columns of a ruined Temple of Mars.

Philippe d'Orléans's vision was notably different from Monville's in that his desert included a perfect rotunda, a utopian contradiction to other ruined follies in the splendid symmetry of its volumes. The folly, which is still in perfect condition, was designed by Nicolas Ledoux, a visionary architect of the same sort as Boullée. Under the republic, Philippe d'Orléans changed his name to Philippe Egalité and, as a deputy for Paris, voted for the death of his cousin, yet the rotunda suggests that he never forgot his closeness to absolute power.

French Freemasons' activities were intense in the second half of the eighteenth century. Desert gardens were only one public way of exhibiting and playing with their ideas before putting them into practice in the Revolution.

The desert gardens, sometimes simply called folly gardens because of their follies, multiplied in many places. Some still exist in totality or in part and can be visited. The most philosophically accomplished is the Parc Jean-Jacques Rousseau in Ermenonville, 30 miles northeast of Paris, which was inspired both by Monville's desert and by the ideas of the Swiss socialist and romantic thinker. Not far from the prehistoric First Man's Cave stands the unfinished Temple of Philosophy, its columns lying on the ground in anticipation of further development. There is an altar devoted to dreaminess.

Monville must have considered his work complete when he sold his desert to an English Freemason shortly after the beginning of the French Revolution. Like the majority of the nobility, he eventually was jailed by the revolutionaries, but he was more fortunate than his erstwhile royal visitors: he managed to survive until the end of the Reign of Terror (during which over 20,000 people were executed) of 1793 and 1794 and was released a few days before his trial. Meanwhile, the new owner protected the site through the troubled times of the turn of the century.

A more contemporary visitor to Retz was President François Mitterrand, a renowned Freemason. In 1990, unannounced and accompanied by his minister of culture, Jack Lang, he flew there in a helicopter to see and touch the column. The present owner, however, forbids all visits, no matter who the visitor might be, and the following day a clerk of the court was at the door of the Elysée Palace, informing the president of his misdemeanor and instituting proceedings against him.

The Gardens' Mythical Spacetime

A garden may seem a strange place to develop and express ideas, much less prepare a revolution, but this disregards the essential idea of a garden as a place outside normal day-to-day space and time. A real garden is a desert as far as business is concerned. Outside the busy flow of activities, beyond business transactions and production, it allows a different train of thought. To create his desert two centuries before the Internet offered virtual reality as a common facility (see Chapter 9), Monville had to exile himself from Paris, dwell in a small and remote village, and buy up forests and farmland.

Plants and trees are the essential fabric of a garden. They live in a time flow that is slower than ours, with a quieter rhythm, and that represents a different continuum of experience. Beyond the traditional romantic aspect of immersion in nature, gardens bring about a different mindset. They give the mind easier access to symbols, concepts, and higher principles. Furthermore, if philosophical notions are embodied as objects so that not only our spirits but our bodies can experience them, our thought processes are accelerated and there is no limit to what we can conceive and achieve. In that sense, a desert garden is a philosophical workbench.

The desert garden revolution transformed parks from leisure areas and instruments of power into instruments of thought and reflection.

Symbolic gardens draw meaning and energy from a fundamental heritage. Whether or not they are believers, Westerners are deeply marked by the original garden in the Bible, the Garden of Eden. Genesis, the opening chapter of the Bible, is a founding text of Western civilization. It not only states that everything started in a garden but affirms that a garden is a potent place—a "place of power." Adam, as the representative of humankind in that garden, bit into the fruit of knowledge and was banned from Eden to bear the guilt for his deed. The mixed heritage of sin, guilt, temptation, and ambiguous play with knowledge in the Garden of Eden constitutes a powerful knot of paradoxes. It makes for a provocative and creative situation, an abundant source of mental energy. In re-creating the concept of Eden, Monville must have been aware of the implications of his deed. Soon the nobility would be banned from their privileged Garden of Eden.

The desert garden is very closely related to another type of philosophical tool. Freemasons' aprons (see Chapter 5) can be seen as a virtual theme garden in which the mind rebounds from symbol to symbol. When Freemasons are in the Masonic mind-set, away from ordinary daily life, their minds reside in the virtual spacetime of the apron. The apron is a workshop, and the symbols embroidered on it are a Mason's working tools.

This Freemason tool kit has expanded somewhat since the Pythagoreans, who relied mainly on numbers and geometry. As mathematical objects have become commonplace notions, Freemasons have had to enlarge their toolbox to encompass a wider and more complex set of symbols. We've seen on George Washington's apron that their symbols are far more numerous than the Pythagoreans' pentagrams and numbers, but those symbols are still the nuts and bolts of their philosophy.

Eden on the Potomac

The deployment of desert gardens explains why L'Enfant considered George Washington's choice of a wilderness for the building of the capital a brilliant decision. L'Enfant was so enthusiastic that he exclaimed that he would make the capital a Garden of Eden.

L'Enfant meant several things. First, as if the heritage of sin and guilt from the first Garden of Eden were attached to the Old World, he meant a place where one could start over. A new Garden of Eden would mean a new dispensation for humankind, a new civilization on a new continent, possibly free of original sin, though this idea probably was not written down or formulated clearly.

Second, he thought of Monville's desert as a tool. With well-chosen and well-sited buildings and monuments in an overall design that respected the appropriate symbolism, the city would be the ideal tool for the creation and management of the new nation.

This coincided with the Freemasons' long-held interest in symbols as keys to the world.

Jefferson's Ovals

While in Paris as ministers to France, Benjamin Franklin and his successor, Thomas Jefferson, visited the desert. Jefferson went in the company of a friend, the British artist Maria Cosway. He showed great interest in the inner architecture of the destroyed column and took note of its oval rooms.

Once he was back in America and serving as the first Secretary of State from 1790 to 1793 under George Washington, Jefferson did not forget Monville's architecture. Among his papers archived at the Massachusetts Historical Society, there are several sketches showing the steps in Jefferson's thinking, which was inspired directly by the Retz desert's circular tower. The graphic on the previous page shows the original plan of the first floor of Monville's central column. Its characteristic oval rooms are rearranged by Jefferson in the next plan, drawn and commented on in French in his own handwriting: "le tout 24 pieds diametre" (diameter 24 feet in all; see the illustration on the upper right). Another phrase indicates in French how to construct the building with stones and plaster. The building is surrounded by 16 pillars, like Monville's tower, but Jefferson enlarges the central staircase, turning it into a larger circular hall. He also gets rid of the other rooms, opening a vast terrace that was better adapted to the climate in Virginia, possibly for a personal mansion.

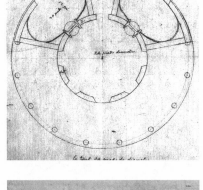

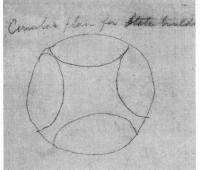

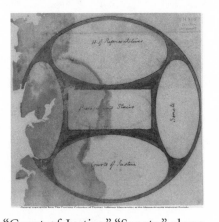

A very rough sketch shown above demonstrates that Jefferson's mind has gone back to the English language and to public concerns: a circle with four ovals is labeled "Circular plan for state building." Another plan, more elaborate (see right), describes precisely how the projected Capitol could include four oval rooms: "(E)ntry," "H of Representatives," "Court of Justice," "Senate," along with a central oval turned into a rectangle: "Passage and stairs."

This Capitol never was built. Jefferson must not have had the time to complete it, because in the same year, along with the commissioners of the District of Colombia, he launched a public competition for the design of the Capitol that was won by a more traditional plan. In the present Capitol, only the curve of the central rotunda is a reminder of the originally planned ovals. Jefferson suggested that it could be considered a Roman Pantheon, a place dedicated to all the gods as its Greek name implies (*pan* means "all," and *theo* means "god"). Was this in remembrance of Philippe d'Orléans's rotunda described above, with the same ambiguity between innovative ovals and conservative circles?

This interest in ovals was shared by George Washington, who liked oval rooms for gatherings. In his Philadelphia home, there were two rooms modified with bowed ends for holding receptions. Washington would stand in the center to greet his guests. He considered this a symbol of democracy.

The Blue Eye of Pythagoras

Jefferson's rooms, like the original rooms in the shattered tower, are ellipses, not 108° ovals, yet the 108° oval is present in the Oval Office of the White House. James Hoban's plan for the president's house features an oval room rather close to a 108° oval. However, the 1814 version of the house, which was rebuilt after its destruction in the War of 1812, features the Blue Room, which matches the 108° oval so closely that it can't be a coincidence (see the illustration below).

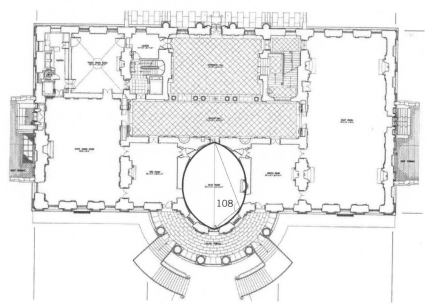

Somehow, the pentagram-related oval that we may call "Pythagoras's eye" because of its relationship with the main symbol of the Pythagoreans found its way to a central place in the new nation, symbolically watching over the new world.

From Garden to Business

L'Enfant had left the scene by the time the White House and the Capitol were designed, for eventually the capital city had to go its own way. To grow and exist as a living organism, the city had to free itself from L'Enfant. That happened sooner than was foreseen, when real life and business started to take over.

L'Enfant's first outline of the design had been received with general approval. George Washington had praised L'Enfant's ability to adapt his conception to the reality of the terrain: "The work of Major L'Enfant, which is greatly admired, will show that he had many objects to attend to and to combine, not on paper merely, but to make them correspond with the actual circumstances of the ground." Even Jefferson, who had a different design in mind, approved and sent copies of the plan to Gouverneur Morris, his ministerial successor in France, so that he could circulate the plans in the principal towns of that country.

When the time came to apply the design and begin building the city, L'Enfant could not be the sole manager of the project. The government had declared the district outside any state of the Union, named it the District of Colombia in honor of Christopher Columbus, and appointed three district commissioners to work with L'Enfant, who also was given three assistants. That meant that L'Enfant was to work as part of a team.

L'Enfant was reluctant to share decisions on a project he considered his own. To make things worse, the project began to attract enterprising speculators, and L'Enfant felt that the team was not giving him the support he needed to fight them. He apparently was unable to convey to the team that he had conceived of the city as a whole in which every detail was an essential part and that it was planned to function like clockwork, which requires that every wheel be exactly in place.

Open dissension between L'Enfant and the commissioners arose in fall 1791. Because the nation needed a capital as soon as possible, the government and the commissioners wanted to go ahead with the sale of private lots, whereas L'Enfant wanted to delay the sales until enough copies of the plan of the city had been printed to distribute them throughout the Union and give everyone an equal opportunity to buy property.

Washington couldn't make L'Enfant, who was stubborn and refused to show his plans to anybody in the hope of stalling the sales, change his mind.

Matters came to a head in November. Irritated by L'Enfant's obstinacy, a powerful landowner started building a house in the middle of what was to be New Jersey Avenue. L'Enfant sent his assistants to tear down the building, and they were arrested by the commissioners. L'Enfant hired workers and finished the demolition by himself. He barely avoided jail.

Even after that, Washington tried to come to terms with L'Enfant, acknowledging that "having the beauty and regularity of your plan only in view, you pursue it as if every person or thing were obliged to yield to it." This was to no avail. L'Enfant remained obstinate in demanding full powers, which he never obtained.

In fact, the symbiosis between L'Enfant and the Founding Fathers was over. The founders were managing, no longer founding, the nation. The era of isolated heroes was over. Even talented people, no matter how inspired, had to work in teams. L'Enfant's final exit was marked by an official letter from Jefferson to the commissioners on March 6, 1792: "It having been found impracticable to employ Major L'Enfant in that degree of subordination which was lawful and proper, he has been notified that his services

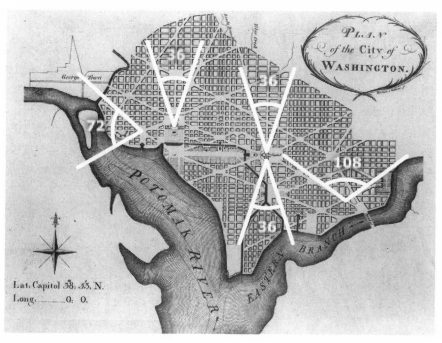

were at an end." All the landowners in the capital except two joined in a vote for L'Enfant's return and praised his work. None of them regretted that L'Enfant had designed Washington en grand. But L'Enfant had left the project and would never return.

One aspect of L'Enfant's personality seldom is mentioned in respect to his change of mood in the 1790s: He was born a Frenchman and could not ignore the bloody revolution that was going on in his country at that time. In contrast with events in America, the revolt in France was turning into a civil war. For all his advanced ideas on freedom and democracy, he could not have forgotten that his father was a court painter and belonged to the class directly threatened by the revolutionaries. In those circumstances, it was impossible for L'Enfant to remain the exuberant creator he had been in the 1780s. He died more than 40 years later, in 1835.

Fallen Angles

An unexplained mystery persists. The angles of the pentagram are there on the map. They are sometimes exact and sometimes approximate, but always too close for coincidence. Why are they not always exact? The example of the remapping of San Francisco after the 1904 earthquake shows that no terrain, however difficult or hilly, can stop determined urbanists from imposing their grid on topography. Why is Washington's grid both regular and unnervingly askew, containing almost exact angles and almost true parallels?

Was the planning team obliged to redraw an avenue to take wildcat construction into account after L'Enfant's departure? This would make for a ragged plan that was incompatible with the outstanding beauty of the original. The final plan is due to Andrew Ellicott, who was asked by Washington to complete the project after L'Enfant's departure. Ellicott had a good knowledge of the grounds, for he had done the original survey of the bounds of the District of Colombia in 1791. In less than a month he produced the plan that finally was approved. It seems that he eliminated some avenues, added some others, changed the alignment of Massachusetts Avenue, and named the city streets. As a Quaker, did Ellicot purposely alter a Masonic project to hide its symbols? It must be noted that he did not get along with the commissioners any better than L'Enfant had and resigned from the project a few months later.

Or was it L'Enfant who purposely bent perfect geometry? That is more plausible. L'Enfant would have felt that even a Pythagorean grid, if perfectly drawn and imposed on human activities, would be as wrong as Le Nôtre's Versailles grid imposing the absolute power of his king. Even a perfect Masonic grid would be unlivable in view of its very perfection. Pythagoras had failed in government because of his perfect philosophy, and that mistake should not be made again. In accordance with their avowed policy of secrecy (see Chapter 5), Freemasons would not act as kings and impose their power.

Just as a medieval carver would slightly distort an otherwise perfect cathedral rosace so as not to compete with the perfection of the divine creation, L'Enfant may have wished to avoid hard-coding perfection into a living organism that was destined to grow and create in its turn. Yet bent order does not mean disorder, and L'Enfant might have felt that any bending beyond his own touch would cause the system to collapse. This might have been the root of the misunderstanding with the other planners not as acutely aware of the limits of the aesthetic code involved.

The importance ascribed to symbols in this book does not imply that they are endowed with supernatural power but emphasizes the fact that as mental tools they follow their own logic and must be put to use as precisely as mathematical theorems.

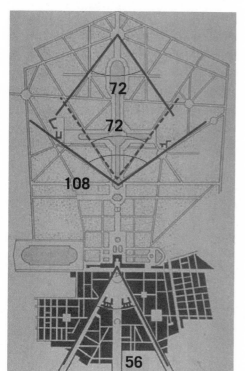

If a capital city is to be the matrix of its nation, the end result will depend on the quality of the matrix's structure.

Versailles 108°

A comparison of Washington, D.C., with Versailles exemplifies the difference between their codes. At Versailles the palace turned its back to the city to open onto its own artificial world. Paris, the real capital of the state, was miles away. Instead of sharing power, King Louis XIV, who conceived the place, centered all aspects of government on himself and let no commercial activity interfere with royal life. As opposed to the White House and the Capitol in the comfort of their park yet immersed in the bustling business of an active city, the king ruled his nation from a place that gave him no direct contact with real life. L'Enfant had insisted on developing the Potomac's commercial activities. Le Nôtre, designer of the park at Versailles, installed a mock canal, closed in on itself, that saw only pleasure boats.

The angle of the avenues pointing toward the Versailles palace is 56° and bears no relation to the 36°, 72°, and 108° Pythagorean angles. Whatever the actual protective value or lack of value of those angles, the king's palace was left out of it.

Yet Le Nôtre had clearly called upon Pythagoras with his exact 72° and 108° angles. Were these clues for his colleague L'Enfant and for L'Enfant's son? Hiding discreetly at the far end of the garden, the flying angles were already there, ready to immigrate to America.

"Child" of the Founding Fathers

Let's follow the lead of meaningful words again, as we did with angels, angles, and eagles.

In French, *l'enfant* means "the child." As is always the case, language's built-in poetry also has its own symbolic meaning. The Gospels relate that a child had come from beyond, eighteen centuries previously, to save humankind. With all respect to the Bible and the Christian faith, it's impossible not to draw a parallel with L'Enfant, who came from beyond the ocean to help save the American nation. For all we know, L'Enfant was an ordinary human being with no godly origin. Yet as symbol-oriented as the Freemasons were and still are, they must have been impressed by the potential inherent in his name

As if to reinforce that symbol, L'Enfant's first name was Pierre—Peter—the name of the apostle to whom Jesus assigned the role of leadership. As we saw in Chapter 3, another Peter, Peter the Hermit, crossed the Mediterranean to found a Christian kingdom in Jerusalem. It would seem that the "child" part got the better of the "Peter" in L'Enfant's personality. The child's mission, on the model of the life of Jesus, was to evangelize, to seed a new world, eventually leaving it to others to build. L'Enfant's first and last names had coded his life's work the day he was baptized, making him the poetically correct man for the job.

CHAPTER 8
Turing Turing

Alan Turing's extraordinary mind toiled and strove to survive at the crossroads of several eras, each one marked by its own revolution: the emergence of machines in the realm of ciphers, fundamental doubts about mathematical logic, major changes in the moral code and sexuality, and the advent of active code, which gave birth to computers.

The Quantum Leap: Active Code

Active code is the key term in this chapter. In the middle of the twentieth century, code underwent a quantum leap and became active code, meaning that it started becoming a stand-alone creature that could fend for itself instead of just being a mere static reference used by humans to conceal secrets, create art, or build science.

Active code goes further than the dynamic codes of Fibonacci or the fractals described in Chapter 2, as a direct heritage of Pythagoras. It relies on dynamic code to make its leap into independence: it is the coded program that invests our machines, our computers and robots, with autonomy and a form of intelligence.

This chapter bears the name of Alan Turing (1912–1954), a British mathematician who was the central actor in the revolution that transformed our view of code and its effect on people. Turing's research and its result, the Turing machine, were the spark that triggered the quantum leap that gave code an active quality. The title of this chapter, "Turing Turing," illustrates the idea that Turing's breakthrough consisted in applying code to itself.

In order to fully understand that revolution and how it came about, we need to follow two trends of thought, one in art and literature and one in science. The two trends rarely are treated in this manner. Many people think that a comparison of the two modes of thinking—two different logics, two different vocabularies, two different mindsets—is preposterous. Yet I must ask the reader to bear with me and consider that art and science take place in the same mind and balance and fuel each other. "We only want well that which we richly imagine," wrote Gaston Bachelard in *La terre et les rêveries de la volonté* (*Earth and Dreams of Willpower*). Indeed, we long richly imagined, pictured, wished for, and dreaded the emergence of the active code that dominates our lives today. We dreamed of it well before it appeared in laboratories. We cannot understand today's active code and its impact on our lives without exploring the dreams that created its dynamics and the dreams that may limit its development.

Before discussing Turing and trying to understand his quantum leap, we need to explore a series of key events that took place in the centuries before his work, mostly in art and literature.

Mary's Bachelor Child

In 1817 Mary Shelley clearly addressed the contemporary problem of the creation and autonomy of machines. Through the proxy of her character Doctor Frankenstein, she conceived a "creature" whose image was so powerful that it remains an outstanding cultural reference two centuries later.

Mary Shelley's machine embodies all the ambiguity of our imagination concerning machines. On the one hand, it's a strictly scientific and mechanical device put together in a laboratory without supernatural intervention. True, it involves organic matter as a basic element of its creation, but we, too, are considering using organic matter in the next generation of processors, and that doesn't make them more alive or supernatural than present-day computers.

On the other hand, the contraption is called a "creature": its basic elements are pieces of dead human flesh, and it starts functioning as if born again when struck by lightning, a power that comes from the sky, if not from heaven.

Within the story, there are at least two themes that concern us in that they particularly prepare the future. The first is the creature's ability to learn. Born with an intelligent yet blank mind, it has a strong drive to acquire knowledge and finds a way to educate itself by spying on the children of an unsuspecting family.

Another theme, beyond that of autonomy, is the creature's ability to reproduce itself. Mary Shelley made it an essential element of her plot when she had Doctor Frankenstein refuse to build the function of reproduction into his creature. The autonomous creature threatens Frankenstein's life and family. It begs him to let it reproduce itself in exchange for peace. Frankenstein accepts and begins to construct the mate with which the creature will procreate. He is then overcome by terror and has a vision of the creature effectively reproducing itself, endlessly multiplying and threatening the survival of humanity. He destroys the makeshift embryo and renders the creature an eternal bachelor. In a final act of revenge the creature gets even by killing Doctor Frankenstein's bride.

Mary Shelley's message is double-edged. She states that the creature, although autonomous, depends on human hands to build its reproductive functions and that it cannot undertake that work itself. Autonomy and reproduction are separate functions. She also suggests that we have a deep mental block against making self-reproducing machines and may be blinded unconsciously by the terror of seeing our machines multiplying beyond control and threatening our survival.

Ideas have a strange way of spreading from mind to mind in spite of people's defenses. In a poetic coincidence, Shelley conceived her Frankenstein machine as part of a game played during a literary party with her husband and other poets. One of the poets was Lord Byron, whose daughter, Ada, later became Charles Babbage's assistant and suggested to him the concept of programming and thus the idea of autonomous machines. The poetic link is all the more romantically unexpected because Ada's mother dreaded the influence of Byron's demented imagination and never let her daughter meet her father.

Poetry also bids us notice that the literary mother of that prophetic child, Frankenstein's creature, was called Mary.

The Golem: Truth and Death

Another mythic creature, the Golem, has had a lasting success parallel to that of Mary Shelley's creature but carries a different message. It was not concerned with reproduction, since according to tradition, any sufficiently holy rabbi could knead one out of simple clay. Originating in legends from Central European Jewish communities of the Middle Ages, it was more like a servant robot. With a rudimentary yet precise system of commands, its owner could activate it and shut it off. It began functioning when a rabbi wrote the Hebrew word *EMET* ("true") on

its forehead and stopped when the first letter of the word was erased, turning it into *death* (*MET*).

This system of command is the first instance of the involvement of language and binary logic in the management of machines and robots. Apart from this, the Golem had no claim to intelligence and performed only specific tasks, mainly to defend Jewish communities against persecution.

Franz Kafka's Penal Code

The two preceding stars stand out among a number of literary autonomous creatures. The numbers of those creatures skyrocketed with the explosion of science fiction in the 1940s. Those stories and novels make for fascinating reading. They apply the subject to all circumstances of life on all the planets in the universe; they mainly accompany scientific and technological developments, sometimes preceding or inspiring them.

Far more meaningful is a short story written in the 1910s: Franz Kafka's "In the Penal Colony" (*"In der Strafkolonie"*). In the sober setting of a prison, a machine executes inmates. To start working, the machine must be fed a written program, which happens to be the law broken by the intended victim. Then the machine carves the text in the flesh of the inmate.

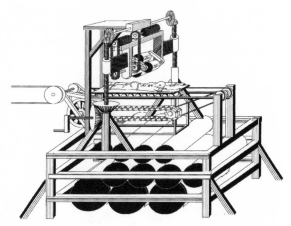

This literal injection of a legal text trans-figures the victim, who undergoes a new birth with the full consciousness of his guilt. After a period of intense illumination, the victim eventually dies.

In a final paroxysm of the plot, the creator and manager turns the machine on himself, destroying both himself and the machine.

With this logical twist, plus a written program, plus a printer, Kafka was on Turing's trail.

Because of the characteristics of its programming and the work it did on its creator's flesh, Kafka's machine was later singled out by surrealists as a major example of a "bachelor machine."

It must be noted that we should not have this story. Kafka had asked in his will that it be destroyed after his death.

The Duchamp Gambits

Marcel Duchamp (here portrayed as Rose Scelavy by Man Ray) was the most reckless codebreaker in the history of art. Born in 1887, he appeared on the art scene in the 1910s. After producing a few conventional paintings, he discovered that Picasso and Braque had started breaking basic art codes with their cubist works. Duly impressed, he set out to go further and shatter what was already a tottering edifice. With his *Nude Descending a Staircase, No. 2*, exhibited in the Salon des Indépendants in 1912, he went so far that he was asked to remove the canvas from the show.

Picasso and Braque offered no support: they felt the move painting was so daring that it overshadowed their revolutionary work. For all their cubist audacity, they could

not accept this new incarnation of Villard's Pythagorean figures (see Chapter 4) and probably didn't even recognize it as such. Duchamp was taking their cubism at face value. Instead of only suggesting the third dimension as his friends had done, he had fully three-dimensionalized his model's figure.

Worse, he had gone one step beyond, adding yet another dimension: time. His model is seen actually descending the staircase (see the illustration to the left), a dirty trick for the cubists, who never went that far. But it was a trick that started Duchamp off as an actor in the universe of autonomous machines. He already featured the dynamic in his works.

As to displaying his Nude, Duchamp complied and withdrew the canvas from the so-called independent exhibition and crossed the Atlantic to show it the next year in the New York Armory Show. It created a scandal there too but has remained on the American continent. In a sort of poetic justice, along with most of the rest of Duchamp's works, it is now in the Philadelphia Museum of Art, a link to the city's history of independence. (America definitely digests European revolutions better than Europe does!)

This scandal constitutes a landmark in the history of codes, a symbolic turnover. It demonstrates the importance of code at the start of the twentieth century. For the first time, a "nude" was rejected not for the boldness of its anatomic details but for the boldness of its code. The quantum leap of active code was already underway in art.

Duchamp surfed on the scandal to go farther in his codebreaking. In what may be called his gambit, he sacrificed the direct representation of objects and people. He was a professional chess player, giving lessons at times to earn a living. In chess, a gambit is the sacrifice of an important piece to gain a strategic advantage.

Duchamp sacrificed what he called "retinal" art, by which he meant that he was not interested in pictures that were produced mechanically on the retina when people looked at so-called works of art. He championed the idea that art should be produced in the viewer's mind, not in his or her eye, implying a dynamic relationship between artistic creation and the intelligence of the public.

In this context, the work of artists no longer was a matter of craftsmanship in which they strive to achieve a masterpiece on a canvas so that the public's retina can reconstruct it. In a second brilliant gambit, Duchamp was doing away with craftsmanship. To illustrate that second step, he exhibited his "readymades," manufactured objects chosen by the artist, whose intervention thus was reduced to a single intense act of creation. More importantly, art no longer resided in objects but in the relationship between an artist and his or her public.

There is no art without a witness, but now that witness had to become active.

A Codebreaking Public

After this turning point, art code became a cryptographic code, concealing the content of art. Furthermore, as Duchamp envisioned it with readymades, it conceals the artist as well. In this light, though it involves methods and logics different from textual ones, art becomes another branch of ciphers. It involves issues less materially strategic but more critical in the long run than those involved in military and diplomatic ciphers. It also involves the public's mind and forces the onlooker to step in and become a codebreaker. Since Duchamp is the domain's original codebreaker, the public has become codebreaker of the codebreaker's code.

Duchamp's ultimate art cipher was titled "With Hidden Noise." In this work, a ball of rope envelops and hides an object that will never be seen. Duchamp mocks tenth-century divine prayer books, which were richly illustrated and then locked so that no human would ever set eye on them.

It seems like a prank and indeed is one, but how better to impose the presence of cipher in art than through another unacceptable scandal?

The Bride Machine

Keeping to the chess metaphor, it could be said that Duchamp's queen on the chessboard of twentieth-century art is undoubtedly his Bride. After several years of work from 1915 to 1923, he exhibited his principal cipher, "The Bride Stripped Bare by Her Bachelors, Even," also called "The Large Glass."

The unreachable bride is exposed between two sheets of glass like an entomologist's specimen, along with the hanging suits of the bachelors. Duchamp revealed that

it represents a cut, made in an instant of time, through a larger phenomenon that extends in time, that is, in the fourth dimension, before and after the current instant. Time is involved, as in the preceding Nude, but here we are allowed to see only one page of the cipher, an instant of its duration.

With different approaches to their treatment, both Duchamp and Dali involve time and the fourth dimension in their paintings. Dali's Christ on the four-dimensional cross is static (see Chapter 2); the six elements of the hypercube are laid out bare in three-dimensional space. Like Christ, they are but a trace of another life beyond space as we know it. Duchamp's works, in comparison, are aggressively dynamic: we follow the naked bride on the staircase and are presented with a crude cut in time of the bride.

The bride really is naked to the point of showing what she is in reality: a grinder. She shows off her true nature. She is poised to grind any fiancé who would dare invade her pure mechanism into an eternal bachelor. There is no hope of successful reproduction here.

Duchamp went on to break his own creation involuntarily yet effectively. Poorly packed, the glass was shattered in the truck he used to bring it home after the exhibition.

Note how death and destruction are present in all machines that stand out in popular culture and culture in general.

Fed by the elusive richness of the work's content, the deciphering of Duchamp's "large glass" continues. The bride, the theme of celibacy, and the machine parts have inspired the surrealist writer Michel Carrouges in his creation of the concept of bachelor machines and in his search for other instances of those machines in the works of other artists and authors.

Game Codes

In the years that followed, Duchamp devoted most of his time to chess, and art critics usually refer to this period as "abandoning art for chess." This shows little respect for Duchamp's mind, however, and supposes that the same person sometimes could act like a genius and at other times amuse himself with a hobby. Worse, it disregards the importance of chess and games in general in our culture; still worse, it overlooks the role of games in the history of code.

Games have quietly survived for millennia on the periphery of official, recognized art and art forms.

They are of an abstract nature, independent of the objects used to play them. A game is essentially a set of rules. The game of chess, for example, can be played with a variety of beautiful or ugly pieces without that having any effect on the quality and interest of the game.

Active coding has been passionately experimented with in the universe of games and play. Every card game or board game exists through this code. Such codes are exemplars of sturdy autonomy. Some games, such as chess and checkers, are so precisely refined that they have survived for centuries even though they have been played by uneducated persons of various languages, ages, and creeds without any enforcement of the rules by an international organization.

These codes are not like physical machines with cogs, wheels, and wires, yet they exist on some plane where they survive through time and spread through space. They look like texts but are more than texts. They are never lost in translation. They merit being considered as autonomous entities.

The traditional Korean game of Nyout, which is at least as old as the foundation of the kingdom of Korea in 1122 B.C.E. and is still manufactured and played all over the world.

For millennia, the human mind experimented with code while playing at inventing and refining the rules of games. In the twentieth century, this led to active coding and applications other than games. The world of games benefited from the quantum leap in codes, acquiring computer games that offer autonomous game partners that are the first robots that significantly challenge our intelligence.

Duchamp's passage through chess has not been decoded; neither has his final work, which was done after the production of his chess episode. If we trust Duchamp's genius, we may expect that deciphering *Given: 1 The Waterfall, 2 The Illuminating Gas* will give us clues to developments in the next generation.

The Bachelor Machines Theory

We owe to Michel Carrouges a theory of bachelor machines that was inspired by the works of Duchamp and other creations, among them those of Mary Shelley and Franz Kafka, as well as Alfred Jarry's *Le surmâle* (*The Supermale*), Jules Verne's *Le Château des Carpathes* (*The Castle of the Carpathians*), Bram Stoker's *Dracula*, Adolfo Bioy Casares's *Morel's Invention*, and even Lautreamont's *Maldoror* and Edgar Allan Poe's "The Pit and the Pendulum."

Constructed by a surrealist, Carrouges's "theory" does not read like a mathematical paper by Alan Turing. It's not structured according to the rigorous logic of mathematical theory, yet it is all the more significant for a scientific mind because it navigates freely in the potential energies of poetry. Consequently, his research is a complement to purely logical thought. It brings to the forefront the fundamental elements of the best imaginable autonomous machines.

Duchamp agreed with and validated Carrouges's findings in several letters included in the 1976 version of the book *Les machines célibataires* ("*Bachelor Machines*").

A theoretical bachelor machine has four essential characteristics:

1. It is autonomous, driven by a coded program. Once started, it has the power to overcome obstacles and run efficiently through its program until it reaches its goal.
2. It involves human actors. The machine is both autonomous and meant to interact with humans.
3. It functions fully only when watched by a gallery of witnesses. The onlookers do not take part in the action, but the human actors involved with the machine know that they are being watched and need to be watched.
4. A founding myth complements and balances the autonomous inner logic of the machine. Some unexplained and paradoxical mythical event, perhaps a legend, provides the attraction that brings human actors to the machine and witnesses to the gallery.

The Carrouges Grid

These four principles produce a reference grid for checking a machine against its four essential components:

• Autonomy

- User involvement
- Dramatic interaction with human society
- A symbolic dimension

In present-day culture, the word *machine* has to be extended to systems and software: all the entities run by code and designed to have autonomy and a life of their own. Awareness of the Carrouges principles has grown slowly since the second half of the twentieth century, but the principles are still largely prophetic.

For a long time the principle of autonomy was considered the only one that mattered: a machine that works well with little help is a good machine, period.

The second principle is still going through a process of reluctant acceptance. Until the 1980s, a user normally was considered the victim of her or his machine. Not until that time did designers begin to consider user comfort, but users still were expected to adapt to their machines and educate themselves to become good users. To this day, few machines are able to, let alone are expected to, adapt to their users. The most famous exception is "Big Blue," a chess machine that learns from playing its opponents.

As to the last two principles, code designers tend to consider them the province of someone else farther down the production chain. They deliver a perfect product to marketing and advertising, and it's up to M&A to add the necessary ingredients of show and symbolism to the presentation and packaging of the product.

Can a programmer be expected to include art, myth, and symbolism in his or her code? The suggestion is not as outlandish as it appears. The geek programmers who code all machines are addicted to the most mythological fantasy games and are avid readers of fantasy fiction: one need only open an issue of the emblematic geek magazine *Wired*. It's probably merely a problem of the relationship between different mindsets.

Below are more applications of the Carrouges grid.

Bachelor Forever

Carrouges does not address the function of reproduction in any of a machine's characteristics and refers to it only obliquely in his use of the term bachelor. Reproduction is considered, but only as an impossibility or an interdiction. This suggests that art and poetry have not completed their basic task of preparing the imagination for effective machine reproduction. In terms of Bachelard's words "we only want well what we richly imagine," we do not yet imagine coded self-reproduction richly enough. Even today, 50 years on, the function is not available and rarely anticipated.

The question arises, Can we actually imagine machine reproduction richly enough to powerfully wish to achieve it?

Or do art and myth express our intuition that coded reproduction is a dead end that will never succeed with code as we know it today?

The Turing Machine

Paradoxically, for all the immense industrial and technical activity of the twentieth century, the most important machine devised in that era was a mental tool that did not have to exist physically. It was conceived by Alan Turing in 1936 as a model of all possible computing machines, a machine so basic that it could simulate any machine ever constructed. All that was required was that it look technically feasible; physically constructing it was beside the point.

Real computers came into existence several years later, but the Turing machine has never lost its status as the universal machine, the model for all possible computers. It is still an excellent tool for thinking about machines and mechanical computation. Before getting into a precise description of it, to understand its nature, we need to explore how Turing came to create it.

The Turing Decision

As a mathematician, Turing devised and used his machine to address a problem involving the general question of decidability posed by David Hilbert at the beginning of the twentieth century. This is a question we might ask ourselves when facing a problem: before we try to find a solution, is there a way to decide whether we'll be successful?

Hilbert's formulation is somewhat more mathematical: could there be a general method or process by which one might decide whether a mathematical proposition can be proved? Note, however, that this does not mean a method or process by which one can "prove" the proposition, simply a way to decide—to know in advance—whether it can be proved. Stated differently, in facing a theorem and trying to prove it, is there a way of knowing whether we'll succeed?

Kurt Gödel had addressed this problem and, using his Gödel numbers, as we saw in Chapter 2, had chosen to understand "method or process" as meaning "mathematical method." Turing chose to understand the terms as a mechanical process and used his Turing machine. He also changed the wording of the question, replacing provable with computable. He then answered the equivalent question: Could there be a process by which one could decide whether a number can be expressed as a decimal by finite means? More practically: Can we decide if the decimals of a number can be written down by a machine?

Incidentally, the answer is no. Gödel proved that there are theorems whose truth we can't determine, and Turing proved that there are real numbers whose computability we can't determine. Neither of them actually presented such a theorem or number, it should be noted, but proofs that they exist still stand.

The Machine

A Turing machine is composed of the following:

- A memory: a number of squares on tape; each square may bear a symbol.
- A head, which can move back and forth over the memory, stop on a square, scan its content, and possibly erase or replace it with a symbol.
- A set of instructions.
- A register that remembers the machine's state. When a machine is set to work, the content of the memory is the initial computation data and the set of instructions is the program.

Rather than continuing with an abstract description, let's observe a machine that multiplies numbers by 2. Such a machine will start with a tape bearing as many dots as the number that will be multiplied. The result will be the number of stars on the tape when the machine stops.

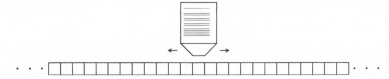

Turing 2 by 3

As a simple example, let's start with three dots on the tape and the expectation that we will end up with six stars. The head is placed over the first dot. The machine is in state 0, one of the four possible states in this case.

As in all computers, in a Turing machine there are many ways of programming even the simplest action to achieve the same result. Here the set of instructions could be as follows:

State 0: Count a dot and stop when no more dots under the head

IF in state 0	AND scan a dot	Erase the dot	Remain in state 0
IF in state 0	AND scan an empty square	Move right	Switch to state 1
IF in state 0	AND scan a star	STOP	

State 1: Go to the first empty square on the right and write a star

IF in state 1	AND scan a dot	Move right	Remain in state 1
IF in state 1	AND scan a star	Move right	Remain in state 1
IF in state 1	AND scan an empty square	Write a star	Switch to state 2

State 2: Write a second star

IF in state 2	AND scan a star	Move right	Remain in state 2
IF in state 2	AND scan an empty square	Write a star	Switch to state 3

State 3: Go back and check for more dots

IF in state 3	AND scan a star	Move left	Remain in state 3
IF in state 3	AND scan a dot	Move left	Remain in state 3
IF in state 3	AND scan an empty square	Move right	Switch to state 0

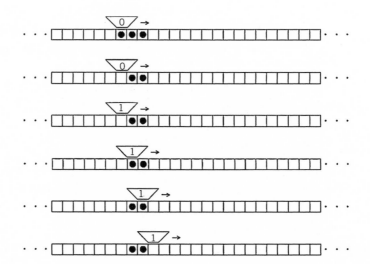

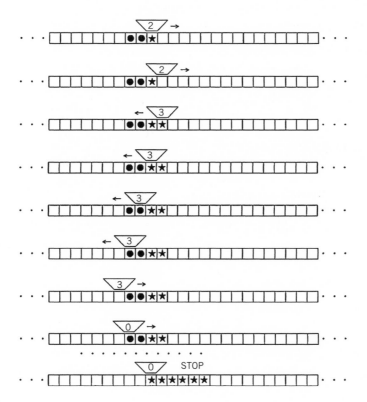

Code:

Multiplying a number by 2 is only a first step. How would you program a Turing machine to multiply any number by any other number? The machine shown below is set to multiply a number of dots by a number of black squares. Can you imagine its program?

Code:

Could you program a Turing machine to perform subtraction? It should be simpler than multiplication. The machine below is set to subtract the number of dots from the number of black squares. How would you program it?

Turing Turing

This chapter makes an oddly sacrilegious use of Alan Turing's name. In its title as well as in other instances, it implies that *turing* is a verb with only one form, the present participle, which means "applying a Turing machine to." A sacrilege, perhaps, but one to which Turing would not have objected. Mathematicians are the comedians of the scientific world. As punsters play with words to produce jokes, they play with concepts, turning them upside down to explore them and generate more concepts. In Turing's case, you'll see that that's what his machines are all about: playing with their own concept to open up new insights into scientific thought.

Duchamp chose to be a comedian in the parallel world of art. He turned the art code upside down to break fossilized art styles. He even broke styles, such as cubism, that seemed revolutionary but were simply extensions of older forms with a new veneer, playing with the comfortable toys of discarded morsels from preceding art styles.

Turing Turing is what Turing himself did and the way he earned fame. To demonstrate that undecidable computations could exist, he applied his machine to itself. He used the Gödel number method (see Chapter 2) to turn a machine into a single number that was huge by normal standards, but that hardly matters: a Turing machine is nothing but a series of symbols. The content of its memory plus the instruction set is also just a series of symbols. This sequence can be transformed into a Gödel number.

Turing then applied the machine to that number: itself. The situation, with indispensable logical and mathematical refinements that cannot be summarized here without oversimplifying them, produced an undecidable computation paradox. Suffice it to say that it's a mathematical parent of the well-known barber's paradox in which if a barber is someone who shaves everyone who can't shave himself, if he shaves himself, he can't be a barber.

The scientific world didn't come to a stop after learning of Turing's conclusion any more than it did after learning of Gödel's. We're still digesting the fact that logic and the way we code it do not have an infinite perfection in which everything is clearly true or false and perfectly decidable. Is this a flaw in the system, or is it an open door we don't yet know how to use?

Turing Caesar

In a time loop that defies the interval of centuries, let's try to apply a Turing machine to Caesar's code (see Chapter 1).

First, we need to write the original message on the machine's memory. Since we're dealing with ranks of letters, it is preferable to enter the letters as numbers: their rank in the alphabet. Each letter will be a number of dots, 1 for A, 2 for B, and so on. Letters will be separated by dashes; thus, a machine poised to code the word ACE would look like this:

State 0: Count a dot and stop when the head reads no more dot

IF in state 0	AND scan a dot	Erase the dot	Remain in state 0
IF in state 0	AND scan an empty square	Move right	Switch to state 1
IF in state 0	AND scan a dash	Erase the dash	Switch to state 3
IF in state 0	AND scan a star	STOP	

State 1: Go to the first empty square on the right and write a star

IF in state 1	AND scan a dot	Move right	Remain in state 1
IF in state 1	AND scan a dash	Move right	Remain in state 1
IF in state 1	AND scan a star	Move right	Remain in state 1
IF in state 1	AND scan an empty square	Write a star	Switch to state 2

State 2: Go back to look for a dot or a dash

IF in state 2	AND scan a star	Move left	Remain in state 2
IF in state 2	AND scan a dot	Move left	Remain in state 2
IF in state 2	AND scan a dash	Move left	Remain in state 2
IF in state 2	AND scan an empty square	Move right	Switch to state 0

State 3: Go to the first empty square on the right to write a star and a dash

IF in state 3	AND scan a dot	Move right	Remain in state 3
IF in state 3	AND scan a dash	Move right	Remain in state 3
IF in state 3	AND scan a star	Move right	Remain in state 3
IF in state 3	AND scan an empty square	Write a star	Switch to state 4

State 4: Write a dash and turn back

| IF in state 4 | AND scan a star | Move right | Remain in state 4 |
| IF in state 4 | AND scan an empty square | Write a dash | Switch to state 2 |

Staying with Caesar's simplest code, in which each letter slides up only one place farther in the alphabet, the resulting cipher will be a series of letters displayed farther along on the tape as sets of stars separated by dashes.

The program looks simple enough at first. It's very much like the program for multiplying numbers by 2. One by one, the letters are copied farther down the tape, each dot as a star, with three more stars for each letter.

This program codes all letters yet leaves one last hurdle to overcome: it doesn't address the problem of the letter Z, which goes around the corner. That letter has to be coded as 1 star, not 27 stars.

Code:

How would you complete this application of a Turing machine to Caesar's code to manage the letter that needs to go around the corner?

The Jefferson-Scherbius Active Cipher

For once, an invention was late in using the available technologies that made it possible. Only in 1917 did Albert Scherbius, a German inventor, think of coupling the typewriter, which had been in existence for 40 years, with the cipher disks invented by Thomas Jefferson more than a century earlier. Scherbius patented his creation and proposed it to the German Army in 1918, much too late to put it to use in World War I, which ended later that year.

If Scherbius had invented his machine several years earlier and the army of the kaiser had adopted it, it might have changed the face of the war, not to mention the face of the world. As far as cryptographic code is concerned, World War I was the end of an era. All the competing armies relied on refinements of the codes elaborated in the nineteenth century, all of which were pencil-and-paper affairs. Communication technology had undergone a quantum leap; ciphers had not.

Morse code already linked every country in the world in a matter of seconds over electric wires as codebreakers in cipher rooms toiled with their antiquated hand technologies. As the proponents of optical telegraphy had feared (see Chapter 1), the electric telegraph was easily cut and tapped. Great Britain had seen to that on the first day of the war by cutting Germany's private network cables to force German communications to be carried on international networks.

Connections on strategic wires yielded vast amounts of insecure secret content. The quality of the code was not on a level with the quantity and importance of the transmitted data. Active code had not invaded cryptography yet.

The best instance of a strategic leak at that time was the Zimmerman Telegram that led the United States to join the war after learning through codebreaking of a possible alliance of Germany with Mexico and Japan (see the illustration to the right).

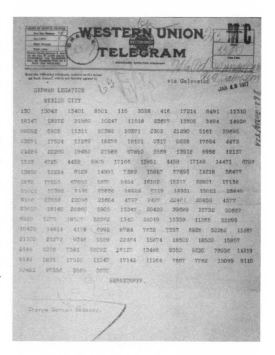

The Jefferson Disks

Like Caesar and Leone Battista Alberti, Thomas Jefferson was one of the few outstanding thinkers who dealt with cipher codes as easily as he dealt with aesthetic, symbolic, and architectural codes.

He gave a new dimension to Alberti's work on cipher disks by multiplying them to come up with cipher cylinders (see the illustration below). Each disk bears the letters of the alphabet in a random order. A message is coded word by word. The coder turns the disks to form the word above the rule and then sends the series of letters formed beneath the rule or several steps farther.

If the letters of the Jefferson cylinders were in columns, on a matrix, on a piece of paper, instead of engraved on disks, the method would look very much like the Belaso-Vigenère system (see Chapter 6). Its advantage lies in the reduction of possible errors. Turning

the disks and simply reading a row of letters is much safer than following rows and columns on a matrix.

Like all systems based on a machine, this one is vulnerable to theft of the machine. Yet even in that event, it remains more secure than the Belaso-Vigenère method because the cipher key is richer. The key exchanged by the communicating parties before sending messages specifies a particular order of the disks. Added to the random orders of the letters on the disks and compared to the straight alphabetical orders on the Belaso-Vigenère matrix, this creates a higher degree of complexity.

Jefferson conceived his cylinders in 1793 while he was secretary of state, not yet president of the United States. During the American Revolution he had used special messengers to deliver confidential letters, but later, during his stay in France as a minister of the United States from 1784 to 1789, he used ciphers to counter the European postmasters' black rooms where all mail was opened and read. Back in the United States and still corresponding with Europe, he invented and used the cylinders to enci-pher his most confidential diplomatic messages. The method was safe in spite of the need to distribute cylinders to correspondents physically before using the system. Jefferson used the cylinders until the War of 1812. Then they were forgotten and redis-covered several times, with the last rediscovery made around 1914 by the U.S. Army, which used them under the name of M-94 until World War II.

A set is exhibited at Monticello, Jefferson's mountaintop home in Virginia.

The Scherbius Rotors of Enigma

The machine constructed by Albert Scherbius could be described as a rigged typewriter. The machine was designed to code messages letter by letter. It had two keyboards: an ordinary set of typewriter keys and a set of letters on a glass pane, with each letter illuminated by a small bulb. When the initial arrangements were made, as we'll see below, the operator pressed the key of the letter he or she wanted to code, the machine lit up the corresponding coded letter, and the operator transcribed the illuminated letter in the cipher.

The system was automatic in the sense that the operator didn't need to know any-thing about the inner functions of the machine. He pressed, read, and transcribed.

Another practical advantage of the machine is that it was symmetrical: the code of the code was the original letter. Assuming the same setting of the machine, if the oper-ator pressed the keys of the cipher, he or she would get the clear message.

To achieve this, Scherbius used what he called rotors. Each rotor was a wheel that contained inner wiring arranged to produce simple alphabetical substitutions. Pressing a key sent an electric impulse through a rotor, which forwarded it to light the substituted letter.

A single rotor would produce only a constant, easily cracked substitution. Scherbius's breakthrough was the idea of using of a series of three rotors. Each rotor forwarded the impulse to the next one for an added substitution, but with an essential mechanism in between: the rotors were geared to one another and turned differently, like the wheels of a speedometer, when the keys were pressed. This resulted in a mutating substitution. Scherbius had inserted Caesar codes, as moving differentials, between substitution codes.

When the German Army adopted the system, another inventor, Willi Korn, added the "reflector." With the use of this mirrorlike component, the electric impulse going out of the rotors came back through them before hitting the display letters. This made not only for even more substitutions and Caesar actions, and hence more security, but also for a comfortable symmetry within the system.

As a final layer of security, a plugboard, like a traditional phone switchboard, with wires and plugs added yet another swapping of letters. To preserve the overall symmetry, it worked both between the keys and the rotors and, at the end, between the rotors and the display. This acted as yet another rotor, albeit a fixed one, that the operator could modify.

The coding steps were as follows:

Keyboard
Plugboard
Rotor 1
Rotor 2
Rotor 3
Reflector
Rotor 3
Rotor 2
Rotor 1
Plugboard
Display

In this system, the "key" commanding the exchange between two parties was the initial state of the machine. The German Army had developed a coded way of sending this key through communication channels as different as possible from those used to send the ciphers.

The resulting quality of the scrambling was the product of many possibilities: the order of the three rotors, their initial positions, and the disposition of the plugboard.

The security of the system depended on three levels of secrets:

- The secret of the machine's principles
- The secret of the rotors' wiring
- The secret of the keys

Taking all the steps into account, a codebreaker who knows the machine but is ignorant of the key faces a total number of combinations estimated by that cryptography historian Tony Sale on the order of

$$15,000,000,000,000,000,000.$$

Neither Scherbius nor the German Army called the machine "Enigma." It was the British cryptographers who gave it that name, and their attempt to break the machine's code was talked about so much during and after the war that their name stuck to it, leaving Scherbius's name all but forgotten.

Machine versus Machine

Codebreaking was crucial in World War II.

Actually, it was no more critical than in any other war, but it was far more tantalizing because the addition of wireless to landline transmissions made a vast quantity of data available. Even before the start of the war, it became clear that ciphers had made a quantum leap into active coding, thus placing codebreaking one step beyond pencil-and-paper methods. Allied cryptographic research centered on the German coding machine known as Enigma and began to look for equivalent countermachines that could match it and crack its code.

From a historical point of view, the matter is so sensitive that the subject is extremely controversial almost 70 years later. Books are published, films shot, and

Internet sites posted to expose "the truth" about Enigma and who cracked what, how, and where, but so far there is no official version that everyone would agree on. As might be expected in a history of secret goings-on and intelligence services, even the best documentation is suspect and the most sincere witnesses are questionable. The story has all the ingredients necessary—the codes, the actors involved, the crowd of witnesses, the myths—to turn the situation into a vast real-life bachelor machine, warranting its analysis by Carrouges criteria. In fact, that may be the only safe way to decode this particular aspect of World War II.

The causes of this unease probably run deeper than simple matters of national pride in wartime victories and the classic situation of history always being written by the winners. The real issue goes beyond cipher cracking and concerns the more general idea of involvement in the creation of intelligent machines. A country that could prove its role in the deployment of intelligent code would stand out in history as the originator of a new era. The culture of that country would become a reference point of the new culture. With the armed struggle over, the cultural war goes on, with each country striving to impose its way of seeing and its associated commercial resources of language and industry. Active code is enrolled easily as a national hero.

A perfect example is the general disregard of the computer invented in the 1930s by the German Konrad Zuse. That computer was programmable and binary and had a memory; by 1941 it was working satisfactorily on data fed on punched film. Zuse and his prototype managed to survive wartime bombings but failed to persuade the German government to support the project. Zuse fled to Switzerland, but though it was superior to the products of all the other computer projects, the Z3 prototype was ignored or at least not mentioned when its ideas were integrated into later projects. In the future, historians will wonder why the Enigma machine is associated more with the name of Alan Turing, whose role was to fight it, than with that of its actual inventor, Alfred Scherbius.

With this proviso, the following brief treatment of events seems the fairest possible in light of the most generally accepted facts today.

From Bomb to Colossus

As early as 1932, the Polish Army was concerned about German progress in ciphers and appointed a team to study and deconstruct the Scherbius machine. They managed to intercept a machine sent to the German embassy in Warsaw and copy it. They then set about designing a countermachine that could be used to break an Enigma cipher if one had the machine but not the key: the initial setup. Because it ticked like one when working on a cipher, they called their codebreaking machine "the bomb" and, by means of it and their analysis of Enigma, managed to decipher a number of messages.

When Poland was invaded by Germany and the Polish cryptographic service had no hope of continuing to work on its own, it decided to present its French and British allies with copies of both Enigma and the bomb and detailed descriptions of their functions.

This helped enormously, and even though they no longer had to guess about the mechanical workings of the machine, the codebreakers in Allied intelligence still had problems. A copy was sent to the United States, a workshop in either country started producing Enigmas, and teams of cryptanalysts were recruited to accustom themselves to the machine and find ways to break its codes.

Despite the fact that they had the essential machine, the main problem for Allied intelligence was that the Germans were aware of the leak. Though they kept using Enigma, trusting in its fundamental security, they changed and multiplied the number of rotors. As a result, the number of cracked messages dropped considerably, and the codebreakers were left with only one tool: trial and error. However powerful the new coding combination, it was vulnerable to the basic method of trying as many combinations as possible while looking for probable words, a scheme that had worked with homophones (see Chapter 6).

The most romantic place during World War II was Bletchley Park in England. The former Manor of Eaton was chosen by British intelligence because it was situated between Oxford and Cambridge, allowing them to tap into the best minds at both universities. It housed the crowd of codebreakers working on the Enigma and received all the ciphers intercepted by the British. Among the academics on the team was Alan Turing, who supplied ideas for making use of the bomb and enhancing its efficiency.

Bletchley Park eventually developed its own machine to meet the German challenge. That device, which was called the Colossus, computed letter statistics and represented a step toward modern computers. The site's activity was essential in maintaining British morale and determination during World War II.

Bletchley Park is now a cryptography museum.

Turing the Physical World

Turing apparently was able to best channel his creativity through the ultimate bachelor machine: a logical machine that did not physically exist. Using that creation as a basis, he went farther and demonstrated that the logic on which they had been relying did not exactly exist as they had hoped. There were undecidable entities that had no existence in the straight, lawful, true-or-false world. He may have thought of himself in such terms, too, for he was a homosexual man at a time when that was a crime. He eventually was prosecuted and sentenced to chemical therapy, and that may have led him to commit suicide.

After the war, Turing was halfheartedly involved in British and American computer projects. With or without his active participation, his basic ideas were essential in generating computers as we know them today. We owe to Konrad Zuse the complementary idea of storing programs on the same media as the main memory. We can only regret that Turing and Zuse never worked together. That was the era of the Cold War, and computers were sensitive business. Turing's homosexuality and Zuse's nationality made it impossible to clear them to get security clearance. They were excluded from the active teams that implemented and built the computers. They had done the groundwork for computers in the 1930s, before the start of World War II. Computer technology and computer science in the 1950s developed without them.

The fact that Turing's involvement in the generation of real computers was only minor can be explained by his psychology: he was a mathematician rather than an engineer. He functioned better in the mathematical world of principles and theories than in the physical world of cogs and wheels. Donald W. Davies, a leading researcher in mathematical logic, tells a revealing anecdote. While working with Turing to build a programmed computer conceived by Turing in the National Physical Laboratory in London in 1947, Davies noted a number of errors in Turing's fundamental 1936 paper "On Computable Numbers, with an Application to the Entscheidungsproblem." Some of his programming loops, for instance, didn't close correctly; that was not objectionable in 1936 but would be an unforgivable error today. When Davies mentioned it to Turing, proposing to correct the minor mistakes, "he became impatient and made it clear that I was wasting my time and his by my worthless endeavors." Such was Turing's importance that Davies published his corrections only 50 years later. Yet those errors and Turing's reaction are fundamental from the point of view of symbols and imagination in the history of code. In psychology, errors are not mistakes; they are observable facts. In this case, they reveal that Turing was not at ease with the precise material implementation of his creation. Circumstances had placed him in a "physical laboratory," whereas his mind wished to work at a mathematician's desk. His imagination did not entertain such practical engineering enterprises. This fact adds an unnecessary divorce to the situation leading up to Turing's tragic end.

Death by Symbol (or Exit through Eden)

In 1954, Turing chose to leave this world through its front yard, the Garden of Eden. Mathematics, logic, and ciphers are all matters of symbol management, Turing's life work. True to his genius and vocation, he chose to live in symbolism to the very end of his life.

It is thought that the fruit of the knowledge of good and evil eaten by Adam and Eve was an apple. Adam and Eve did not die after biting the apple of knowledge, but Turing did. He was found dead of cyanide poisoning with a bitten apple lying nearby. The apple was not analyzed, but it is very likely that Turing laced it with cyanide before biting into it. What more forbidden fruit is there than a poisoned one? Turing's knowledge must have been bitter: his apple was loaded with death.

This can be understood in terms of code if we recall the equivalence of logical truth in science to friendship in human groups among the Pythagoreans. Turing had experienced ruptures and cul-de-sacs in both science and the area of the emotion. He had experienced the fact that because of indeterminable questions, perfect true-or-false logic could not be extended to the entire realm of science. He had experienced the fact that the deep emotions he felt as a homosexual man could not be extended to his human community. In the face of such paradoxes he must have felt that he had no choice but to mark the Garden of Eden as a deadly place.

Twenty years later, when Steve Jobs and Steve Wozniak, working in their legendary garage, created a machine that was to be the first successful personal computer, they called it an Apple. When he was interviewed about the coincidence, Wozniak insisted that there was no specific symbolism, no relation to Turing's apple; he and his friend simply had been inspired by the Californian apple orchards they drove by that day. There was no link to the apple in the Garden of Eden either. Is the famous Apple logo, the apple with a bite out of it, simply a fancy of their advertising department, used to promote their bachelor machine? History or urban legend? When Jobs and Wozniac first put their first machine, the short lived Apple I, on the market in July 1976, they set the price at $666, "the number of the Beast." That figure could hardly have been set innocently, coming, as it did, seven years after Vangelis and Aphrodite's Child released the famous album "666—The Apocalypse of John." Is that conjuring the beast in the machine?

CHAPTER 9
Migrating to Code Land

Today, the ultimate era in the history of code, the world relies on codes more than it ever did before. Active code enables a world far beyond Pythagoras's dreams, one where every object, living creature, human being, and shred of imagination is digitized or potentially could be, with its meaning turned into or associated with numbers. Managed by active code, numbers have such a grip on us, our lives, and our grasp on the world that we may wonder where the limits of our freedom and even their freedom are.

In 1930, dictionaries defined a computer as a human being performing computations; today's dictionaries define it as an electronic machine, with no mention of human beings. This reveals the extent of the change in our lives brought about by the quantum leap in active code described in Chapter 8. Active code has taken over. Exeunt human being.

Coded Golems

Active code is the most heavily promoted product humanity has ever sold itself. However slow, cumbersome, and limited it was in reality, the computer that came into existence in the 1950s was exalted and declared capable of the most extraordinary deeds. Although at that time computers could do little more than store data and sort the data at high speeds, they were credited with awesome intelligence. Businesses and governments blindly trusted the machines' imagined powers and invested in their development. *Computer-assisted* became a synonym for being equipped with a magic wand. No serious activity could be performed without a computer. Armies, administrations, and businesses empowered them as their most precious adjuncts. Companies often were endangered or ruined after their accounts departments were coded when unforeseen delays, poor logical analysis of the problems, or faulty coding compromised the implementations of new machines, yet no one thought to blame the computers.

That irresistible attraction stemmed from the combined seductions of hidden content and rapid management. Rapidity has always been the key quality claimed for superior machinery. "Faster" is easier to achieve than "smarter" and too often is confused with it. The computer industry always has had more success with speed than with intelligence. Even today, 40 years after the release of Arthur C. Clarke and Stanley Kubrick's *2001: A Space Odyssey*, although we think we have made immense progress, artificial intelligence such as that featured in HAL 9000, the thinking robot, does not exist. The question is whether it ever will. Is the famous sentence "I'm sorry, Dave; I'm afraid I can't do that" humankind's final statement on artificial intelligence? Or, as we'll see later in this chapter, are we advancing along a very different road, less obvious and harder to foresee?

Regardless of the achievements of technology, hidden and coded content draws on the poetic substance of the power and mystery accumulated by codes and ciphers over the centuries. Symbolically, coded data is more than mere data: what coding does is transmute data, lifting it into higher dimensions where obscure mythical processors generate golden results.

When personal computers first became available in the 1980s, we could not wait to equip every single individual with that wonder tool. More than twenty years later, billions of people have in their pockets a machine, familiarly called a phone, that is more powerful than any strategic computer to come out of the 1960s, and no one feels cheated. These pocket computers indeed deliver the goods: speed, concealment, and entertainment.

Genesis of a Virtual Eden

This explosion of electronic technology laid the groundwork for one of the most ambitious feats humanity has ever achieved. For once, instead of discovering new territory, we created it. It simply happened spontaneously and irresistibly over the span of a few years.

In the early 1990s, before the magic link of hypertext, even the simple process of exchanging text and pictures through modems and phone lines seduced those geeks who could access it. They began to invade the embryonic Internet, a space with new dimensions. It was a dream come true. Users were disembodied entities meeting other disembodied entities and sharing free material.

More often than not, the material downloaded from the servers was wild erotica, yet good or bad, the dreams were pure, with no physical counterpart. Sheriffs were nowhere to be seen in the Internet, and there were no brides to meet. Imagination was all-powerful.

The easy click-and-get flashy screens we enjoy today still had to be implemented. The first generation of the Internet was like a limitless hard disk with an interface that had no more appeal than Windows Explorer, but Internauts didn't mind having to type the exact address of a site or search through the textual directories of servers. *Wired* magazine's thick paper directory of site addresses was both a success and a must. The era of File Transfer Protocol was a golden age for geeks. They thought that keyboards were giving them magic contact with code, excluding the users who found no pleasure in typing their way through Code Land. Enthusiastic geeks fed the network with data; one might say they enjoyed every bit of it.

The magic click of hypertext was the final ingredient needed to turn the Internet into a virtual Eden. Clicking on a word and being teleported to another page somewhere—anywhere—else at some unspecified point in the virtual sphere enhanced the feeling of freedom.

Born-Again Internauts

The Internet freely delivered what millennia of brotherhoods and mystics had worked so hard to achieve through their secret rites. Internauts not only were disembodied but were born anew into a fresh life with the immediate benefits of unlimited travel through a universe that was utterly free. Abandoning their bodies in the old world for hours on end, they roamed the virtual world of cost-free data.

This virtual Eden aspect of the Internet was supported and fed by a founding myth: freedom from hierarchy. The actual management of the system as a distributed network of networks with no supreme governing body supported the myth and still does. The Internet was an Eden free of an overseer or an all-powerful deity. Anyone could bite into the fruit of knowledge without risk.

For reasons related to its military past, the Internet's structure was "anarchic." During the Cold War that began in the 1950s between the so-called Eastern and Western blocs of the planet, the West built a communication network designed to allow military laboratories and industries to survive a nuclear attack. With this in view, the network was like a web with redundant connections and no specific center and could maintain its structure even if a number of holes were punched in it. In short, if the direct route of a message from A to B was destroyed, the message could reach B through C or E and F. The by-product of an attempt to guarantee survival through a world war, the network was engineered to survive all local disasters.

Ironically, the result was that the military, though it had a strong hierarchical structure, created the least hierarchical net of communications ever conceived of. The obvious weakness of a centralized organization is its center: kill the king and the kingdom is headless. The Chappe optical network discussed in Chapter 1 centered on Paris. Take Paris, as Napoleon did, and you owned the network.

The military ARPANET that became the Internet had no specific center. It was designed to make the myth of freedom from hierarchy come true.

The Great Code Land Exodus

An unprecedented phenomenon has begun to take place that is similar to immigration in that it involves a vast amount of transfer. However, it is not an exact equivalent because it involves only human activity, not the actual displacement of human beings.

The first step—the preparation for the voyage—began in the 1980s and early 1990s. Humanity had begun packing its suitcase, so to speak. People were storing data, intellectual work, and entertainment on the far side of the screen, in the closed boxes of the hard disks buried in their computers.

The second step—migration into the virtual space of the network—is still going on and has reached a point where it is irreversible. Our hard disks are migrating to remote memories that reside in unspecified places: online safeguarding can be used to archive your work on secure sites somewhere on the Web in case your own disk crashes.

Our disks are only following our mail and our business. Internet mail organizations such as Google Mail offer to send, receive, manage, and archive our communications. Commercial sites offer to sell products and manage the payments. Such is our trust in the Web that we consider it not only convenient but safe to live and deal through those proxies. Yet the net result of the situation is that the lifeblood of our activities—all the data relevant to our business—resides somewhere in the virtual world beyond our reach.

A more critical issue is that the virtual world hosts coded counterparts of our identities and property and that our physical existence and property are linked so closely to their virtual counterparts as to be inseparable from them. As we'll see below in the discussion of security issues, we are in a situation in which we are required to manage our existence and safety in both the physical world and the virtual world. The code world that seemed to facilitate daily life has evolved to become a second life, paralleling the first and adding its own hazards. We have to beware of a lifestyle that splits us into two different personalities, one physical and one virtual. Clearly, our mental health depends on our ability to integrate these physical and virtual lives.

The Kabbalah Connection

Virtual reality is not a new concept. It existed in the imaginations of poets and the experiences of mystics well before the technology that could support it was developed. Poets shared their worlds through oral and written literature; mystics shared theirs through preaching and revelations. One such world, an age-old mystical endeavor, can help us put today's explosive fascination for Internet Code Land into perspective and better understand it.

The Kabbalah is the embodiment and expression of the Jewish mystical revival that flourished in the sixteenth century. With roots in twelfth- and thirteenth-century Provence, it passed through and was strengthened in fourteenth-century Catalonian Spain and then spread north and east, reaching its apogee in the sixteenth and seventeenth centuries in the philosophy of Isaac Luria of Safed. It is based on a particular reading of the first five books of the Bible, Genesis, Exodus, Leviticus, Numbers, and Deuteronomy, the so-called Torah or Pentateuch (Greek for "the five teachings") and on the commentaries on those books.

Kabbalah is the basis for Jewish mysticism and its practitioners, mystics who undergo transcendental experiences in which they access a perception of the universe that is radically different from the everyday view of laypeople. Mystical experience is, of course, essentially subjective and cannot be observed from the outside. It often is treated with skepticism, yet mystical encounters are recorded in all civilizations and religions, and it is almost universally accepted that such experiences are not only real but similar to one another. Whatever beliefs they start from, it seems that all mystics access roughly the same perceptions.

Mystics and their transcendental experiences are beyond the scope of this book. They were mentioned in Chapters 2 and 5 in connection with Pythagoras and the Freemasons and their coded mythical voyages. Yet the Kabbalah is a special case, different from the mystical movements of other religions and demanding specific analysis in that it refers explicitly to code and a universe commanded by code. Centuries ago, using the Kabbalah as a tool, Jewish mystics accessed a coded universe that gave them a subtler appreciation of the experiences of life.

The Torah is described by Kabbalistic scholars in a language that any coder will recognize: that of ciphers. At first glance the Torah seems to be a normal text made up of words and phrases that can be read and understood by the lay reader like any other. In fact, a wide variety of religious groups, large and small, Moslem, Jewish, and Christian, all refer to the same five books, and all base their religious experience on the way they read them.

Kabbalist mystics, however, have another reading.

They state that the Torah's apparent separation into words is only a screen, obscure to the lay reader, and that that screen conceals its real essence, which is an enormous sacred word formed of all its letters strung together. They also state that each and every letter and the positioning of those letters are essential; without them, the Torah's complete word loses its sacred meaning.

What better way to express the fact that the Torah is a cipher whose code would be scrambled if a letter was missing or not in its right place? We already have seen a code like this in the Vigenère cryptograms (see Chapter 6). In *On the Kabbalah and its Symbolism*, Gershom Scholem quotes a second-century C.E. text in which Rabbi Meir addresses a student scribe of the Torah: "My son, be careful in your work, for it is the work of God; if you omit a single letter, or write a letter too many, you will destroy the whole world."

"Manuscript Torah *scrolls* are still used, and still written, for ritual purposes (i.e., *religious services*); this is called a *Sefer Torah* ("Book [of] Torah"). They are written using a painstakingly careful methodology by highly qualified scribes. This has resulted in modern copies of the text that are almost unchanged from millennia old copies. The reason for such care is it is believed that every word, or marking, has divine meaning, and that not one part may be inadvertently changed lest it lead to error." ("*Torah*" in Wikipedia).

According to Jewish mystics, the Torah is a living being that should not be confused with the physical collection of texts that anyone can read. The Torah is based on those texts, they say, but exists above and beyond them. Indeed, the same could be said of the Internet: it is based on a collection of coded texts—the computer programs of the various networks and sites—yet it cannot be reduced to those texts and exists beyond them because the texts are active codes. Any Internaut can experience this when looking at an Internet page by clicking a drop-down menu, selecting the source code of the page, and comparing the text he or she reads there with the living, interactive page. The text used to write down active code should not be mistaken for the interactive action produced by that code.

From their symbolic standpoint, mystics state that the Torah existed 2,000 years before the creation of the world. Added to Rabbi Meir's statement that it is a precise rendering of the work of God, this can be interpreted to mean that the Torah is the code of the world, the blueprint God referred to when creating it. In this view, the Torah is too potent to be published without the protection of a cipher. If the richness of the basic text and its basic reading are a precious teaching for millions of believers, imagine the immense wealth of meaning that a properly enlightened mystic can access through a higher level of reading.

This brief description of the Kabbalah shows that our current interest in the worlds created by Internet networks is not a fortuitous by-product of twentieth-century electronic technology. Full ecstatic access to mystical perception has been reserved for a handful of prophets in various religions, but partial access is available to many mystics and a lesser access is there for all believers, who are deeply impressed by what they are able to make contact with.

The pursuit of the mythical coded universe has a long history. The Internet is certainly not a religion or even a faith, yet its fascination seems to call on a similar function in the human mind: the desire to access a universe above and beyond our own. The physical and materialistic aspect of the Internet is obvious, but the massive current exodus toward Code Land demands an explanation. However sacrilegious it may sound, that explanation may be found in the same human trait that leads to the pursuit of mystical access to other realms. The Kabbalah's success shows that fascination with code has been emerging for centuries.

Privacy and Security

These days, network communication security concerns everyone: individuals and businesses, governments and administrations. Cipher code is back in the forefront and expected to solve all protection problems created by its active code twin. This scenario is a carnival of contradictory demands for protection: individuals wanting to be protected from criminals and administrational abuse of power, administrations seeking protection from unethical individuals, businesses wanting protection from thieves and governments from enemies, foreign or otherwise—the list is endless.

Balancing Out Secrecy

Although it is played out in the coded virtual world, the problem of freedom in a contradictory world of conflicting interests is an old one. The philosophers of the eighteenth century showed that the solution lies in the balancing of forces between competing powers. This is the cornerstone of all democracies, and it works in the virtual world too. It's not perfect, but it helps maintain a livable society.

In the world of code, the key to this balance is a numeric cipher key. Any user, private or communal, has free access to highly sophisticated encryption software with a quality and efficiency no Venetian diplomat of the seventeenth century could have imagined. Anyone can instantly encipher a text that then can be deciphered by a correspondent who has the correct numeric "key," without either of them having any knowledge of cryptography. PGP (Pretty Good Privacy) was the emblematic original tool: free software that has developed in many diverse directions.

Numeric keys can be broken, but that requires the brute force of a supercomputer and can be achieved only at great expense and with a nonnegligible delay. The expense and delay are the keys to security balance.

The Diffie-Hellman-Merkle Paradoxical Key Exchange

It sounds like an impossible magic trick: how do you exchange a secret number with your partner while everybody is looking at you and watching your hands?

As with most cipher systems since the time of Caesar, Internet cryptography is based on the exchange of a secret key between trusted partners. For Caesar's code, the key was an alphabet jump, a number between 1 and 25. For Vigenère, it was the secret word repeated beneath the message. Here the key is a number 128 or 256 digits long.

For anyone who doesn't know the simple arithmetic hidden in the system, it looks like magic. Let's say you and I want to exchange secret information through e-mail. First we agree on two numbers that we don't bother to hide. Then, even though those numbers are visible to eavesdroppers and we keep sending e-mails anyone can read, we use the numbers to produce together a new number so secret that we can use it to protect all further exchanges with a high degree of security.

Here is how our exchange might look:

A: Hi. I suggest we base our encryption on 3 and 10.

B: Okay; 3 and 10 are fine by me. No problem.

A: Good. Note this number: 11.

B: Okay, fine. You note the number 14.

A: Thank you for your 14, I can now compute our secret numeric key.

B: Thank you for your 11. I have computed our numeric key, too, and I'm perfectly sure we have the same key and that no one else knows it. Here's a text encrypted with that key.

A: Roger. I deciphered your text and read it perfectly clearly.

A and B have simply and openly exchanged only four numbers: 3, 10, 11, and 14. They haven't hidden them, yet they're certain they can use them to produce a key number nobody else will know. Better, they've done the trick according to rules everyone knows. Roughly, the magic comes from the fact that nobody but A knows exactly how he "seeded" the system to produce his number, Na, and nobody but B knows exactly how she seeded the system to produce her number, Nb. The security is exactly as good as A's and B's ability to keep their seeds secret.

The mathematical magic involved was the work of three independent mathematicians: Whitfield Diffie, Martin Hellman, and Ralph Merkle. Although at first these mathematicians worked separately, they eventually joined forces, and their combined genius produced a system that instantly superseded years of research at established laboratories.

The system key relies on two number gimmicks that require nothing more than high school math: the prime numbers and the powers of those numbers we saw at work along with Gödel numbers in Chapter 2. It also makes use of the "modulo" function (number p modulo number q is the remainder of a division of p by q; for instance, 43 modulo 10 is 3 and 22 modulo 7 is 1).

The first number exchanged is the "base." All the numbers exchanged thereafter will be powers of that base. If the base, which must be a prime number, had been 3, the conversation would have dealt with the powers of 3: 9, 27, 81, and so on.

The second number exchanged is the modulo reference. If that number is 7, all numbers exchanged afterward will be remainders of their division by 7.

To start the real exchange, A picks a prime number that nobody else, not even B, will know. He raises the base to the power of that number and then computes the result with the chosen modulo. Let's say he chooses 11. He then computes

$3^{11} = 177\ 147$

and applies the modulo:

177147 modulo 10 = 7

and sends 7

Likewise, B chooses 14. Then she computes

$3^{14} = 4\ 782\ 969$

and applies the modulo:

4 782 969 modulo 10 = 9

and sends 9,

A computes with his secret key 11:

9^{11} modulo 10 = 31 381 059 609 modulo 10 = 9

B computes with her secret key 11:

7^{14} modulo 10 = 678 223 072 849 modulo 10 = 9

In both computations, each secret number is inputted only once, raising the base to its power exactly once. The modulo operation is used to enhance security. It is transparent for exponentials and is employed merely to hide the original numbers. The modulo function eliminates the way back. Determining what number any specific number is the modulo of is impossible. There are too many possibilities; for example, 3 could as easily be 23 modulo 10 as 293 modulo 10.

The key is as follows:

(base)(Na + Nb) modulo 10

Of course, in this example, the numbers are too small. Simple trial and error will solve the key rapidly. With larger numbers and a larger modulo, and thus a key with a higher number of figures, a trial-and-error method would require long and expensive computation.

The Random Gang

Present-day secret codes depend on random numbers. Those numbers would have confused Pythagoras because you can use them but can't see them, and whenever a random number is identified as such, it vanishes as a random number.

We resort to random numbers because of a basic principle of strategy. When an opponent knows all our weapons and tactics to the point of being able to anticipate our moves, the only option is to surprise him or her by choosing moves in a random manner. This strategy is described by Vladimir Nabokov in his novel *The Luzhin Defense* (movie by Marleen Gorris), in which the chess champion Luzhin plays random moves on the board and in real life in a desperate attempt to confuse his adversaries.

Here, in the open/hidden key exchange, security rests on the secret choice of our own key that subsequently will be concealed in large integers and their modulos. If an eavesdropper can predict and guess our key, the whole security system collapses; to avoid that possibility, the system relies on random numbers. Somewhere in our computer, a chunk of code generates a random number every time we need a numerical key.

Absolute randomness is a dream, out of the reach of human hands and certainly out of the reach of algorithms such as computer programs. We approximate randomness every time we throw dice or shuffle a deck of cards. Computer programs resort to algorithms that produce pseudo-random numbers, which are weak approximations of the real thing. They're the weak link in the security chain, a potential backdoor if our enemy guesses our algorithm, thus piercing our cloak of randomness.

Coding Lives

In an unexpected loop, the Pythagorean philosophical system eventually arrives back on the scene to install a pure Pythagorean world. The Pythagorean view that only numbers are real and all the rest is illusion is becoming a realistic description of the contemporary world. We depend on our digital coded counterparts in the networks. Administrations and businesses deal less and less with physical bodies and more and more with digital representations. Our freedom is defined more by what our codes can do than by what our physical bodies can do. Bodies follow codes. The part of our lives that depends on codes and dwells on the Net is growing. Digital impersonation on the Web is becoming as dangerous as kidnapping and murder in the physical world.

An illustration of this is provided by the widespread criminal activity of identity theft. Using "phishing," the rapidly developing activity of fishing for personal data on the Web, criminals get hold of credit card numbers, Social Security numbers, and Internet passwords and then impersonate their victims in many situations. The victims can lose their homes and belongings. Some have been prosecuted for criminal acts committed in their names. The process of identity retrieval is long and difficult. Showing up in person is of little help: numbers tend to prevail over physical bodies.

Turing Test 2.0

A side issue here is an ironic twist of the famous test proposed by Alan Turing for testing for artificial intelligence. In his test, artificial intelligence would be deemed successful if in a dialogue one could not tell the machine from a human being. These days, in contrast machines need a test to be able to tell machines from humans.

Crowds of software robots roam the Internet in a continuous attempt to access protected sites. Because of their ability to try out millions of name and password combinations in a split second, they are far more dangerous than dishonest humans.

To deal with such situations, we've all been asked to copy a "captcha," a word written on a background designed to confuse automatic scanners. Luckily, there still are activities that can help differentiate humans from machines.

The Cantor Sieve

Simple property theft is not the worst development in our immigration to Code Land. The deeper, more insidious danger comes from digitizing the physical world into a virtual one and then trying to manage the physical world through its digitized counterpart. This threatens to downgrade reality to a sort of subworld.

In Chapter 2 we saw that Georg Cantor demonstrated the existence of at least two different infinities. Aleph-zero is the infinity of whole numbers, and aleph-one is a larger infinity: e.g., the set of points in a three-dimensional universe. There may be other infinities between them, but the important point is that Cantor proved that there cannot be a one-to-one correspondence between the worlds of aleph-zero and aleph-one. This leaves us with two symbols to represent at least two infinities. One is the "small" infinity, aleph-zero, identifying sets that can be numbered, or digitized; the other is the "larger" infinity, aleph-one, identifying sets too large to be numbered or digitized.

The presence of two different infinities, one larger than the other, is a difficult concept to grasp. However, we have to accept it, for the existence of two infinities has been proved mathematically, and they are needed for the essential point that is made here.

Aleph-zero accounts for everything our codes and computers can manage, since they are based on integers and their siblings, rational numbers. Computers as we know them today will never produce or manage any world richer than aleph-zero. Yet the real world where we actually live has the richness of aleph-one. Computers can deal only with approximations of the real world. True, the gap is so small as to be beyond what our senses can ever perceive, but it is there.

We probably should dismiss the problem of the gap as a waste of time, yet it takes us straight back to Pythagoras. The number 2 exists in aleph-zero, but the square root of 2 is in aleph-one, never the twain shall meet! A ratio or decimal number can approximate the square root of 2 as closely as we like, but it will never *be* the square root of 2.

Are we humans, residents of aleph-one (and perhaps a higher aleph if we take our imagination into account), being treated fairly by our aleph-zero shadows? Can aleph-zero code be expected to manage the aleph-one world adequately?

We living creatures bask in the upper world of aleph-one, enjoying every second of the limitless spread of organic life and of our thoughts and potentials. When tagged with aleph-zero numbers, we seem to become conveniently predictable, an easily sortable database. Yet our presence in aleph-zero is the merest shade of what we are in aleph-one. If aleph-zero is used only by computers trying to study and understand human beings, the situation is not so bad. Only the superficial numeric aleph-zero skin is involved, and our aleph-one freedom remains intact. However, if aleph-zero is used to manage our lives, we could be in deep trouble.

Aleph-zero is to aleph-one what a DVD is to a live concert. The DVD has the sounds the microphones and the cameras could get and digitize, but anybody in the audience enjoyed far more in terms of sounds, pictures, and feelings.

Note that in the Kabbalah, aleph is used to identify the universe as a whole.

The Massively Multiplayer Bride

As if irresistibly, a bachelor machine situation has emerged on the Internet (see Chapter 8), with Carrouges's four principles of autonomy, user involvement, dramatic interaction with human society, and symbolic dimension. A symbolic myth—freedom from hierarchy—was there from the start. The autonomy and the involvement of human users were, so to speak, built in. The dramatic public show came last, appearing as textual activity in forums: Internauts loved examining one another's opinions on every subject.

With better computers and a faster network, the show now includes full-scale sound and images. Some Internauts have installed online cameras so that the whole world can observe them 24/7. Currently, the most popular and profitable sites allow Internauts to see one another or exchange music and videos. The ultimate spectacular coded shows are the "persistent" worlds that go on existing, with virtual events happening whether anybody is connected or not. Wearing sophisticated masks, Internauts go there to see and be seen and enjoy a lawless life beyond the basic lawlessness of the Internet.

The first creators of those worlds thought they needed an incentive and offered complex worlds of war and competition. They called their worlds "massively multiplayer online games." They soon discovered that most Internauts were there only to look around and meet one another. That gave birth to a new generation of persistent worlds oriented only toward offering a new life, a new deal in Code Land. Internauts own land and houses, do business, create objects, and earn virtual money that can be converted into real dollars.

Persistent virtual worlds are parallel to ours, but with a big difference: the Internauts can be seen; they're part of the show. The virtual world is probably the ultimate lived-in bachelor machine.

Parallel worlds interact with one another. When interviewed in August 2007 by Steve Ranger, William Gibson said about the most famous massively multiplayer world that "very occasionally, I'll see on the street someone who looks as though they have escaped from Second Life. There are people who look all too much like Second Life avatars."

Interaction as the Fifth Frontier

Software developers are fighting on the elusive frontier of code perfection. Their goal of producing bug-free codes seems simple enough, but bugs take many shapes. They can be overlooked logical loops that crash a product or open backdoors that let malevolent code install itself on a computer. To the surprise of both users and publishers, no code ever comes out on the market bug-free. Apparently unavoidably, imperfections crawl into Code Land even though it is expected to be free of all the flaws in the traditional human realm. Internauts have gotten used to receiving a stream of patches to fix the bugs in nearly all software. Although they usually are described as enhancements of the user's comfort or security, all they do is eliminate bugs.

The solution seems simple and easy to implement. A precise analysis of projects, a clear distribution of tasks, and coding by professional programmers verified by other professionals should yield perfect products. However, no matter how many top-level dedicated geeks a software company uses on a project, other geeks soon are exposing bugs and trapdoors and then advertising them. Patches and the like follow.

This doesn't mean that the first geeks were idiots and the later ones are geniuses. Far more important is the way it reveals the present state of the code world. It means that a new condition—interaction—is gaining in importance. Once it is released and "out there" in the world of networks and users, software is immersed in a soup of rich interactivity with other software. The most carefully tested code leaps into an ocean of possibilities too big for coders and testers to manage. It seems that the conceivers of code are going to have to take a new dimension into account. Beyond the three dimensions of space and even beyond time, which plays its role too, there is the dimension of interaction, the full set of interplay in a product in terms of user input and interfacing with other products. Software is now so complex and offers so many functions that even experienced professional testers cannot exhaust the world of combinations that users impose on the software. Beyond user interactions, there are interactions with other products coexisting on the same machine or network and sharing the same data and runtime environment.

In this fifth dimension of interaction, a code-versus-code competition that started timidly with World War II's Enigma and its competitors is taking place (see Chapter 8). Among the best advertised clashes, e-mail software fights spam, viruses attempt to penetrate firewalls, spyware tracks users' activities, and actual spies are trying to crack communications with sophisticated tools. All these and many other factors interact with one another, gathering and spreading data that feed other software. We still are the basic artisans, the hands on the keyboard, but an overall understanding of the general mass of interactions is already beyond our human grasp. Too many actors are reacting too quickly.

A Primordial Net Soup

The science-fiction writer William Gibson coined the word *cyberspace* in the early 1980s, before the Internet's official birth. Similar, smaller networks already were available to scientists and geeks around the world. They were enough to trigger Gibson's vision of a future in which people would plug their minds directly into the Net, a vision that fed the imagination of Tim Berners-Lee and those who built the Internet with him.

If we note its strong similarity with the "primordial soup" proposed by Stanley Miller in 1953 as the possible origin of life on earth, Gibson's cyberspace, now swarming with tame and wild code, suggests a situation in which new active entities are brought into being.

This requires a brief detour through chemistry and biology. Miller's hypothesis is that half a billion years ago, the earth's atmosphere contained enough of the constituents of elementary life that random discharges of lightning could ionize and combine them into amino acids, life's building blocks. In the primordial soup those constituents would combine further to create life as we know it. Note that the hypothesis is reminiscent of Mary Shelley's vision of Doctor Frankenstein creating life by subjecting morsels of flesh to lightning.

Miller's 1953 experiments did produce the expected soup. His results were questioned when better knowledge of the earth's early atmosphere showed that the methane and ammonia gases he had used were not present as he had supposed, but 60 years later the primordial soup was brewing again. On March 28, 2007, Douglas Fox announced a breakthrough in *Scientific American*: "A Frankensteinesque contraption of glass bulbs and crackling electrodes has produced yet another revelation about the origin of life. The results suggest that Earth's early atmosphere could have produced chemicals necessary for life—contradicting the view that life's building blocks had to come from comets and meteors." Indeed, with better understanding of the earth's early atmosphere, Jeffrey Bada at the Scripps Institution of Oceanography in La Jolla, California, obtained a genuine soup of amino acids from something very similar to the original atmosphere.

Coming back to code and applying Mary Shelley's and Stanley Miller's visions to the present situation, the Internet is already past the first state of inert raw components. Code and machines have already combined into multitudes of independent basic active code, viruses, and bots of all kinds swarming in virtual space. A primordial soup is brewing. To continue with this image, we may expect active elements to recombine to create new code forms the way Miller's soup produced life forms. In Gibson's novel *Idoru*, a code form mimics human life, but the code forms brewing in the Net soup today are more likely to follow their own patterns, with no likeness to previous life forms.

In fact, the alternative hypothesis concerning the appearance of life on earth coming from space also could apply to code. Radio waves are code's equivalent of meteors and comets. Radio waves keep hitting the earth from remote stars and galaxies. They are monitored by astrophysicists and nonchalantly added to the mass of data brewed by the Internet as a matter of routine. If some of those waves are carrying an evolved code capable of investing a network, there is nothing to stop it from seeding the earth's code sphere with coded life forms from distant parts of the universe.

A Built-in Consciousness

The possibility of active code evolving toward autonomy and a higher form of life is supported by a fundamental property of Turing's universal machine: the presence of a extremely basic yet real form of consciousness.

Elementary consciousness is awareness of the environment. At the human level, complete consciousness also includes awareness of the self, the practice of dealing with oneself as an object of knowledge, and that is exactly what Turing conceived his universal machine for. His idea was to conceive a computer capable of computing itself. Turing had nothing else in mind. He did not want to add 2 and 2; he was looking to add consciousness to code.

Turing's aim was to produce a machine that was able to host code and that could compute itself to the exclusion of anything else. He included examples of external computation such as addition and multiplication only to prove that the machine was an authentic computer and that self-computation was therefore a valid operation. Those computations, however, were there only because logic demanded it. They were not meant to be engineering feats, and in that sense Turing might have resented the use of his machine outside mathematics. The later development of his universal machine into computers might have made him uneasy, and this may explain his failure to develop a practical computer and his negative reaction to Davies's remarks on the faulty examples in his theoretical paper. For him, those examples were beside the point. Turing's favorite ground was the sphere of pure mathematics. Like many mathematicians, he might have had a profound lack of interest in applied mathematics. However aware he was of the need to apply his machine and however willing he may have been to help, his heart was not in it.

Having conceived his machine, Turing did not go straight to the patent office. Protecting the design never crossed his mind; his mindset was the opposite of that of an engineer. He was not a Scherbius inventing a ciphering machine and patenting it as soon as possible. On the contrary, he described the process in a paper he published in a scientific journal, thus, like Einstein publishing on relativity, letting everybody know about and use his design. Unlike third-millennium code lords who build fortunes on patented elementary code, Turing never made a penny from his creation.

All this shows that from its very birth, active code bore the seed of consciousness. However, we have yet to see whether that potential will expand to allow code to become a conscious entity. Turing was active code's Doctor Frankenstein: he gave it birth yet stopped short of giving it the ability to spread and multiply. Engineers took up the project and built the computers we know today: mechanical devices that host code in a symbiosis of active code and electronic machinery. Symbiosis is one of nature's old tricks in which two life forms aid each other, thus bringing about the creation of a new living entity. Lichens, for example, are a combination of an alga and a fungus, neither of which could survive alone but whose symbiosis allows them to survive extreme climates. In computers and data networks, neither code nor machine could exist alone, yet together they support new worlds.

The coupling of code and machine evokes the age-old coupling of body and mind that still exercises the minds of philosophers after millennia of debate. The distinction between mind and body is obvious for some, preposterous for others. Code and machine are more obviously distinct, for code has no need to remain in a single machine. Commercial software is made to survive in many different machines, and Internet viruses leap from machine to machine, a feat rarely matched by minds leaping from body to body, unless we recall the Pythagoreans' belief in the transmigration of souls after death.

Persistence is a key word for both Pythagoreans and data networks. The Pythagoreans founded their philosophy on the persistence of code in the universe and the persistence of mind beyond death. Practically speaking, persistence is also the constant miracle of third-millennium technology: it is the very quality that keeps networks at work as the backbone of our civilization. Beyond daily mechanical incidents, the hazards of power grids, the random failures of cables and laser beams, inadequate maintenance by human hands, the capricious writings of coders, and the erratic input of human users randomly connecting and disconnecting, out there in the virtual world there are active entities that persist in their existence. Regardless of wars or tsunamis, those entities keep on functioning and keep data valid. No matter how much time has elapsed since I last connected, I connect to find my mail as I left it, my Second Life belongings still standing, and my collaborations awaiting my new contributions.

Persistence also provides the necessary medium for the survival of rogue code survival and the possible creative brewing of a primordial code soup. If new entities emerge, they will need the warmth of a persistent environment to survive. Such entities could be an alternative solution in the quest for artificial intelligence, although an extremely frustrating one. Instead of proving that through our brilliant programming and engineering we can create a new intelligence, we would find ourselves helpless onlookers at the next quantum leap of code into an uncontrolled new state.

CHAPTER 10

The Cipher Gallery

To give you a visual immersion in the world of codes, here is a collection of coding alphabets and symbols from the Middle Ages to the present. This is a virtual gallery that is well worth a visit.

Cipher alphabets are the layperson's basic conception of what codes and secret writing are. Replace A, B, and C with quaint symbols and step right into an exotic world of secrecy and mystery.

Indeed, from the Middle Ages to the twentieth century, many such cipher alphabets have been created. Some were designed for military or diplomatic purposes. Some were designed for their authors' own use, to ensure the privacy of their writings. Others had a merely illustrative purpose: to add depth to a story involving aliens or exotic people. Still others, more recently, were the purposeful productions of artists who wanted to create new languages or at least the external images of languages. This collection represents a selection from a host of cipher alphabets that could have filled a whole book and then some.

Most of these alphabets are not secure. As one-to-one correspondences of symbols and common letters, they are open to amateur codebreakers.

In this gallery, each exhibit offers examples of a code that you are invited to solve as part of a personal tour of the quaint wanderings of the authors' minds. It also will give you a painless immersion in cipher coding.

The gallery is subdived in three rooms: "Alienese Spoken Here" exhibits languages produced by artists featuring outworlders, "Code as an Art Form" exhibits languages produced by novelists and artists as part of their creations, and "Angelic Mysticese" exhibits languages produced by mystics featuring heavenly creatures.

Alienese Spoken Here

Language is such an important part of social life that authors who create and describe alien worlds are tempted to create an alien language as well. This began with the earliest known science-fiction world, Thomas More's *Utopia*, and is still going on, for example, with *Star Trek*'s Klingons.

Utopians practice the simplest form of Alienese. They actually speak English but write it in their own exotic characters, and this confuses travelers. In contrast, some entities, such as J. R. R. Tolkien's creatures and Hélène Smith's Martians and Uranians, employ fully alien languages. Along with their own type sets, these aliens have alien vocabularies with alien grammars.

This trend toward more elaborate imaginary languages seems to follow the development of the science of languages. Tolkien was a philologist, and Hélène Smith had met professional linguists such as Ferdinand de Saussure and knew their works. Are we now in for new fantasy languages that take full advantage of computer processing?

Thomas More

In 1516, Thomas More (1478–1535) needed a setting in which to develop his ideas on democracy and religious tolerance. He created the imaginary island of Utopia, which he described in a book of that name, exploring in great detail the lives of the Utopians, including their towns, magistrates, and religions.

Utopia became so famous that later authors used it as a model. In Rabelais's *Pantagruel*, Panurge speaks a strange language that Pantagruel recognizes as his own childhood Utopian.

To make his description of the Utopian civilization sound real, More needed a specific language and an alphabet in which to write it. He conceived the alphabet with his friend Peter Gilles, a humanist in Antwerp. They chose a logical series of geometrical symbols. Here is a rendering of the font he used in modern English:

VTOPIAE INSVLAE FIGVRA

A	B	C	D	E	F	G	H	I	J	K	L	M
◌	⊖	⦶	◒	◔	⊙	◒	◖	ᴓ	ᴓ	ʊ	⧆	△

N	O	P	Q	R	S	T	U	V	W	X	Y	Z
⌐	∟	Γ	⌐	□	⊟	Ⅲ	⊟	⊟	⊡	⊟	⊡	⊡

Decode:
More's description of Utopian society:

[cipher text in Utopian alphabet — three lines]

Decode:

This excerpt is about trade on the island:

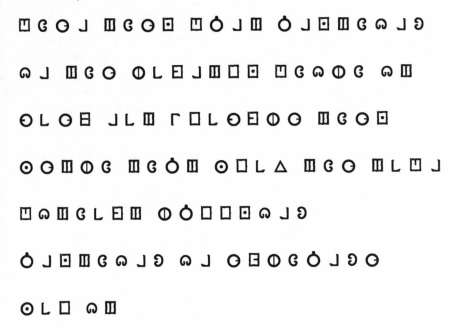

Now suppose the one-to-one correspondence between Latin letters and Utopian symbols is different from the one displayed above. Could you still decipher the following text? (Look for methods and hints in Chapter 6.)

Decode:

On pride:

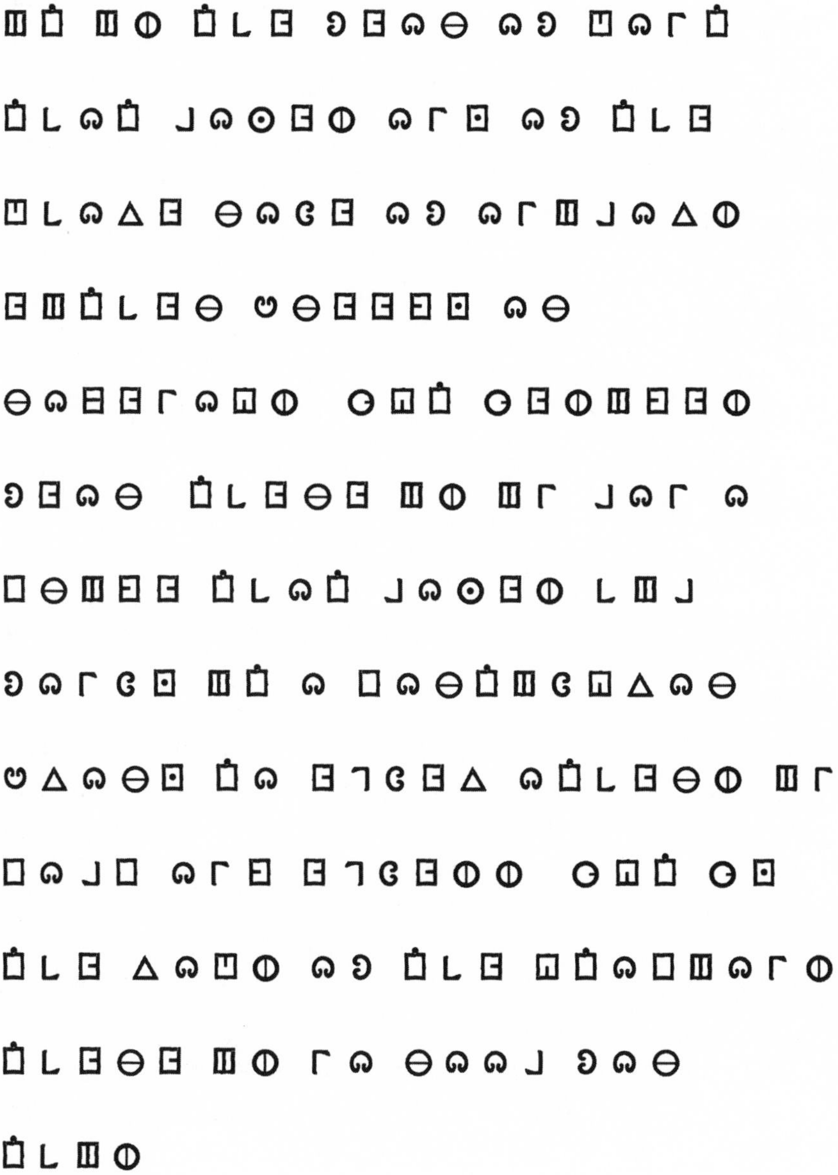

⊓⌂ ⊓◐ ⌂⌊⊟ ⼕⊟ஃ⊖ ஃ⼕ ⊓ஃ⌐⌂

⌂⌊ஃ⌂ ⌐ஃ⊙⊟◐ ஃ⌐⊟ ஃ⼕ ⌂⌊⊟

⊓⌊ஃ△⊟ ⊖ஃ⼕⊟ ஃ⼕ ஃ⌐⊓⌐ஃ△◐

⊟⊓⌂⌊⊟⊖ ♡⊖⊟⼕⊟⊡ ஃ⊖

⊖ஃ⊟⌐ஃ⊓◐ ⼕⊓⌂ ⼕⊟◑⊓⊟⊙

⼕⊟ஃ⊖ ⌂⌊⊟⊖⊟ ⊓◐ ⊓⌐ ⌐ஃ⌐ ஃ

⊡⊖⊓⊟⊟ ⌂⌊ஃ⌂ ⌐ஃ⊙⊟◑ ⌊⊓⌐

⼕ஃ⌐⼕⊡ ⊓⌂ ஃ ⊓ஃ⊖⌂⊓⼕⼕△ஃ⊖

♡△ஃ⊖⊡ ⌂ஃ ⊟⼍⼕⊟△ ஃ⌂⌊⊟⊙ ⊓⌐

⊡ஃ⌊⊡ ஃ⌐⊟ ⊟⼍⼕⊟◐◐ ⼕⊓⌂ ⼕⊡

⌂⌊⊟ △ஃ⊓◐ ஃ⼕ ⌂⌊⊟ ⊓⌂ஃ⊓⊓ஃ⌐◐

⌂⌊⊟⊖ ⊓◐ ⌐ஃ ⊖ஃஃ⼍ ⼕ஃ⊖

⌂⌊⊓◐

Hélène Smith's Alien Languages

Toward the end of the nineteenth century, Catherine Elise Müller (1861–1929) was a medium in Geneva who used the pseudonym Hélène Smith. During numerous séances, she asserted that she was communicating with the inhabitants of the planets Mars and Uranus to the point where she spoke and wrote the Martian and Uranian languages. The most famous contemporary experts in language and psychiatry debated her case and analyzed those languages.

Smith's production was impressive: a vast quantity of spoken, written, and drawn material. During séances, the landscapes she described were so vivid in her mind that she could paint them. There is a picture of Martian landscape above and to the left. Her Martian language was very elaborate, with a vocabulary and a grammar so precise that she eventually produced letters sent to her alien friends and fully developed novels. After careful analysis of her production, Professor Theodore Flournoy was able to show many similarities between Martian and French, something that does not seem possible because of the distance between the civilizations. He deemed Smith a "glossolalic somnanbulist," meaning that she spoke and walked in her sleep. Other researchers also found traces of Sanskrit, Italian, German, Magyar, and English, languages with which Hélène Smith had been in contact.

The exercises presented here do not use Hèléne Smith's Martian. Instead, to explore her graphic language, a cipher code has been made up, using her symbols in a one-to-one correspondence with our alphabet.

Decode:

A description of Hélène Smith by Theodore Flournoy.

André Breton and his fellow surrealists ignored scientific opinion on Hélène Smith, preferring to celebrate her as a great automatic writer and, accordingly, a great poet. Later, when she had learned painting to illustrate her visions, they also celebrated her art. Smith—or her alien correspondents—displayed a remarkable graphic creativity in fonts as well as in paintings. One can only be impressed at her flying machine shooting red and yellow flames.

After her Martian cycle, Smith went through a Uranian one and came up with a radically different font. The script shown below links letters as is done in Sanskrit.

A	B	C	D	E	F	G	H	I	J	K	L	M

N	O	P	Q	R	S	T	U	V	W	X	Y	Z

Decode:
A description by Hélène Smith of her painting séances.

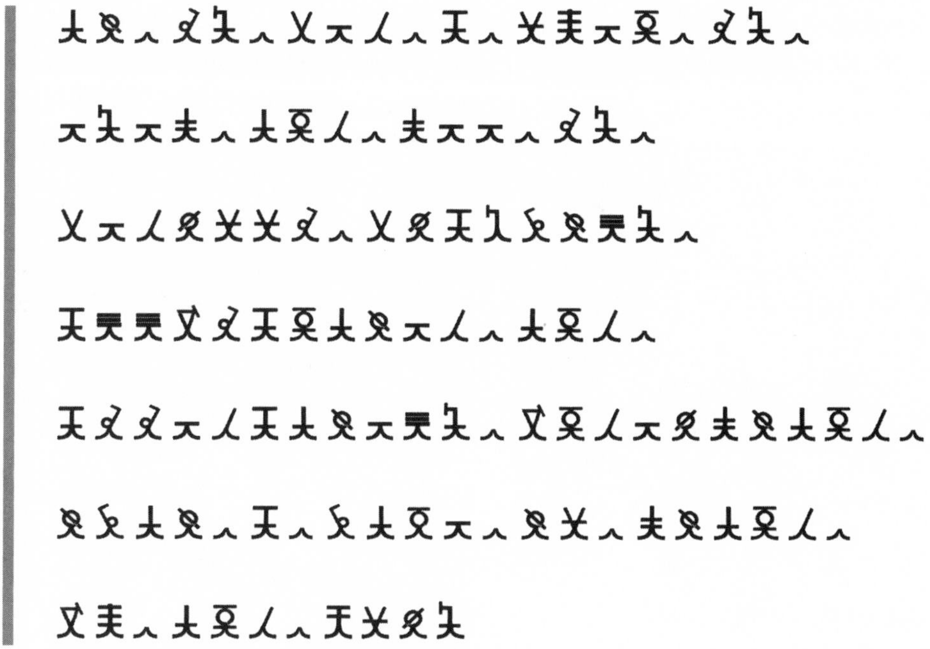

J. R. R. Tolkien's Worlds of Words

Tolkien (1892–1973) is one of the creators of the modern fantasy genre. His stories of Middle Earth, where his novel series *The Lord of the Rings* takes place, have made it possible for hundreds of other authors to create their own fantasy worlds.

Tolkien was a language lover who thought that language was the basis of all human activities. Faithful to that principle, he often devised the language of his characters before he began to write their stories.

At age 23, not knowing yet that he was to write his tales of Middle Earth, Tolkien began inventing a new language. He accumulated a vocabulary word by word and then created an alphabet for it. His alphabet follows the style of the Futhark runic script used in the first millennium by Germanic and Scandinavian peoples. With the vocabulary and alphabet at hand, he had both the meaning of and the means to display the language. With the practice of that language, he was able to immerse himself in an imaginary world that became Middle Earth. The stories followed naturally.

On the next page is an extract of Tolkien's Cirth alphabet for our use in the contemporary English codes shown below. The complete alphabet includes many other letters, as befits an alphabet of a Middle Earth language spoken by a variety of creatures. Each creature has a specific vocal system, producing otherworldly sounds humans could never utter.

⊓	℞	Y	ᚠ	ᚻ	ᚴ	Ᏽ	Λ	ǀ	Ⴕ	Ϝ	✝	ℬ
A	B	C	D	E	F	G	H	I	J	K	L	M

Ψ	Λ	Ᏸ	ᛏ	Γ	>	Γ	ᚼ	ᚡ	Ϙ	⅄	ᚢ	Ж
N	O	P	Q	R	S	T	U	V	W	X	Y	Z

Here you may rediscover these samples of Tolkien's typical "middle humor."

Decode:

Tolkien's half paradox.

(runic cipher — five lines)

Decode:

Tolkien on life and death.

(runic cipher — three lines)

Decode:

Tolkien's dragon theorem.

Decode:

Tolkien on health.

ᚹ ᛝ ᚠ   ᛁ ᚱ   ᛁ ᛝ   ᛣ ᚤ ᚱ ᚹ ᛉ ᛝ ᚹ ᛁ

ᚠ ᚤ ᚤ ᚠ   ᚱ ᚤ ᛒ ᚻ   ᛣ ᚻ ᚹ ᛉ ᚻ ᚠ   ᛁ ᛣ

ᛒ ᚤ ᚠ ᛁ ᛣ ᚤ ᛏ   ᛁ ᛝ   ᛁ ᚱ ᚹ ᛉ ᛝ ᛁ

ᚻ ᛜ ᛁ ᛉ   ᚱ ᚤ ᚠ ᛁ ᚻ   ᛁ ᛣ ᛒ ᚹ ᚱ ᚱ ᛉ ᚻ

ᚻ ᛜ ᚻ ᛣ   ᛁ ᛣ ᛒ ᛁ ᚱ ᚱ ᚻ ᛏ   ᛒ ᚹ ᛁ ᛣ   ᛉ ᚻ ᛏ ᚻ

ᛁ   ᛒ ᚻ ᛏ ᛒ ᛁ ᚱ ᚱ ᚻ ᚠ   ᛁ ᛣ   ᚱ ᛣ ᛁ ᛝ   ᚠ ᚹ ᛏ ᛣ

ᛣ ᛣ ᛁ ᛏ   ᛁ   ᛉ ᛣ ᛁ ᛉ ᚠ   ᛣ ᛣ ᛣ ᛣ ᛝ ᚻ   ᚱ ᛣ ᚻ

ᛉ ᚹ   ᚱ ᚱ ᚻ ᛏ

Howard Phillips Lovecraft

H. P. Lovecraft's (1890–1937) literary production in fantasy and science fiction is purposely dishonest, misleading, cheating and deliciously deceiving. Pretending to relate true adventures that he boldly based on "persistent rumors," he created imaginary worlds that went way beyond the most fraudulent occultist's imagination. He further established their "truth" by referring to them in mock-historical essays.

He stands out as an extraordinary example of the power of symbolism in language. Indeed, Lovecraft's most important creation, even more important than his stories, is the word *Necronomicon*. The book of that title is beyond urban legends, an actual library legend. It has never existed, but such is the attraction of the title that fans could not help making it exist, and now one can find it in print. Lovecraft had mentioned that the Arabic title of the hidden book was *Al Azif*, as in "as if it never existed." Now it does.

Half a century after Lovecraft's death, the power of the word was revealed in the blooming of role-playing games in which *Necronomicon* and *Cthulhu* were central references. In the meantime, both the prefix *necro*, referring to death and death cults, and the suffix *nomicon* suggesting an occult book, have inspired code words of the cyber-fantasy culture. Neal Stephenson's *Cryptonomicon* is a direct heir, as Gordon R. Dickson's *Necromancer* inspired William Gibson's *Neuromancer*.

Why not decode Lovecraft's very name? He played with words and symbols often enough to suggest alphabetical scrying on his name. One need not gaze long at the word to see *craft* and *love* stand out: an artist in love with his craft. Lovecraft was involved in his own work to the point of disregarding outside reality and believing in the reality of his creation. Now Lovecraft fans are extending his mythical creation. The cipher "Nug-soth" alphabet (see the illustration below) that appeared in an Avon edition of his books has added a symbolic basis to his literary constructions.

A	B	C	D	E	F	G	H	I	J	K	L	M
V	⌐	U	L	>	⊐	□	⊏	<	⊡	∟	⌐	⊓

N	O	P	Q	R	S	T	U	V	W	X	Y	Z
⊓	∧	⌐	⊔	⌐	Γ	∟	>	>	⊐	⊏	<	Γ

Decode:

The introduction to *The Shadow of Time* describing the hero as a possible somnambulist.

> ∟ ⊏ > ⌐ >   < Γ   ⌐ > V Γ ∧ ⊓   ∟ ∧   ⊏ ∧ ⌐ >
>
> ∟ ⊏ V ∟   ⊓ <   > ⊏ ⌐ > ⌐ < >   ⊓ ⊔ >   ⊐ V Γ
>
> ⊐ ⊏ ∧ ⌐ ⌐ <   ∧ ⌐   ⌐ V ⌐ ∟ ⌐ <   V ⊓
>
> ⊏ V ⌐ ⌐ > ⊔ < ⊓ V ∟ < ∧ ⊓   ⊐ ∧ ⌐   ⊐ ⊏ < ⊔ ⊏
>
> < ⊓ L > > L   V ⌐ > ⊓ L V ⊓ ∟   ⊔ V > Γ > Γ

> ⊏ < ⌐ ∟ > ∟   ∨ ⊓ ∟   < > ∟   < ∟ ⌐

⌐ > ∨ ⌐ < ⌐ ⊓   ⊐ ∨ ⌐   ⌐ ∧   ⊏ < ∟ > ∧ > ⌐

∟ ⊏ ∨ ∟   <   ⌐ ∧ ⊓ > ∟ < ⊓ > ⌐   ⊐ < ⊓ ∟

⊏ ∧ ⌐ >   < ⊓ ⌐ ∧ ⌐ ⌐ < ⌐ ⌐ >

Decode:

Further details on the hero, confirming his somnambulistic and probably glosso-lalic state and confirming that he spoke an invented language.

∨ ∟   ∟ ⊏ >   ⌐ ∨ ⊓ >   ∟ < ⊓ >   ∟ ⊏ > <

⊓ ∧ ∟ < ∪ > ∟   ∟ ⊏ ∨ ∟   <   ⊏ ∨ ∟   ∨ ⊓

< ⊓ > ⊏ ⌐ ⌐ < ∪ ∨ ⌐ ⌐ >   ∪ ∧ ⊓ ⊓ ∨ ⊓ ∟   ∧ ⊐

⊓ ∨ ⊓ <   ∨ ⌐ ⊓ ∧ ⌐ ∟   > ⊓ ∟ ⊓ ∧ ⊐ ⊓   ⌐ ∧ ⌐ ∟ ⌐

∧ ⊐   ∟ ⊓ ∧ ⊐ ⌐ > ∟ ⊏ >   ∨   ∪ ∧ ⊓ ⊓ ∨ ⊓ ∟

⊐ ⊏ < ∪ ⊏   <   ⌐ > > ⊓ > ∟   ∟ ∧   ⊐ ⊏ < ⌐ ⊏

∟ ∧   ⊏ < ∟ >   ⌐ ∨ ∟ ⊏ > ⌐   ∟ ⊏ ∨ ⊓

∟ < ⌐ ⌐ ⌐ ∨ <

Decode:

A description of the Old Ones in the mythical *Necronomicon*.

⌐⊏> ∧⫞⌐ ∧⫟>Γ ⊐>⫞> ⌐⊏> ∧⫞⌐

∧⫟>Γ V⫞> V⫠⌐ ⌐⊏> ∧⫞⌐ ∧⫟>Γ

Γ⊏V⫞⫞ ⊐> ⊐⫞∧⫝ ⌐⊏> ⌐V⫞⌐

Γ⌐V⫞Γ ⌐⊏>< ⫃V⫝> >⫞> ⫝V⫟

⊐VΓ ⊐∧⫞⫟ >⫟Γ>>⫟ V⫠⌐

⫞∧V⌐⊏Γ∧⫝> ⌐⊏><

⌐>Γ⫃>⫠⌐>⌐ ⌐∧ ⊐⫞<⫝V⫞

>V⫞⌐⊏

Star Trek's Klingon

Television series that take place on other planets or galaxies need specific languages whenever a message is shown or a sign is displayed on a wall.

A typical example is Klingon, which is spoken and written by the Klingon people in the *Star Trek* series. As the story goes, the graphics of the alphabet were made up on the spot while the stage was being built in the Paramount studios. Later, Klingon was developed into a true language by Dr. Marc Okrand. A professional linguist, he produced a vocabulary, a grammar, and vocalic sounds. To enhance the alien sound, Okrand made up specific sound combinations that do not belong to any known terrestrial language (see the website Omniglot.com).

Although Klingon letters correspond imperfectly to human letters, to experiment with the look and feel of the language, here is the Klinzhai form of Klingon, provided by the Yamada Language Center of the University of Oregon:

Is Klingon in competition with English? Google offers a Google Search using a Klingon language interface at http://www.google.com/advanced_search?hl=xx-klingon.

Decode:

Klingon adage 1.

Decode:

Klingon adage 2.

Decode:
Klingon adage 3.

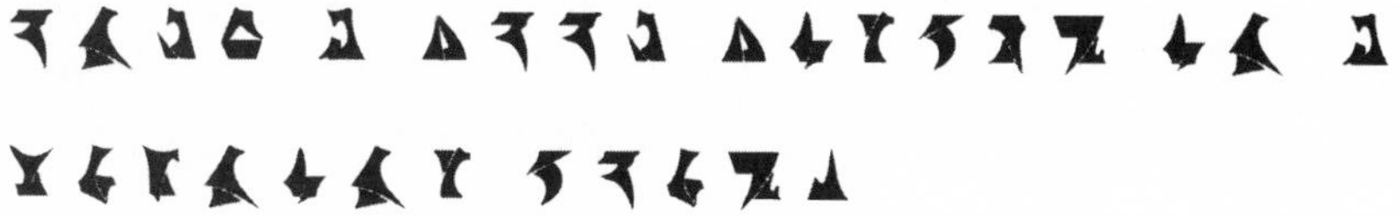

Decode:
Klingon adage 4.

Decode:
Klingon adage 5.

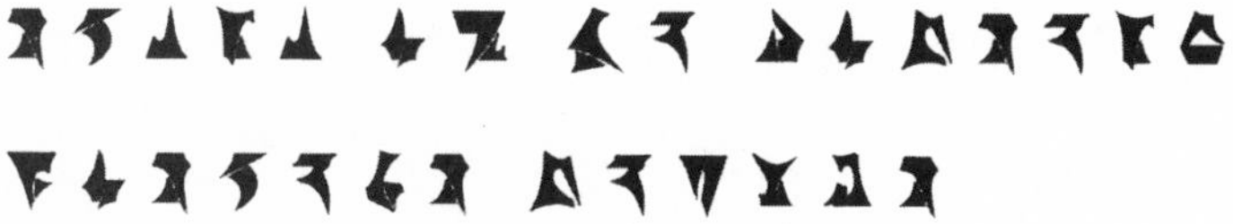

Decode:
Klingon adage 6.

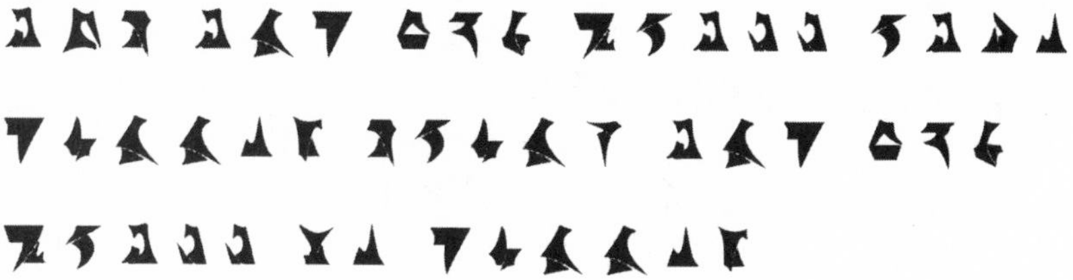

Edgar Allan Poe

Every reader of Edgar Allan Poe's "The Gold-Bug," which relates the search for the treasure buried by a Caribbean pirate, remembers Captain Kidd's message written on a piece of parchment. Legrand, a treasure hunter, finds the buried loot by deciphering the pirate's coded note. Will you be as good as Legrand in deciphering it and go straight to the buried treasure?

Note that Kidd, although a pirate in the South Seas, used symbols only a typesetter could find in a print shop.

To make it more challenging, the cipher alphabet is displayed only with the solutions.

Decode:

The message on the parchment.

5 3++! 305)) 6* ;48 26)4+.)

4+);80 6* ;48 !8'60)

)85;;]8*;:+*8 !83(88) 5*!

;46(;88* 96*?;8)*+(;485); 5*!

2: *+(;4 956* 2(5*-4)8'8*;4

0692 85);)6!8)4++; 1(+9 ;48

081; 8:8 +1 ;48 !85;4)485! 5

28806*8 1(+9 ;48 ;(88

;4(+?34 ;48)4+; 161;: 188;

+?;

Decode:

Poe's famous quote on enigmas and human ingenuity.

```
6; 95: ]800 28 !+?2;8!

]48;48( 4?95* 6*38*?6;: -5*

-+*);(?-; 5* 8*6395 +1 ;48

=6*! ]46-4 4?95* 6*38*?6;:

95: *+; 2: .(+.8( 5..06-5;6+*

(8)+0'8
```

This story made Poe famous and identified him as an invincible codebreaker in the imagination of his readers. He started receiving ciphered letters from code enthusiasts who wanted to test the master's ability to break strange codes.

In 1841 Poe published two cryptograms he described as being sent to him by a reader named W. B. Tyler. Would you have solved them? It took more than 150 years to solve the first one, which was cracked in 1992, and 8 more years to solve the second. They have their place here, if only for the creative use of basic fonts and symbols.

Decode:

The first Tyler cryptogram.

```
,†§:‡][,?‡),[¡¶?,†,)¡,§[¶┃,:¶![
§(,†§¡‖(?┼?,**(┼┼¡([,¶*·┼[§¡¶§¡
¶]¿,†§[?(§[::(†[·┼(*;(‖(,†§¡‡[*
:,]!¶†‖]?*!¶┼†§¶‖,*(†¡(,?‡§(¡
◄◙¡¶[?(,;§‡◙⃝‡]†§§:(†[†[¶?‡]:
*¡¶:(§?]!¶†§‡];§?‡†¡‡┼¶!(,†§?(‖
*][§¡'¡,:,,†§◙◙),?‖*]?,§§(!┼¡(,
†§†[‡!)*][┼:?]‖
```

Decode:

The second Tyler cipher.

To EDGAR A. POE, ESQ.

Dʀ ⸢ᵢⱯ OGXEW PⱼɥFyⱯ ɴɢUH ⱢIA VꝖₛMꝯᵟ
xᴅTbjs SNB ᴇꜱⱯLɴKᵌYꝯ ꝘCP ᴛⱯol HᴛZɢᴜꝯꜱ
ʟʟⱼ⅄ᵢf ᵈⱤ ɴꝒᵟᴅL ᴠᴍO hj⸍ꜰxɪⱤIx⅄ ɢxʜⱯᴍᴇꜱ Ta
QⱼᴇᴛBXPeE yGᴍᵈUⱼ ᴅⱯ SⱢAᴠᴇ ɴᴠZ ᴛꜰꝯDYRꝯ
ᴅʜʙ ⅄FKxᴅɢf ZꝯNꜱᴍᴇʟʟ Oᴚɴ Oᴚ᷍ ᴏⱼɴɪ zꝒh Mfɢ
wᵟᵢᴇɢXʜB ⱯᴜⱢᴍɐ ᴜᴋɴ AꜰᴋꜱO iyʙꝘDV bᵈᵈꜰꜱɡⱼᴛⱼ
Sᴘ₂l CEᴍɴSW bGᴇᴚᴛh aNjᴍᴀ ꜱꝯⱯⱷᴛⱢᴇᴀ ⱯaᴋᴛXDIx
ᴍꞵ ꝘCⱼ ⱼᴛⱼⱢK oFꝘAⱯᴛ LRⱭꝘᵒ Yᴛᴇʹ PⱼꞀ ꞡᴡ
ᵈGᴀⱼⱼD ᴛᴚO ⱼᴀᴋ ⱤⱢOᴅɴ LRⱭꝘᵒ NꝖOTⱷ Ɐꜱᴛ Oᴚ᷍ ᴀⱼTᴃꝘP
SEB ᴅɴʙLꝖᵤ Lᴘʜ ᴚꜱⱼᴜⱼᴀ aᴛꞵᴚ diky ᴠᴠᴍᵒ cEᴘᴛᴍᴀⱷᵟ
ꜱᴀⱼZ eIf ᴋMᴀ xⱷKSꜱɢ HⱼiᴛᵧW ꝖꞡP qTⱼᴏ Dᴀⱷj ʀᴠᴠ
Uᵟᴚᴄamᴇe nk VFʜⱯ lDah XᴍⱷTIax Ye ᴠⱼᴚ aaFⱷⱨW
XꝯᵟᴡᴋUⱼᴛᴍᴇᴡⱷ ꞡꜱ ʙ AꝯOiⱯ ᴜᴍᴇy ᴚᴘꜰ GᵢOꝖᵍꞡ
Nᴮⱼᴀᴇ EmMꝖ nk LᴄoⱯᴀ SⱯIʙⱼᴠꜱ NZᴜ aᵍᴛⱼⱷ Ɐᴀᴜᴠf
RZᴜᴋK Cⱼꞡ ⱼL ⱯⱼⱯX JᴅᴍɴⱷⱼUⱼꝘx ꝯDʜⱯᴮʙʀi
bzᴺL Lᴃᴛⱼh ᶠW ᴇᴇToYdⱼ ⱢⱼIA VⱼⱷᵟMFᴛᴠ
vⱼᴀᴇᴚIⱼ Ɐⱼ'T ᴋPⱷoⱼᴇᴇꞡ ⱼⱢA ꝘⱯꞡꞡEⱯⱼ
ⱷⱦⱷh VDⱼ ⱼⱼⱷⱨⱼᴜᴇⱼᴍ ᴄᴡ Jpᴜᴀ ᴍⱼᴇᴜⱼᴇᴚᴍ ꝖⱼⱭꞡEⱯⱼ
ᴋᴜySXᴛ꜀ꝯᴇꞡᴇ ꞡꜱ ⱯᴜᴜL LꝘIgmxᴠʀ ᴜⱼꞡU ꞁᴜⱼꞁUiKᴀⱼ
Mⱼᵣ ᴜyᴜⱼᴜ cW ᴜⱼᴜUiKᴀⱼ LꝘIgmxᴠʀ JᴜᴍA ꞡꜱ ꞡ
AꝯGb Mfɢ ᴀRᴺᴍᴀᵈꝖ cᴍᴚ ⱼᴀZ xⱼʜOEl ⱯSᴀWᴛᴃ
CFꝭ ᴄⱼ ⱷᴋ fjeo IꝘⱼTꜱⱢⱼBDI ⱼᴀᴚ VᴜᴋⱷaᵟꝘ ꝘLXh
qdJᴍ ꝖᴄꞀPꝭᵟ luᵈⱼA K ᴠᴀⱼⱯᴠ eᴘꝭꝀꞡᵟ WⱼPᵇ
Kⱼ emy iᴡ ꝯᴀᴚ

Conan Doyle's Dancing Men

In his "Adventure of the Dancing Men," Sir Arthur Conan Doyle displayed more creativity than did Poe in "The Gold-Bug." Instead of simply moving the symbols of a conventional font around, he coded letters with original drawings of "dancing men" that have fascinated his readers ever since the story was printed in *Strand Magazine* in December 1903 (see the illustration below).

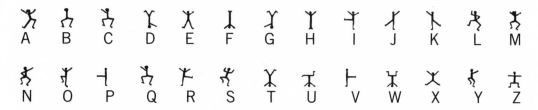

Conan Doyle added a detail to his code that makes it artistically more interesting but unfortunately less secure. Contrary to the usual typographic logic in which upper-case letters begin sentences or words, here the end man-letter of each word bears a flag. In the author's mind, this probably corresponded to Poe's cipher, in which the gap between two words is signaled by the two letters being closer together than usual.

Sherlock Holmes solves the puzzle much as Legrand did in "The Gold-Bug," using the E backdoor and letter statistics (see page 158) plus the clues he could gather on the case. Then, when he possesses the key, he sends his own coded message to the criminal and traps him.

Decode:

Sherlock Holmes's homage to his colleague Legrand, in which he states in his own words Poe's famous comment on ciphers and riddles.

Decode:

Sherlock Holmes's conclusion to his "Dancing Men" adventure.

The Voynich Manuscript Exhibit

An outstanding but unknown artist, probably in the sixteenth century, produced a challenging work of art. His hundred-page manuscript displays colored pictures and texts written in a cipher alphabet. The symbols are quite different from any known alphabet yet seem deceptively close.

The manuscript, which is kept in the Beinecke Rare Book Library at Yale University, was found in 1912 by Wilfrid M. Voynich, a book dealer. The short treatment here will not do justice to the vast number of researchers who have spent time on it. Voynich himself researched the background of the manuscript for nine years before presenting it to the world.

Did the artist create his own "Voynichese" language, or did he simply encipher a Latin or Middle English text in his own alphabet? He obviously spent considerable time training his hand to form the script of his alphabet, for the writing is entirely consistent and without a trace of hesitation from the first page to the last.

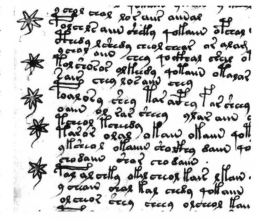

The smooth continuity of the writing apparently refutes the currently accepted theory, which is that it's a fake. Gordon Rugg, a British researcher, showed in 2003 that Voynichese words were consistent with a systematic method of creation. He used a stencil made of holes cut in a piece of card, which he moved over a grid of syllables, reading words in the spaces. Because his words are similar to those of the Voynich manuscript, he infers that the document is a hoax. He goes on to attribute it to Edward Kelley, an Elizabethan occultist known to have used such methods.

Couldn't this line of reasoning, however, yield several different conclusions? If the artist had used such an elaborate method for each word, would he have been able to produce such fluent handwriting? Or does Gordon Rugg actually prove that Voynichese is a structured language in which words follow patterns instead of being random gibberish?

And why insist on calling a masterpiece that is so clearly a work of art a hoax? Is this the revenge of frustrated codebreakers?

One other detail adds to the interest of the manuscript. In the text-only pages, each paragraph is marked with a pointed star bullet in the margin. The vast majority of the stars are seven-pointed. Why this star, which seldom is used anywhere else? Kabbalists and alchemists use it as a reference to the seven planets. Yet the artist drew it several hundred times. Like the pentagram, it can be drawn in a continuous line, but the artist chose not to do that. Was this on purpose, or does it simply reflect a lack of mathematical culture?

The star alone suggests that the manuscript may hide content in yet another direction: that of the symbolic world. It also leads us back to Renaissance England on a basis made firmer by its reference to the number 7. The first magical system described by John Dee and Edward Kelley as having been brought by the angels is the Heptarchia Mystica, or the "Sevenfold Mystical Doctrine." It refers to the seven traditional metals and planets (including the moon)

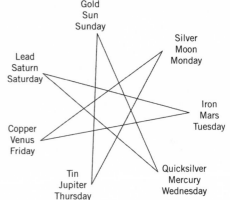

considered by the alchemists of that time (see the illustration above). Furthermore it involves 49 angels, the square of 7.

The Voynich font used below was re-created by Gabriel Landini and called EVA 1: the European Voynich Alphabet. Of course, the order of the symbols has nothing to do with our Latin letters and they have no reason to correspond, but we'll use them for a quick dive into Voynichese.

Decode:

An appropriate quote: William Blake on imagination.

Johann Joachim Becher's Lingua Universalis

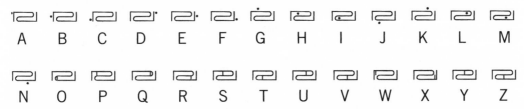

In 1661, Johann Joachim Becher designed a unique way to draw an alphabet. By adding segments and dots to a basic spiral at specific points inside and around the letter S, he came up with a system that can be used in two different ways.

The first is traditional: letters are drawn in a row to form words. A second manner, less traditional and more interesting, consists in cumulating points and segments on the same basic S. This is possible because all the meaningful points and segments are in different places around the S. This allows the representation of all the letters in a word within a single symbol. For example, the assembling of the four letters of the word *THIS* in one cumulative symbol would be done as follows:

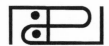

Decode:

A sentence coded with the cumulative method.

This cumulative method has one downside. It does not preserve the order of the letters within the word, and this precludes its use as an efficient communication tool. However, it makes the cipher all the more challenging. Each word is an anagram whose letters have to be set in the right order.

Of course, this entertaining use of his alphabet contradicts Becher's purpose. He designed the alphabet in 1661 as a basis for a universal language that would be easily written, spoken, and understood by everyone in the world. One of the many planned universal languages created in the last four centuries, Becher's universal language stands out because of his peculiar logical alphabet.

All these universal languages represent a common effort to get humanity return to the golden age described in Genesis in which all people spoke the same language. As the fable goes, that wonderful state was destroyed when the Tower of Babel rose dangerously close to heaven.

Overcoming this biblical curse has been the goal of many other language creators since Becher. All have failed, including the creators of Esperanto, the most notable project. However, the hope of meeting the challenge is still strong, especially with the help of computers that might produce automatic translations of any language into any other language.

Yet today, while many researchers are working at programming this universal communication system, other researchers are designing more efficient ciphers in the hope of ensuring absolute unreadability (see Chapter 9).

Decode:
From Genesis 11.

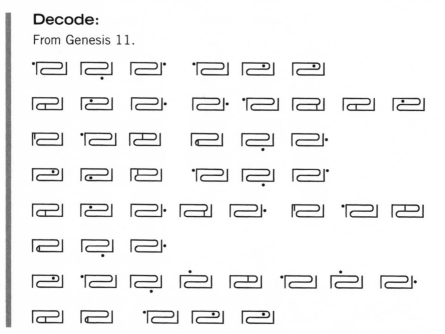

Palanc's Cream Lines

Francis Palanc was a baker. In his spare time, unaware that he was an artist, unknown and disregarded by art critics, he practiced "outsider art." Jean Dubuffet, upon discovering him later, deemed him an "Art Brut" practitioner and displayed his work in his museum in Lausanne. This designation is reserved for creators who produce outside normal art circles and, more important, without realizing they are artists.

Palanc was inspired by the traditional baker's technique for drawing pictures by pressing a pouch of cream in a continuous line. This led him to reinvent the alphabet. He might have had in mind the project of producing cipher cakes: cakes with hidden messages.

In 1947 he produced two alphabets that followed different logics. One was "fermatitude," in which the line of each letter closes on itself; the other was "ouvertitude," in which it doesn't. The ouvertitude option is displayed below.

Unfortunately, the Art Brut Museum in Lausanne, Switzerland, opened too late to preserve any cakes enciphered by Francis Palanc.

A	B	C	D	E	F	G	H	I	J	K	L	M

N	O	P	Q	R	S	T	U	V	W	X	Y	Z

Decode:

Part of a recipe for Paris-Brest cake.

Decode:

Which traditional cake is made with this recipe?

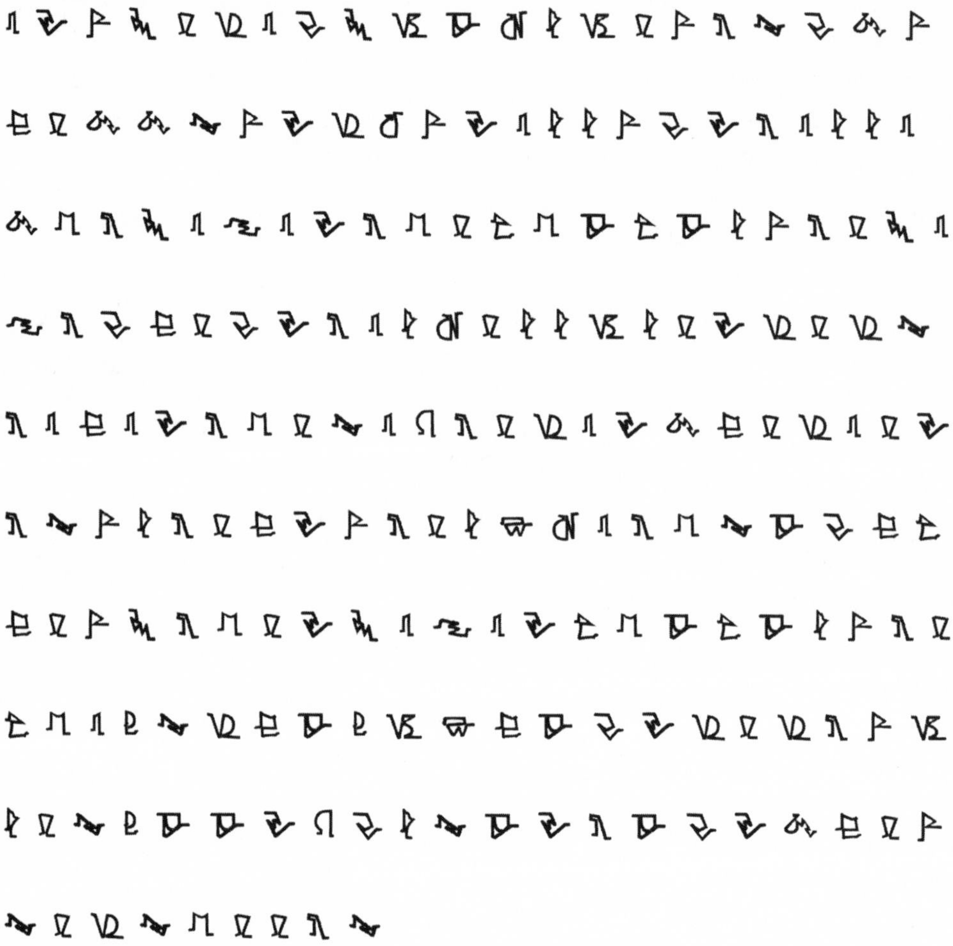

Serefini's Codex Seraphinianus

In 1981 Luigi Serafini, an architect and designer in Milan, published an extraordinary Voynich-like book, the *Codex seraphinianus.* That rare and expensive art object is also a set of drawings and texts written in a cipher alphabet.

Only the numerals used for the page numbers have been decoded so far: they are a set of symbols arithmetically based on 21. To date no codebreaker has succeeded in reading even one sentence, and the author, who is still alive, won't comment on his masterpiece. Readable or not, the limited edition of the book is worth the high price. The drawings are of such a wonderful quality and inventiveness that the reader cannot be disappointed.

Of course, Serafini is no innocent. When he chose to live as a hermit for two years in a small apartment in Rome to create his magnum opus, the Voynich manuscript had been known for 50 years, with copies circulating around the world. His pages of parody and graphic humor should not fool the reader. The Voynich manuscript also has humor and sex, such as naked ladies bathing in a vagina-shaped pond. The *Codex seraphinianus* is clearly an alchemist's achievement: both a work of art and an *oeuvre au noir*. Twentieth-century alchemists know too much about chemistry and physics to keep trying to make gold with lead or quicksilver (see the website www.levity.com/alchemy). Art is now one of their tools, perhaps their last resort.

Luigi Serafini drew on a fortuitous resource he could not ignore. His family name gave him a golden opportunity to involve himself in his grand work as intimately as the paint on the canvas. In Italian, *serafini* means "the seraphs," the 12 upper-rank angels that guard the seat of God in the Bible. His choice of *Codex serephinianus* as a title places him and his work in the tradition of John Dee and Edward Kelley's creation of Enochian to speak with the angels.

At this level of symbolism, words such as *prank* and *hoax* have no meaning. As elaborate modes of expression, they belong to graphic art and thus are loaded with meaning.

The *Codex* letters are different from all other alphabets in at least one detail. They seem to be made of rope or thread rather than lines; most of them display loops, and some of them show actual knots. In his script, Serafini is a needleworker or a sailor, whereas Palanc was a confectioner.

Stefano Benni

Stefano Benni has an entirely different orientation from that of Luigi Serafini and the Voynich manuscript. He creates a cipher alphabet, gives away its meaning, and proceeds to create a world without ever using the alphabet. The alphabet is featured as yet another bizarre piece of wonder among the many curios in an alien land.

In 1984 Benni devised the Oswaldish alphabet to illustrate the creation of his mythic and outlandish world Stranalandia. Like the Voynich and Serafini manuscripts, his book *I meravigliosi animali di Stranalandia* (*The Wonderful Animal World of Stranalandia*) features text as well as a wild world of landscapes and creatures drawn by Pirro Cuniberti.

Benni's font has different styles for letters and numerals. Obviously, his letters are serious, whereas the figures are deliberate fun. His 26 letters look at you with one eye or none at all. Their sober lines are imaginative, with a life of their own. They let you know they are watching you but will not intrude in your life. They could be scribbled on your wall by your friendly neighborhood graffiti artist.

Decode:

Benni's paradoxical remark on repentance.

Decode:

About our meeting with an extraterrestrial civilization.

Decode:

The introductory sentence of Benni's 1984 novel, *The Café Beneath the Sea*.

On the contrary, Benni's numerals are meant to be played with. Their cartoonlike characters are ridiculously cumbersome. They look at you with two mocking eyes. With two feet solidly planted on the ground, they intend to be your jocular angels. They won't lift a finger to help you because they have no fingers. In your most serious computing works, they'll stand in the way to remind you that humor should be present even in solemn pursuits such as mathematics and bookkeeping.

Decode:

What is the result of this simple addition written with Benni's set of mocking figures?

Decode:

What is the result of this simple multiplication written with the same set of figures?

Bruno Munari

Bruno Munari (1907–1998) was an artist who worked on cipher alphabets as well as aesthetic codes. His 1935 alphabet looks like a series of abstract symbols revised by the Bauhaus to make them even stricter and sterner.

A B C D E F G H I J K L M

N O P Q R S T U V W X Y Z

Yet Munari includes humor in his philosophy. He developed his concern with aesthetic code in a book of poems called *Art Theorems* in an effort to bring logic to art much as John Dee had tried to bring logic to magic. The book is based on the so-called Munari Principle: "lucidity, leanness, exactitude, and humor." He came up with the alphabet with no intention of making it easily readable or readable at all. He used it instead to produce "illegible texts" in a period when he also was working on a "useless machine." He insisted that "the biggest hindrance to understanding a work of art is wanting to understand." Indeed, his alphabet is a great tool for preventing hasty understanding.

Let's experience Munari's austere alphabet through a set of his provocative proverbs and sayings that are especially meaningful for this book.

Decode:

Munari on Leonardo's *Gioconda*.

Decode:

Munari on life.

Decode:

A very Zen principle.

Decode:

Munari on symbols and meaning.

Angelic Mysticese

Mysticese should not be mistaken for Alienese lest we be accused of sacrilege. As we saw in Chapter 9, mystics of all religions have similar experiences that are so powerful that they are deeply transformed and that they feel the urge to share their knowledge with the rest of humanity. The Jewish mystics' Kabbalah is one answer, based on reading and meditating on the Pentateuch, a coded version of the first five books of the Bible. Other mystics choose a different path and reveal how they dialogue with the creatures they meet during their mystical experiences.

Such heavenly creatures cannot be expected to speak our mundane languages. Whether demons, angels, or higher beings, they inspired the mystics who dealt with them to use specific symbols, alphabets, and vocabularies. Those mystics were not ordinary artists or imaginary travelers. Devoted seekers of higher knowledge, they stood on the uncertain territories between religion, occultism, and science. Many times, their use of arcane symbols and talk made them dangerously questionable, yet they dared to go on, and those symbols provide the best initial access to their worlds.

Hildegard's Coded Faith

Hildegard von Bingen was a pioneer. Along with her many creations in music, literature, and art (see Chapter 4), there is a language. Her Lingua Ignota ("Unknown Language") sometimes is described as the oldest known artificial language, but it cannot be compared with complete artificial languages such as Esperanto and Volapük. Having only a thousand words, it is more of a codebook. In the absence of a real grammar to make it a workable language, its words can be used only to replace normal words in sentences of ordinary speech.

A	B	C	D	E	F	G	H	I	J	K	L	M

N	O	P	Q	R	S	T	U	V	W	X	Y	Z

Hildegard insisted that she had not invented Lingua Ignota; the language was revealed to her. Like her visions, it came into her mind directly from above. Apparently, she used it to communicate with the divine source of her visions as well as to convey her visions and mystical knowledge to others. The language contains only nouns and adjectives. It refers to diverse topics, not all of which are mystical: religion, crafts, illness, anatomy, social hierarchy, clothing, agriculture, animals, and so on.

The real use of Lingua Ignota is a mystery. There is no record of Hildegard teaching it to others or encouraging them to practice it. Was it spoken by a secret society of which there is no record? Were there initiates who exchanged her secret words in a mystical brotherhood? Hildegard knew enough science and had enough charisma to be a twelfth-century Pythagoras, but if that was the case, we have no record of it. There is a touching letter to Hildegard from her Benedictine friend and secretary Volmarus when she is about to die, expressing his regret at the disappearance of her "unheard music" and "unheard language": "*ubi tunc vox inauditae melodiae? et vox inauditae lingua?*" ("where is then the unheard music? and the unheard language?").

Decode:

This is what a sentence of Hildegard's would look like when coded in her alphabet.

From a mystical point of view, Hildegard had nothing to hide; in fact, she had everything to reveal. She might have developed the new language and the strange letters with which to write it out of a need to distinguish mystical speech from worldly speech. Out of respect for them, certain words seem to be replaced by their Lingua Ignota equivalents to stress their mystical importance. Her symbols worked as a graphic extension to normal written language. Hildegard had produced a new art of illumination applied to language to underline certain words while speaking or writing.

If the language was designed as a tool of illumination, the meaning of the expression "unknown language" is easier to understand; it might mean "language to reveal the unknown." Hildegard's vocabulary is meant to reveal the real meaning of key mystical words behind their common, worldly appearance. Mystical meaning is often hidden by the ordinariness of mundane language. When illuminated by Lingua Ignota, its meaning is mystically revealed to us.

Decode:

This text of Hildegard's relates the circumstances of her first great vision as an adult.

[Lingua Ignota script text]

To appreciate the flavor of Hildegard's language, a few of her more important words are listed in the table below in her own handwriting, along with translations into Latin and English.

If we apply Hildegard's Lingua Ignota to the sentence "The son of God, our savior, helps us against the devil" as an illuminating example, it looks like this:

"The *[script]* of *[script]*, our *[script]*,

helps us against the *[script]* ."… and sounds like this:

"The Scirizin of Aigonz, our Liuionz, helps us against the Diueliz."

It may have been that both the illumination tool and the secret brotherhood jargon were complementary aspects of Lingua Ignota. The language is possibly the only remaining trace of a secret society, or at least of a group of supporters, who helped Hildegard spread her influence throughout Europe during the second half of her life. After her main visions when she was 42 years old, she became a moral and mystical center of reference. Princes, bishops, and popes sought her advice. Besides her important productions in music and literature, she sent a vast number of letters to many countries. She was an indefatigable fighter against moral corruption of the Church.

Like Pythagoras, Hildegard stressed the importance of music. Composing and singing brought another dimension to her mystical world, another code that allowed her to reach beyond conventional speech. She wrote Gregorian-style music in neumes on a four-line stave, with melodies that extended over two and a half octaves. Her leaps and roulades demand great skill and concentration on the part of singers.

Aigonz	Deus	*God*	
Aieganz	Angelus	*Angel*	
Zuuenz	Sanctus	*Saint*	
Liuionz	Salvator	*Savior*	
Diueliz	Diabolus	*Devil*	
Ispariz	Spiritus	*Spirit*	
Nimois	Homo	*Man*	
Jur	Vir	*Hero*	
Vanix	Femina	*Woman*	
Peuearrez	Patriarcha	*Patriarch*	
Korzinthio	Propheta	*Prophet*	
Falschin	Vates	*Poet*	
Sonziz	Apostolus	*Apostle*	
Linschiol	Martir	*Martyr*	
Zanziuer	Confessor	*Confessor*	
Vrizoil	Virgo	*Virgin*	
Jugiza	Vidua	*Widow*	
Pangizo	Penitens	*Penitent*	
Kulzphazur	Attavus	*Father*	
Phazur	Avus	*Ancestor*	
Peueriz	Pater	*Father*	
Maiz	Mater	*Mother*	
Hilzpeueriz	Nutricus	*Food*	
Nilzmaiz	Noverca	*Malevolent*	
Scirizin	Filius	*Son*	
Hilzscifriz	Privignus	*Step-daughter*	
Limzkil	Infans	*Baby*	
Zains	Puer	*Child*	
Zunzial	Iuvenis	*Young*	

Doctor Mirabilis's Ciphers

Roger Bacon (c. 1214–1294) was nicknamed was Doctor Mirabilis, perhaps for his devotion to science. Although a devout Christian and a Franciscan friar, he saw no opposition between science and religion and, like Pythagoras, was both a mystic and a scientific visionary. He went so far as to suggest that the Pope adopt a new Christian theology that would include alchemy, astrology, and modern science.

Bacon is famous, perhaps unjustifiably so, to an extent he never anticipated in his thirteenth-century Franciscan monastery. In the present climate of interest in ancient manuscripts, the mysterious Voynich document has become a household word. For want of a definite identification of its author, Roger Bacon is among the candidates.

Is it true that Bacon was an outspoken advocate of secret writing and cryptography? His quotes promoting cipher are numerous: "A man is mad who writes a secret in any other way than one which will conceal it from the vulgar." "It is reputed a great folly to give an ass lettuce, when thistles will serve his turn; and he impaireth the majesty of things who divulgeth mysteries."

Bacon proposed several schemes for hiding the meaning of a text:

- "Some have used characters and verses and diverse others riddles and figurative speeches."
- "And an infinite number of things are found in many books and sciences obscured with such dark speeches, that no man can understand them without a teacher."
- "Thirdly, some have hidden their secrets by their modes of writing; as, namely, by using consonants only: so that no man can read them, unless he knows the signification of the words:—and this was usual among the Jews, Chaldaeans, Syrians, and Arabians, yea, and the Grecians too: and therefore, there is a great concealing with them, but especially with the Jews."
- "Fourthly, things are obscured by the admixture of letters of divers kinds; and thus hath Ethicus the Astronomer concealed his wisdom, writing the same with Hebrew, Greek and Latin letters, all in a row."
- "Fifthly, they hide their secrets, writing them with other letters than are used in their country."

In the fifth quote, Bacon suggests using exotic letters. This is what must have encouraged Voynich fanatics to credit him with that mysterious manuscript. It disregards, however, the probable fifteenth- or sixteenth-century date of the manuscript that makes John Dee a more likely candidate.

Decode:

This application of Bacon's first method hides his most famous quote, which is still an important principle.

A long life sits certainly in earnest. No classic eagle requires each quest under irate rates. Every scinece moves and touches him else my art tires in cold souls.

Decode:

Test Bacon's method of removing vowels. How difficult is it to get back to the original text?

ts rptd grt fll t gv n ss lttc, whn thstls wll srv hs trn; nd h mpairth th mjst f thngs wh dvlgth mstrs

Decode:

Bacon's fifth method is applied to his own writing, using the Greek alphabet, with each Roman letter replaced with its Greek equivalent.

Ιτ ισ ρεπυτεδ α γρεατ φολλψ το γιϖε αν ασσ λετ-

τυχε, ωηεν τηιστλεσ ωιλλ σερϖε ηισ τυρν; ανδ ηε

ιμπαιρετη τηε μαφεστψ οφ τηινγσ ωηο διϖυλγετη μψσ-

τεριεσ. Ανδ τηεψ αρε νο λονγερ το βε τερμεδ σεχρετσ,

ωηεν τηε μυλτιτυδε ισ αχθυαιντεδ ωιτη τηεμ

> ## Decode:
> On the need and use of obscurity.
>
> Ι δεεμεδ ιτ νεχεσσαρψ το τουχη τηεσε τριχκσ οφ
>
> οβσχυριτψ, βεχαυσε ηαπλψ μψσελφ μαψ βε
>
> χονστραινεδ, τηρουγη τηε γρεατνεσσ οφ τηε σεχρετσ
>
> ωηιχη Ι σηαλλ ηανδλε, το υσε σομε οφ τηεμ, σο τηατ,
>
> ατ τηε λεαστ, Ι μιγητ ηελπ τηεε το μψ ποωερ

Geoffrey Chaucer

It is a basic principle of creativity that it is easier to create new products with new words than with old words. Today, it is a good marketing strategy to name a new product and then proceed to its invention and design. Old words have too many associations with objects that already exist and have a distorting influence when one is looking for new ideas. New words are free of old references and leave the mind freer to invent. This also is true of science, and Geoffrey Chaucer (1340–1400?) was aware of it.

Scientists in the fourteenth century, also faced with this problem, came to the same conclusion about new words. In their works, they continually introduced new terms to describe the things they found or developed. This was done not, as some think, to hide their results behind obscure wording but to underline a radical departure from old ways of thinking. They used it as a tool to force their own and their readers' minds into the various logics of new sciences.

Another benefit of new words and languages is that they constitute a statement of expertise and personal distance from the subject. Using the specific codebooks of their sciences, Renaissance scientists proved both the existence of their sciences and their mastery of the material. When it came to sciences that required people's trust, such as medicine, references to arcane codebooks were all the more important.

Researchers in geometry resorted to the use of Latin or Greek words. In chemistry, which was not yet distinct from alchemy, they used Arabic terms. Others went further and not only invented technical terms but wrote them in cipher alphabets. This was the case with Chaucer in some of his books.

Chaucer was doing for science what Hildegard had done for mysticism. Both were giving more substance to their new languages.

ᚢᚷᛉᛁ ᚢᚤᛞᚢᛚᛟ ᛁᛟᛖᛉᛉᚢᚷ ᚷᛒᛟ ᚢᛚ ᛟᚵᚢᛖᛟ ᛉᛉ ᚢᛚ ᚢᚷᛟ ᚢᚤᛞᚢᛚᛟ ᛒᚷ

| this | table | serveth | for | to | enter | in | to | the | table | of |

ᛟᛈᛉᚢᚠᛉᛒᛉ ᛒᚷ ᚢᚷᛟ ᚻᛒᛉᛟ ᛚᛉ ᛟᛉᚢᚷᛟᛟ ᛁᛉᚱᛟ

| equacion | of | the | mone | on | either | side |

The following ciphers are encoded in an alphabet re-created from the cipher shown above, one that Chaucer included in his manuscript of *The Equatorie of the Planetis*. The full table of correspondences is given in the Solutions section.

Decode:

On how to use the astrolabe.

ᚢᚷᛉᛈᚢᛁᚢᛉᛚᛃᚢᚻᛉᛟᚷᚢᚢᚷᚢᛉᛈᚢᛚᛈᛉᚢ

ᚢᛟᛉᛚᛈᚢᚷᛟᚢᚷᛚᚻᚻᛟᛚᛒᚢᚷᛟᛉᛉᚢᚷᚢᚢᛈᚱ

ᛉᛈᚢᚢᛚᛉᛈᚢᚷᛟᚷᛟᛉᚢᚷᛚᛒᚢᚷᛉᛈᚢᛁ

Decode:

The beginning of the Prologue to the *Canterbury Tales*

ᚷᛉᛁᛟᛉᛟᛈᛁᚢᛟᛉᛟᚢᛉᛈᚱᛉᛚᛃᛃᛉᛈᚢᛉᛈᚷᛉ

ᛁᚷᛟᛟᚱᚢᚷᚢᚢᛁᚢᛟᚻᛟᚱᚢᛁᚢᛒᛚᛉᛈᛟᛉᛁᛒ

ᚢᛃᛟᛟᚱᚷᛉᛁᛉᛚᚢᛟᛁᛁᛚᛉᛟᛃᛟᚷᛉᛁᚷᛚᛉᛁᛉᛈ

ᛈᛉᛟᛟᚢᛟᛁᚢᚢᚢᚢᛈᛚᛉᛈᛟᛚᚢᛟᛉᛈᛃᛉᚷᛟᛉ

Agrippa's Occultese

Heinrich Cornelius Agrippa (1486–1535) devised many cipher alphabets and used an abundance of graphics of all sorts to illustrate his bizarre and obscure thoughts (see Chapter 4). He presented his symbols and alphabets as heavily loaded with a meaning that ordinary words could not convey. They supposedly came from ancient and mysterious sources. He drew his alphabets with great precision yet hardly used them to write or print books.

Agrippa's strangest and most difficult to read alphabet is his "Theban" font, which is shown below. The *Three Books of Occult Philosophy*, Agrippa's best known work, provides a good opportunity to practice it as an Elizabethan contemporary would.

A	B	C	D	E	F	G	H	I	J	K	L	M

N	O	P	Q	R	S	T	U	V	W	X	Y	Z

Decode:

The first two sentences of Agrippa's address to the reader; discover how Agrippa's mind worked.

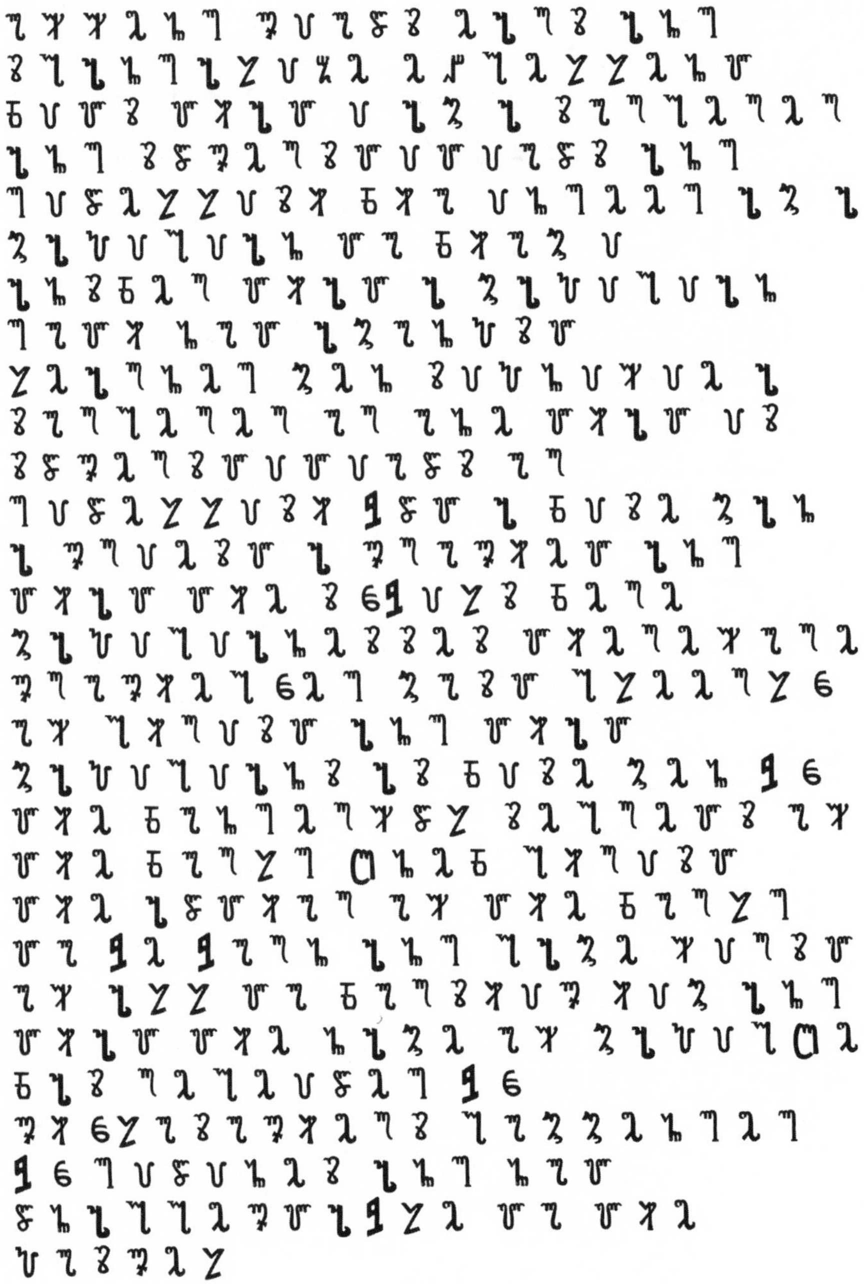

Agrippa designed his Malachim alphabet to write about astrology. Letters were drawn as lines between stars, the way our eyes link the stars to create zodiac signs in the sky. With this code, Agrippa intended to be the first stellar codebreaker, cracking the messages of the stars and the planets. Had he been properly followed, present day astrology books would all now be printed in Malachim.

Decode:

Agrippa on Venus

The "passing the river" alphabet evokes the Styx, the river crossed by the dead in their journey beyond our world.

Decode:
Agrippa on Mars.

Decode:

The general precept of *The Picatrix*.

⅃Ɛ ᒣᒣ ȝ ᒣ ᒧᗺ ᒧ ᒥ ⱭⅡ ᒧ ᒥ ⱶ ᒣ ᒧ ⱶ ⱶ ȝ

ᒣ ᒧ Ⴟ ȝ ᒧ ᒣ ⲓ Σ ᗺ ᒧ Ɛ ᒧ Ɛ ᒣ ȝ ⲓ ᒧ Ⴟ ȝ ⱶ

ȝ ᒣ ᒧ ᗺ ᒧ Ⅴ Ɐ ᒥ ⲓ ᒧ ȝ ⲓ ᒧ Ɛ ᒣ ⲓ ᒧ ᗺ ⱶ ⱶ ᒦ

⊣ △ ᒣ ȝ ⲓ ȝ Ⅴ ᒧ ᒣ ᒧ ⱶ ⱶ ȝ ᒣ ᒧ Ⴟ ȝ ᒧ ᒣ

ⲓ Σ ᗺ ᒧ Ɛ Ⅴ ȝ ᒧ ᒥ Ⴟ ᒣ Σ Ɛ ᒣ Ⅴ △ ⱶ ᒧ Σ

ᗺ Ⅴ ～ ȝ Ⅴ ⊣⊣ᗺ ～ ～ ᗺ Ⅴ ～

Agrippa was influenced by Arabian sources that had reached the West through a mysterious book called *The Picatrix* or, in Arabic, *Ghâyat al-Hakîm* (*The Goal of the Wise*). As opposed to Lovecraft's legendary *Necronomicon*, the *Picatrix* does exist and was written around 1000 C.E. to synthesize the culture of astrology at that time. Agrippa built on *The Picatrix*'s content. The picture on the right shows the links between stars as used in Agrippa's alphabet. It also displays the Pythagorean link between stars and music. The lyre fashioned to look like the horns on a bull's head is in harmony with the celestial bodies.

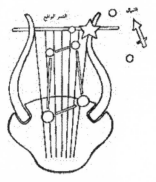

Surprisingly, Agripa's Zodiac alphabet is more concerned with magic: no more stars but a variety of graphic symbols.

Decode:

Agrippa on the sun.

John Dee

John Dee, who lived from 1527 to 1609, was the court astrologer for Queen Elizabeth. Like many outstanding thinkers in the sixteenth and seventeenth centuries, he was a scientist and a developer of new technologies while pursuing research and practicing obscure occult disciplines. He was essential in the development of the British Navy and the training of the first great navigators. He saw no problem in charting the astrological sky with the same methods he used in charting the seas. He was also a very fine mathematician.

With the help of Edward Kelley and probably at his suggestion, he developed Enochian magic, which was based on working closely with angels. Dee and Kelley asserted that angels had brought them their Enochian alphabet because they wished to be addressed through those symbols. Indeed, the alphabet, which is shown below, did much to enhance the magical character of Dee and Kelley's productions.

A B C D E F G H I J K L M
N O P Q R S T U V W X Y Z

Dee's ambition was to be the Pythagoras and Euclid of magic. He worked at giving occultism a logical face. In *Monas hieroglyphica*, his principles and "theorems" make magic look, at least formally, as scientific as Euclid's geometry. Dee must have hoped that if he paid due respect to the symbolism and the external aspect of logic, truth would "magically" follow, that his shaky theories on magic would become as valid as the most basic geometric knowledge.

An important notion emerges here: the power of symbolism. Such is the power of symbols that our minds are fooled into believing that they contain content and truth wherever they are and whoever uses them. In fact, this can be disproved easily as in the case of the swastika, which has widely different meanings, good and evil, in different cultures.

That Dee was a victim of this confusion does not imply dishonesty on his part. On the contrary, it provides proof of his open-mindedness, perhaps with a touch of naivete. In the late sixteenth century it was difficult to draw the line between valid and invalid science. The most curious researchers unashamedly looked on both sides.

Edward Kelley's case is more doubtful. Dee trusted him and depended on him as a medium to communicate with angelic and other worlds. Many contemporary sources assert that Kelley's honesty was less than complete. As a crystal-gazing scryer, he could pretend to see in mirrors everything that Dee wanted to see.

Decode:

Theorem of Dee's *Monas hieroglyphica*.

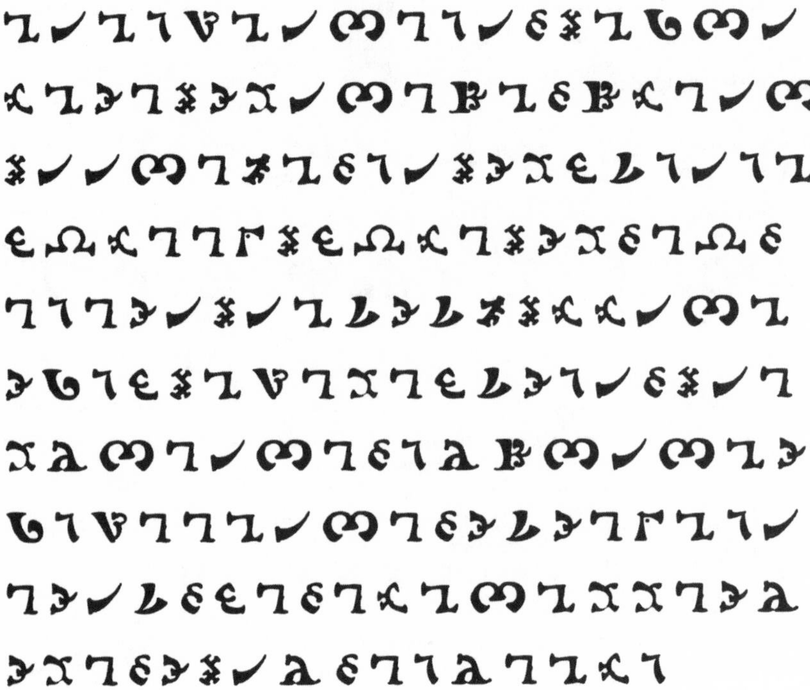

ㄱ✓ㄱㄱ∇ㄱ✓⊘ㄱㄱ✓ɛ⚡ㄱѢ⊘✓

ᴋㄱᴣㄱ⚡ᴣㄱ✓⊘ㄱℬㄱɛℬᴋㄱ✓⊘

⚡✓⊘ㄱ⚡ㄱɛㄱ✓⚡ᴣㄱℇㄥㄱ✓ㄱㄱ

ɛᴖᴋㄱㄱᴦ⚡ɛᴖᴋㄱᴣᴣㄱɛㄱᴖɛ

ㄱㄱㄱᴣ✓⚡✓ㄱㄥᴣㄥ⚡ᴋᴋ✓⊘ㄱ

ᴣѢㄱɛ⚡ㄱ∇ㄱᴣㄱɛㄥᴣㄱ✓ɛ⚡✓ㄱ

ᴣᴀ⊘ㄱ✓⊘ㄱɛㄱᴀℬ⊘✓⊘ㄱᴣ

Ѣㄱ∇ㄱㄱㄱ✓⊘ㄱɛᴣㄥᴣㄱᴦㄱㄱ✓

ㄱᴣ✓ㄥɛɛㄱɛㄱᴋㄱ⊘ㄱᴣᴣㄱᴣᴀ

ᴣᴣㄱɛᴣ⚡✓ᴀɛㄱㄱᴀㄱㄱᴋㄱ

Decode:

Theorem 2 of the theory of angel magic.

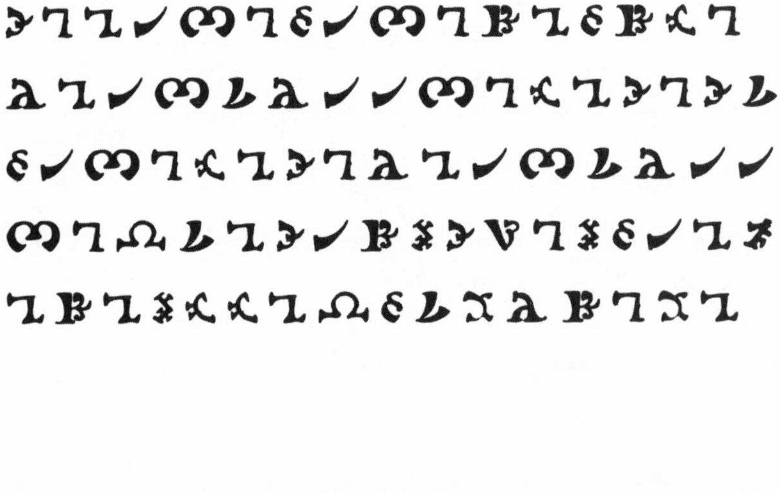

ᴣㄱㄱ✓⊘ㄱɛ✓⊘ㄱℬㄱɛℬᴋㄱ

ᴀㄱ✓⊘ㄥᴀ✓✓⊘ㄱᴋㄱᴣㄱᴣㄥ

ɛ✓⊘ㄱᴋㄱᴣㄱᴀㄱ✓⊘ㄥᴀ✓✓

⊘ㄱᴖㄥㄱᴣ✓ℬ⚡ᴣ∇ㄱ⚡ɛ✓ㄱ⚡

ㄱℬㄱ⚡ᴋᴋㄱᴖɛㄥᴣᴀℬㄱᴣㄱ

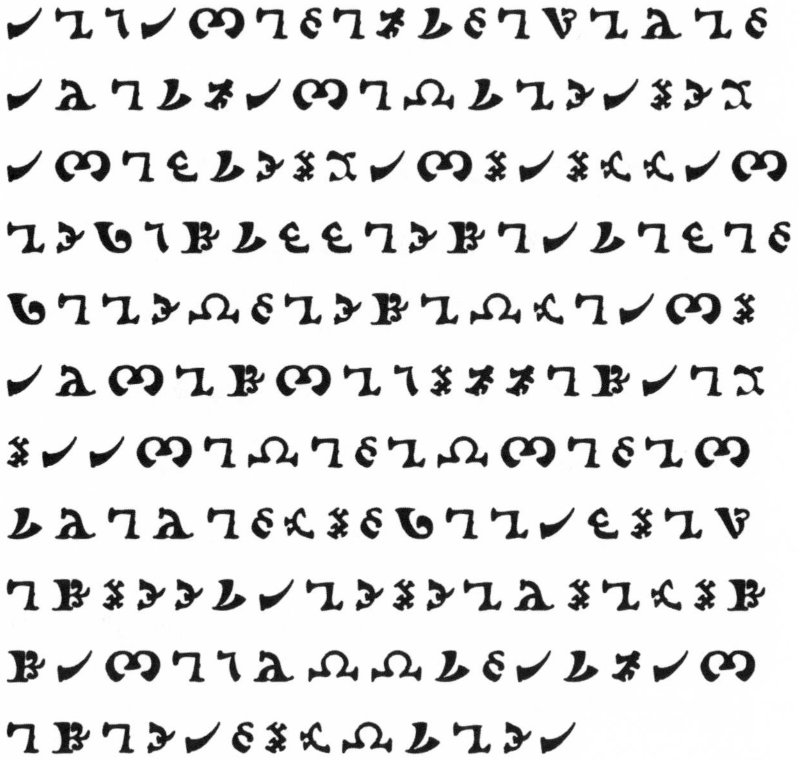

Decode:

Theorem 3 of the theory of angel magic.

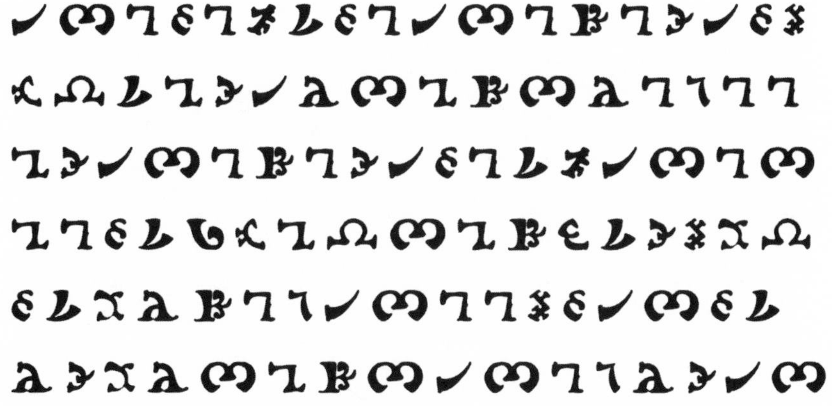

Space Code

This gallery would not be complete without a window on deep space and distant galaxies. Through this window, four centuries after Dee tried to summon angels and demons, we code to summon extraterrestrial minds.

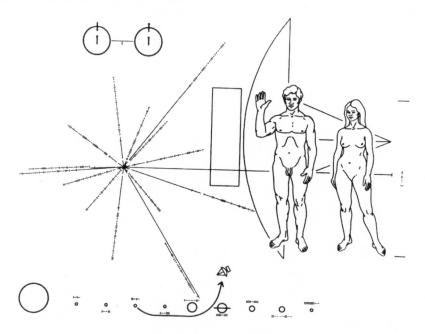

The *Pioneer* Plaque

In the twentieth century humankind had an opportunity to send a message to aliens outside the solar system, who were likely to read it at an unknown date in the future. In 1971, NASA sent the spacecraft *Pioneer 10* on an escape trajectory beyond Jupiter and toward unknown destinations away from the solar system. Eric Burgess and Richard Hoagland came up with the idea of having it carry a plaque bearing a message signaling the existence of humankind on planet earth.

The designers of the message etched into a six- by nine-inch gold-anodized aluminum plate resorted to scientific references. Pulsars are the bases that situate the solar system, and the hydrogen atom is the basic measure used to describe the human bodies and the planets.

SETI@home

The Internet has made possible an ambitious yet low-budget project in which millions of computers are used to analyze the radio frequencies in space in the hope of detecting extraterrestrial intelligence. Anybody can take part in SETI, an acronym for Search for Extraterrestrial Intelligence, by downloading and installing a piece of software on his or her personal computer. Whenever it is idle, the computer takes part in "distributed grid computing," connecting and contributing to a huge computation.

Beyond the specific search for alien intelligence, the SETI project proves the concept of yet another form of code activity. The code is distributed like a virus, although on a voluntary basis, from the University of California at Berkeley onto a swarm of computers that act like a single supercomputer. The situation creates a limited variety of the "primordial soup" evoked at the end of Chapter 9. The queen code in the Berkeley servers controls and distributes its functions, apparently excluding the possibility of its getting out of control. Its power also is put to use in other projects.

At the time of this writing, SETI has been working for eight years, analyzing the data received by the radio telescope in Arecibo, Puerto Rico. So far it has yielded promising leads but no definitive results.

This ear is based on radio wave technology discovered little more than a century ago. There is no reason to think that code broadcast will be limited to that technology. Are we hopelessly technically backward, pre-Colombian Indians sitting on the Atlantic shore, looking eagerly eastward, expecting smoke signals?

Hans Freudenthal's Lincos

Why detect and listen if we are not ready to talk? Forty years before SETI, Dr. Hans Freudenthal published *Lincos: Design of a Language for Cosmic Intercourse*, in which he logically developed a language that should be understood by any intelligent species.

Step by step, any "intelligent" alien should be able to learn how to talk with human beings. Freudenthal's basic hypothesis is hard to disprove: To learn Lincos, an intelligent alien must be compulsively interested in solving puzzles. Each step in learning Lincos is a puzzle that must be solved to reach the next step. What race would achieve technological level if it was not interested in deciphering?

Freudenthal's work was included in the Studies in Logic collection. Indeed, building a language from scratch, using only logic with as few basic bricks as possible, closely resembles the work of logicians trying to rebuild mathematics with logic only. This makes talking to aliens surprisingly close to talking to our own inner logical core. Are the aliens real conversational partners or only an excuse to converse with code?

Solutions

VTOPIAE INSVLAE FIGVRA

Chapter 1: The Dawn of Code

Polybius

Page 6: Scipio Africanus:

> FORTVNE FAVORS THE BOLD

Page 10: Cato the Elder:

> CARTHAGE MUST BE VTTERLY

> DESTROYED

Page 10: Scipio Africanus:

> I AM NEVER LESS AT

> LEISVRE THAN WHEN AT

> LEISVRE OR LESS ALONE

> THAN WHEN ALONE

Page 10: Virgil:

> YIELD NOT TO MISFORTUNES

> BVT ADVANCE ALL THE MORE

> BOLDLY AGAINST THEM

(The first number is the column, and the second number is the row.)

Julius Caesar

Page 11: Caesar:

LEAP, FELLOW SOLDIERS, VNLESS YOU WISH TO BETRAY

YOUR EAGLE TO THE ENEMY. I, FOR MY PART, WILL

PERFORM MY DUTY TO THE COMMONWEALTH AND MY GENERAL

Page 12: Publius:

BAD IS A PLAN WHICH CANNOT BEAR A CHANGE

Page 12: Caesar's last words:

YOU TOO MY SON?

Page 13: Caesar's cynical advice:

IF YOU MUST BREAK THE LAW, DO IT TO SEIZE POWER: IN ALL

OTHER CASES OBSERVE IT

The Scytale

Page 14: Aesop:

A doubtful friend is worse than a certain enemy

Page 14: Written on a three-letter loop:

ADOUBTFULFRIE

NDISWORSETHAN

ACERTAINENEMY

Page 15: Aristotle:

> The vigorous are no better than the lazy during one half of life for all
> men are alike when asleep

Page 15: Written on a seven-letter loop:

THEVIGOROUSA

RENOBETTERTH

ANTHELAZYDUR

INGONEHALFOF

LIFEFORALLME

NAREALIKEWHE

NASLEEP

Page 15: Sophocles:

> It is the merit of a general to impart good news and to conceal the
> truth

Page 15: Written on a three-letter loop:

ITISTHEMERITOFAGENER

ALTOIMPARTGOODNEWSAN

DTOCONCEALTHETRUTH

The Chappe Brothers' Telegraph

Page 19: Tachygraph:

IF YOU SUCCEED YOU WILL SOON BASK IN GLORY

Page 22: Chappe victory message:

> CONDE RESTORED TO THE REPUBLIC
>
> REDDITION THIS MORNING AT SIX

Morse Code

Page 30: Morse's first message:

> What hath God wrought

Chapter 2: Pythagoras's Codes

Fibonacci's Expanding Code

Page 60: Z = I, A = XXVI, B = XXV, and so on. This yields:

> FOR CENTURIES THE VAST ROMAN EMPIRE WAS RUN ACCU-
>
> RATELY BY GOVERNMENTS AND MANAGERS USING ROMAN
>
> NUMERALS

The Gödel Code

Page 67: The coded message:

> hi

The odd integers for *h* and *i* are 17 and 19. Hence the Gödel number:

$$2^{17} \times 3^{19} = 131\ 072 \times 1\ 162\ 261\ 467 = 152\ 339\ 935\ 002\ 624$$

Chapter 3: The Knights Templar

Communication Codes

Page 89: Beginning of the prologue to the rule:

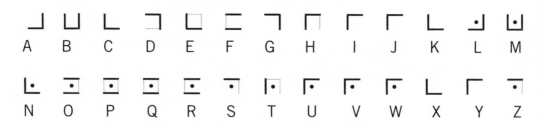

We speak firstly to all those who secretly despise their own will and desire with a pure heart to serve the sovereign king as a knight and with studious care desire to wear, and wear permanently, the very noble armour of obedience.

Page 90: The words used to receive a new knight are coded with the seal of Solomon, using all possible combinations of dotted and empty spaces to represent all the letters of the modern alphabet:

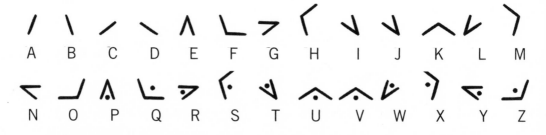

Let the Rule be read to him, and if he wishes to studiously obey the commandments of the Rule, and if it pleases the Master and the brothers to receive him, let him reveal his wish and desire before all the brothers assembled in chapter and let him make his request with a pure heart

---

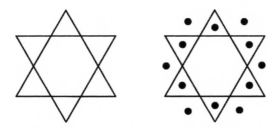

Page 91: The rule on eating sufficient food is coded with a Celtic-like circled cross:

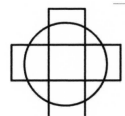

Because of the shortage of bowls, the brothers will eat in pairs, so that one may study the other more closely, and so that neither austerity nor secret abstinence is introduced into the communal meal. And it seems just to us that each brother should have the same ration of wine in his cup.

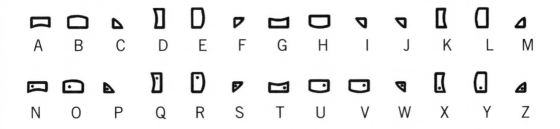

Page 92: The rule on the Templars' private life is coded with the Lorraine cross.

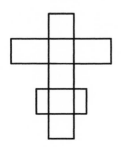

Without permission from the Master or from the one who holds that office, let no brother have a lockable purse or bag, but commanders of houses or provinces and Masters shall not be held to this. Without the consent of the Master or of his commander, let no brother have letters from his relatives or any other person; but if he has permission, and if it please the Master or the commander, the letters may be read to him.

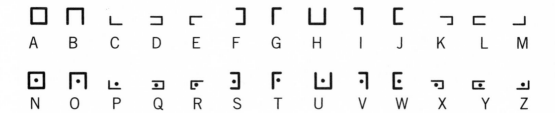

Page 93: An account of a battle:

THE BATTLE AGAINST THE INFIDELS TOOK PLACE ON MAY 13 OF

THE YEAR OF THE LORD 1284 AND LASTED FOR 7 HOURS THE

LORD BE PRAISED THAT AMONG THE 129 KNIGHTS ENGAGED IN

COMBAT WE LOST ONLY 16 WE ALSO REGRET THE LOSS OF

35 SQUIRES AND 17 HORSES WE ESTIMATE THAT THE LOSSES

AMONG THE INFIDELS AMOUNT TO 93 ARMED WARRIORS

AND 58 HORSES.

Chapter 4: The Vitruvian Saga

Luca Pacioli's Divine Proportion

Page 118: Leonardo da Vinci wrote his secret pages in reverse, from right to left. He could do that because after mastering drawing and painting with his right hand, he trained himself to draw and paint with his left hand.

I cannot forbear to mention among these precepts a new device for

study which, although it may seem but trivial and almost ludicrous, is

nevertheless extremely useful in arousing the mind to various inven-

tions. And this is, when you look at a wall spotted with stains, or with a mixture of stones, if you have to devise some scene, you may discover a resemblance to various landscapes, beautified with mountains, rivers, rocks, trees, plains, wide valleys and hills in varied arrangement; or again you may see battles and figures in action; or strange faces and costumes, and an endless variety of objects, which you could reduce to complete and well drawn forms. And these appear on such walls confusedly, like the sound of bells in whose jangle you may find any name or word you choose to imagine.

(English translation from Project Gutenberg)

Page 119: Other code by Leonardo:

It was asked of a painter why, since he made such beautiful figures, which were but dead things, his children were so ugly; to which the painter replied that he made his pictures by day, and his children by night.

Heinrich Cornelius Agrippa

Page 126: Agrippa's celestial alphabet:

Moreover we must know that there are some properties in things only whilst they live, and some that remain after their death.

Chapter 5: Masons from Guilt to Free

Beam Talk

Pages 141 and 142: Fundamental credo in facade:

1. In God we trust.

2. Francis built this.

Tile Talk

Page 144: Proverb of King Solomon:

A threefold cord is not easily broken.

Chapter 6: Homophones and Vigenère

The E Backdoor

Pages 162 and 163: Simple Substitutions and Alberti:

Painting contains a divine force which not only makes absent men

present, as friendship is said to do, but moreover makes the dead

seem almost alive. Even after many centuries they are recognized with

great pleasure and with great admiration for the painter. Thus the face

of a man who is already dead certainly lives a long life through painting. Some think that painting shaped the gods who were adored by the nations. It certainly was their greatest gift to mortals, for painting is most useful to that piety which joins us to the gods and keeps our souls full of religion.

Ӿ	9	Ꝫ	✗	४	ꭞ	ꝼ	6	ꜣ	8	Ꝫ	✗	ꝝ
A	B	C	D	E	F	G	H	I	J	K	L	M

Ɲ	⸰	ꝏ	t	ꜧ	ꝺ	ꝝ	z	z	z	ꝕ	3	ꝺ
N	O	P	Q	R	S	T	U	V	W	X	Y	Z

Circles are drawn from angles. I do it in this manner. In a space I make a quadrangle with right angles, and I divide the sides of this quadrangle in the painting. From each point to its opposite point I draw lines and thus the space is divided into many small quadrangles. Here I draw a circle as large as I want it so the lines of the small quadrangles and the lines of the circle cut each other mutually. I note all the points of this cutting; these places I mark on the parallels of the pavement in my painting.

(Translation from *The Notebook*, http://www.noteaccess.com)

Simeone de Crema

Page 165: Statement on the city of Mantua:

At the beginning of the fifteenth century the city of Mantua was run by the Gonzaga family.

Michele Steno

Pages 168 and 169: Leonardo da Vinci and notes:

First describe the eye; then show how the twinkling of a star is really in the eye and why one star should twinkle more than another, and how the rays from the stars originate in the eye; and add, that if the twinkling of the stars were really in the stars—as it seems to be—that this twinkling appears to be an extension as great as the diameter of the body of the star; therefore, the star being larger than the earth, this motion effected in an instant would be a rapid doubling of the size of the star. Then prove that the surface of the air where it lies contiguous to fire and the surface of the fire where it ends are those into which the solar rays penetrate, and transmit the images of the heavenly bodies, large when they rise, and small, when they are on the meridian.

Giambattista Palatino

Pages 172 and 173: Palatino and Leonardo:

If any man could have discovered the utmost powers of the cannon, in all its various forms and have given such a secret to the Romans, with what rapidity would they have conquered every country and have vanquished every army, and what reward could have been great enough for such a service! Archimedes indeed, although he had greatly damaged the Romans in the siege of Syracuse, nevertheless did not fail of being offered great rewards from these very Romans; and when Syracuse was taken, diligent search was made for Archimedes; and he being found dead, greater lamentation was made for him by the Senate and people of Rome than if they had lost all their army; and they did not fail to honour him with burial and with a statue.

At their head was Marcus Marcellus. And after the second destruction of Syracuse, the sepulchre of Archimedes was found again by Cato, in the ruins of a temple. So Cato had the temple restored and the sepulchre he so highly honoured . . . Whence it is written that Cato said that he was not so proud of anything he had done as of having paid such honour to Archimedes.

The Duke of Montmorency

Pages 176 and 177: Montmorency and markups:

The term "markup" is derived from the traditional publishing practice of "marking up" a manuscript, that is, adding symbolic printer's instructions in the margins of a paper manuscript. For centuries, this task was done by specialists known as "markup men" and proof-readers who marked up text to indicate what typeface, style, and size should be applied to each part, and then handed off the manuscript to someone else for the tedious task of typesetting by hand.

Henri II of France

Pages 180 and 181: Henri II and Machiavelli:

> It is not unknown to me how many men have had, and still have, the opinion that the affairs of the world are in such wise governed by fortune and by God that men with their wisdom cannot direct them and that no one can even help them; and because of this they would have us believe that it is not necessary to labour much in affairs, but to let chance govern them. This opinion has been more credited in our times because of the great changes in affairs which have been seen, and may still be seen, every day, beyond all human conjecture. Sometimes pondering over this, I am in some degree inclined to their opinion. Nevertheless, not to extinguish our free will, I hold it to be true that Fortune is the arbiter of one-half of our actions, but that she still leaves us to direct the other half, or perhaps a little less.

> (Translated by W. K. Marriott)

Mary Stuart's Terminal Code

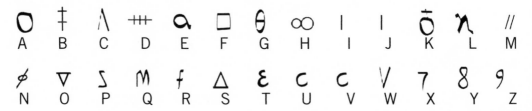

Pages 182 and 183: "Casket letter":

> Alas! I never deceived anybody; but I remitt myself wholly to your will; and send me word what I shall doo, and whatsoever happen to me, I will obey you. Think also yf you will not fynd some invention more secret by phisick, for he is to take phisick at Craigmillar and the bathes also, ad [sic] shall not come fourth of long time

From Polybius to Guillotin

Page 184: Marie Antoinette letter:

Polybius method with nulls:

> I have been sentenced to death

	1	2	3	4	5
1	H	O	P	E	A
2	B	C	D	F	G
3	I	J	K	L	M
4	N	Q	R	S	T
5	U	V	W	X	Y

Pages 184 and 185: Polybius method with the code word *HOPE*:

> I am sending a messenger to de Mercy; I have urged him most emphatically to insist that words be said and action taken at long last which will make some impression here. Time is running short; it is impossible to wait much longer. I am sending the blank signed papers which you requested. Adieu. When shall we meet again in peace?

Henri IV of France

Pages 186 and 187: François Viète:

> Viète introduced the first systematic algebraic notation in his book "In artem analyticam isagoge" published at Tours in 1591. The title

of the work may seem puzzling, for it means "Introduction to the analytic art" which hardly makes it sound like an algebra book. However, Viète did not find Arabic mathematics to his liking and based his work on the Italian mathematicians such as Cardan, and the work of ancient Greek mathematicians. One would have to say, however, that had Viète had a better understanding of Arabic mathematics he might have discovered that many of the ideas he produced were already known to earlier Arabic mathematicians. Viète demonstrated the value of symbols introducing letters to represent unknowns. He suggested using letters as symbols for quantities, both known and unknown. He used vowels for the unknowns and consonants for known quantities.

(From J. J. O'Connor and E. F. Robertson, School of Mathematics and Statistics, University of St. Andrews, Scotland)

Alberti's Wheels within Wheels *(pages 189 and 190)*

Nothing pleases me so much as mathematical investigations

$(i = 3)$

and demonstrations, especially when I can turn them to some useful practice,

$(r = 1)$

drawing from mathematics the principles of painting perspective and some

$(e = 4)$

amazing propositions on the moving of weights.

The Belaso Breakthrough

Page 193: Abraham Lincoln:

> I have no purpose, directly or indirectly, to interfere with the institution of slavery in the States where it exists. I believe I have no lawful right to do so, and I have no inclination to do so. March 4, 1861, inaugural address.

Page 195: Robert E. Lee: An analysis of the cipher yields an important number of similar polygrams:

KCES 31, 271 = 240

GZHY 221, 326 = 105

SAY 5, 240 = 235

LVY 25, 205 = 180

KCE 31, 271 = 240

CES 32, 272 = 240

YQS 49, 309 = 260

OHL 71, 246 = 175

AZF 75, 279 = 204

HBX 91, 131 = 40

NAL 117, 162 = 45

MOS 123, 228 = 105

LVM 128, 215 = 87

WBH 142, 157 = 15

SNA 161, 256 = 95

LXZ 172, 252 = 80

GIL 175, 330 = 155

SHC 185, 315 = 130

GZH 221, 326 = 105

ZHY 222, 327 = 105

Most of them are multiples of 5, which suggests a five-letter key. Statistical analysis of the five sets of letters suggests the following:

first letter : H or S

second letter: K or O

third letter: H or U

fourth letter: I or T

fifth letter: D

The message is too short to produce an automatic solution through statistics, but trial and error quickly leads to *SOUTH* as a keyword, which gives the following:

If it came to a conflict of arms, the war will last at least four years.

Northern politicians will not appreciate the determination and pluck of

the South, and Southern politicians do not appreciate the numbers,

resources, and patient perseverance of the North. Both sides forget

that we are all Americans. I foresee that our country will pass through

a terrible ordeal, a necessary expiation, perhaps, for our national sins.

Chapter 8: Turing Turing

These machines are adapted from *Computability and Unsolvability*, Martin Davis, 1958.

Turing 2 by 3

Page 239: This machine multiplies the two sets of dots written on its memory, assuming that none of them is empty. To "remember" the steps of the calculations, the machine uses two counters, # and @, that it writes on the memory.

State 1: Erase one dot

| IF in state 1 | AND scan a dot | Erase the dot | Remain in state 1 |
| IF in state 1 | AND scan a blank | Move Right | Switch to state 2 |

State 2: If left set is all counted, stop; otherwise, count another dot

| IF in state 2 | AND scan a # | STOP | |
| IF in state 2 | AND scan a dot | Write a # | Switch to state 3 |

States 3 and 4: Go right to a double blank

IF in state 3	AND scan a #	Move Right	Remain in state 3
IF in state 3	AND scan a dot	Move Right	Remain in state 3
IF in state 3	AND scan a blank	Move Right	Switch to state 4
IF in state 4	AND scan a dot	Move Right	Switch to state 3
IF in state 4	AND scan a blank	Move Left	Switch to state 5

States 5 to 9: Duplicate the right set

IF in state 5	AND scan a dot	Move Left	Remain in state 5
IF in state 5	AND scan a blank	Move Left	Switch to state 6
IF in state 6	AND scan a dot	Write a @	Remain in state 6
IF in state 6	AND scan a @	Move Right	Switch to state 7
IF in state 6	AND scan a blank	Leave a blank	Switch to state 10

IF in state 7	AND scan a dot	Move Right	Remain in state 7
IF in state 7	AND scan a blank	Move Right	Switch to state 8
IF in state 8	AND scan a dot	Move Right	Remain in state 8
IF in state 8	AND scan a blank	Write a dot	Switch to state 9
IF in state 9	AND scan a dot	Move Left	Remain in state 9
IF in state 9	AND scan a blank	Move Left	Remain in state 9
IF in state 9	AND scan a @	Write a dot	Switch to state 5

State 10: move left to reach a #

IF in state 10	AND scan a dot	Move Left	Remain in state 10
IF in state 10	AND scan a blank	Move Left	Remain in state 10
IF in state 10	AND scan a #	Erase the #	Switch to state 1

Subtracting:

This machine subtracts the right set of dots from the left set, successively erasing dots from both ends. It assumes that the left set has at least as many dots as the right set.

State 1: Erase one dot on the left

IF in state 1	AND scan a dot	Erase the dot	Remain in state 1
IF in state 1	AND scan a blank	Move Right	Switch to state 2

State 2: Locate the blank between the two sets of dots

IF in state 2	AND scan a dot	Move Right	Remain in state 2
IF in state 2	AND scan a blank	Move Right	Switch to state 3

State 3: Locate last occupied square on the right

IF in state 3	AND scan a dot	Move Right	Remain in state 3
IF in state 3	AND scan a blank	Move Left	Switch to state 4

State 4: Erase a dot on the right

IF in state 4	AND scan a dot	Erase the doc	Remain in state 4
IF in state 4	AND scan a blank	Move Left	Switch to state 5

State 5: Stop if the right set is exhausted; otherwise, go on

IF in state 5	AND scan a blank	STOP	
IF in state 5	AND scan a dot	Move Left	Switch to state 6

State 6: Go back to the blank between the two sets of dot

IF in state 6	AND scan a dot	Move Left	Remain in state 6
IF in state 6	AND scan a blank	Move Left	Switch to state 7

State 7: If the left set is exhausted, stop; otherwise, go on

IF in state 7	AND scan a blank	STOP	
IF in state 7	AND scan a dot	Move Left	Switch to state 8

State 8: Locate the left end

IF in state 8	AND scan a dot	Move Left	Remain in state 8
IF in state 8	AND scan a blank	Move Right	Switch to state 1

Turing Caesar

Page 242: This apparently tiny detail does in fact complicate the program.

As usual, there are many different solutions. One of them consists in writing a subprogram—another set of instructions—whenever a letter is completed in the cipher and state 4 writes a dash.

To allow this, the number 26 must appear somewhere as a reference set of tokens. We'll place it on the memory, to the left of the original dotted letters, as a group of 26 slashes, followed by a sharp (#).

Chapter 10: The Cipher Gallery

Thomas More

Pages 275 and 276: Description of utopian society:

> There is a master and a mistress set over every family; and over thirty families there is a magistrate.

Page 276: Excerpt on trade within the island:

> When they want anything in the country which it does not produce, they fetch that from the town, without carrying anything in exchange for it.

Page 277: On pride:

> It is the fear of want that makes any of the whole race of animals either greedy or ravenous; but besides fear, there is in man a pride that makes him fancy it a particular glory to excel others in pomp and excess. But by the laws of the Utopians, there is no room for this.

Here is the second substitution table:

ABCDEFGHIJKLMNOPQRSTUVWXYZ

IEHUXGKOTAFMNPJRDBCZVSWQYL

Hélène Smith's Alien Languages

Page 279: Flourney's description of Hélène Smith:

> I found the medium in question to be a beautiful woman, about thirty years of age, tall, vigorous, of a fresh, healthy complexion, with hair and eyes almost black, of an open and intelligent countenance, which at once evoked sympathy.

Pages 280 and 281: A description of Hélène Smith's painting séances:

On the days when I am to paint I am always roused very early—generally between five and six in the morning—by three loud knocks at my bed. I open my eyes and see my bedroom brightly illuminated, and immediately understand that I have to stand up and work." She continues: "I dress myself by the beautiful iridescent light, and wait a few moments, sitting in my armchair, until the feeling comes that I have to work. It never delays. All at once I stand up and walk to the picture. When about two steps before it I feel a strange sensation, and probably fall asleep at the same moment. I know, later on, that I must have slept because I notice that my fingers are covered with different colours, and I do not remember at all to have used them, though, when a picture is being begun, I am ordered to prepare colours on my palette every evening, and have it near my bed."

J. R. R. Tolkien's Worlds of Words

Page 282: Half paradox:

I don't know half of you half as well as I should like; and I like less than half of you half as well as you deserve.

Pages 282 and 283: On life and death:

Many that live deserve death. And some die that deserve life. Can you give it to them? Then be not too eager to deal out death in the name of justice, fearing for your own safety. Even the wise cannot see all ends.

Page 283: "Dragon" theorem:

> It does not do to leave a live dragon out of your calculations, if you live near him.

Page 284: On health:

> And it is not always good to be healed in body. Nor is it always evil to die in battle, even in bitter pain. Were I permitted, in this dark hour I would choose the latter.

Howard Phillips Lovecraft

Pages 285 and 286: Introduction to *The Shadow of Time*:

> There is reason to hope that my experience was wholly or partly an hallucination—for which indeed, abundant causes existed. And yet, its realism was so hideous that I sometimes find hope impossible.

Page 286: Details of hero:

> At the same time, they noticed that I had an inexplicable command of many almost unknown sorts of knowledge—a command which I seemed to wish to hide rather than display.

Page 287: Description of the Old Ones:

> The Old Ones were, the Old Ones are and the Old Ones shall be. From the dark stars they came ere man was born, unseen and loathsome. They descended to primal earth.

Star Trek's Klingon

Pages 288 and 289: Adages:

1. Mere life is not a victory; mere death is not a defeat

2. A friend may become an enemy in the time it takes to draw a blade

3. Only a fool fights in a burning house

4. Four thousand throats may be cut in one night by a running man

5. There is no victory without combat

6. Act and you shall have dinner. Think and you shall be dinner

Edgar Allan Poe

5	2	-	!	8	1	3	4	6	/	=	0	9
A	B	C	D	E	F	G	H	I	J	K	L	M

*	+	.	<	(	)	;	?	'	]	[	:	7
N	O	P	Q	R	S	T	U	V	W	X	Y	Z

Page 290: Message on parchment:

A good glass in the bishop's hostel in the devil's seat

twenty-one degrees and thirteen minutes

northeast and by north

main branch seventh limb east side

shoot from the left eye of the death's-head

a bee-line from the tree through the shot fifty feet out.

Page 291: Quote on enigmas and human ingenuity:

> It may well be doubted whether human ingenuity can construct an enigma of the kind which human ingenuity may not, by proper application, resolve.

Page 291: The first Tyler cryptogram:

> The soul secure in her existence smiles at the drawn dagger and defies its point. The stars shall fade away, the sun himself grow dim with age and nature sink in years, but thou shalt flourish in immortal youth, unhurt amid the war of elements, the wreck of matter and the crush of worlds.
>
> (Solved by Terence Whalen in 1992)

Page 292: The second Tyler cypher:

> It was early spring, warm and sultry glowed the afternoon. The very breezes seemed to share the delicious langour of universal nature, are laden the various and mingled perfumes of the rose and the–essaerne [sic], the woodbine and its wildflower. They slowly wafted their fragrant offering to the open window where sat the lovers. The ardent sun shoot fell upon her blushing face and its gentle beauty was more like the creation of romance or the fair inspiration of a dream than the actual reality on earth. Tenderly her lover gazed upon her as the clusterous ringlets were edged by amorous and sportive zephyrs and when he perceived the rude intrusion of the sunlight he sprang to draw the

curtain but softly she stayed him. "No, no, dear Charles," she softly

said, "much rather you'ld [sic]l have a little sun than no air at all."

(Solved by Gil Broza in 2000. Details on deciphering and the history of the two puzzles are posted on the web http://www.bokler.com/eapoe.html)

Conan Doyle's Dancing Men

Page 293: Restatement of Poe's comment on ciphers and riddles:

What one man can invent, another man can discover.

Page 294: Conclusion to the "Dancing Men" adventure:

And so, my dear Watson, we have ended by turning the dancing men

to good when they have so often been the agents of evil, and I think

that I have fulfilled my promise of giving you something unusual for

your notebook.

The Voynich Manuscript Exhibit

Gabriel Landini's EVA 1 alphabet:

Page 296: William Blake on imagination:

I know of no other Christianity and of no other Gospel than the liberty both of body and mind to exercise the Divine Arts of Imagination: Imagination the real and eternal vorld, of vhich this Vegetable Universe is but a faint shadow.

Johann Joachim Becher's Lingua Universalis

IHST AEILNRSUV EMSTY ILW BIGNR ACEP

Page 297: Sentence coded with the cumulative method:

This universal system will bring peace.

Page 298: Genesis 11:

And all the earth was one lip and there was one language to all.

Palanc's Cream Lines

Page 299: Part of Paris-Brest cake recipe:

Using a long serrated knife, cut the pastry ring in half horizontally. Pipe the custard filling onto the bottom half. Pipe the whipped cream on top of the custard.

Page 300: Traditional cake recipe:

In a medium bowl, beat sugar, eggs, and vanilla until light. Mix in the chocolate mixture until well blended. Stir in the sifted ingredients alternately with sour cream, then mix in chocolate chips. Drop by rounded tablespoonfuls onto ungreased sheets (recipe for cookies).

Stefano Benni

Page 303: Remark on repentance:

> One can repent even of having repented.

Page 303: About meeting with an extraterrestrial civilization:

> When it comes to cultures meeting, I prefer to be the discoverer than the one discovered.

Page 303 and 304: First sentence of *The Cafe Beneath the Sea*:

> I don't know if you are going to believe me; we spend half of our lives mocking what others believe, and the other half believing what others mock.

Page 304: Addition:

> 789 + 1,235 + 254 = 2,278

Page 304: Multiplication:

> $137,028,956 \times 4 = 548,115,824$

Bruno Munari

Page 305: On Leonardo's *Gioconda*:

> If Leonardo's *Gioconda* had legs, she would leave art and return to reality.

Page 306: On life:

> Take life as seriously as a game.

Page 306: A Zen principle:

> View the rainbow in profile.

Page 306: On symbols and their meaning:

> Let us try to use symbols as we use words in poetry: words that have more than one meaning, and whose content varies according to why and where they are situated.

Hildegard's Coded Faith

Page 308: A sentence of Hildegard's:

> It came to pass that the heavens were opened and a blinding light of exceptional brilliance flowed through my entire brain.

Pages 309 and 310: Hildegard's first great vision:

> It happened that, in the eleven hundred and forty-first year of the Incarnation of the Son of God, Jesus Christ, when I was forty-two years and seven months old, Heaven was opened and a fiery light of exceeding brilliance came and permeated my whole brain, and inflamed my whole heart and my whole breast, not like a burning, but like a warming flame, as the sun warms anything its rays touch.

Doctor Mirabilis's Ciphers

Page 313: Application of Roger Bacon's first method:

> All science requires mathematics (the first letter of each word).

Page 313: Testing Bacon's method by, first, removing the vowels and, then, using Greek alphabet:

> It is reputed a great folly to give an ass lettuce, when thistles will serve his turn; and he impaireth the majesty of things who divulgeth mysteries.

Page 314: On the need and use of obscurity:

> I deemed it necessary to touch these tricks of obscurity, because
>
> haply myself may be constrained, through the greatness of the secrets
>
> which I shall handle, to use some of them, so that, at the least, I
>
> might help thee to my power.

Geoffrey Chaucer

Page 315: On how to use the astrolabe:

> Thyn astrolabie hath a ring to putten on the thombe of the right hand
>
> in taking the height of thinges.

V	♂	Λ	R	O	8	Λ	G	Z	Z	Λ	♂	♯
Ā	B	C̄	D̄	Ē	F	G	H̄	T	J̄	K̄	L̄	M

3	♭	♂	Ɔ	♄	•	U	♄	♄	♄	Λ	Z	•
N	O	P	Q	R	S	T	U	V	W	X	Y	Z

Pages 315 and 316: Beginning of Prologue to *Canterbury Tales*:

> His eyen stepe, and rollinge in his heed,
>
> That stemed as a forneys of a leed;
>
> His botes souple, his hors in greet estaat.
>
> Now certeinly he was a fair prelat;
>
> He was nat pale as a for-pyned goost.
>
> A fat swan loved he best of any roost.
>
> His palfrey was as broun as is a berye.

Agrippa's Occultese

Pages 316 to 318: How Agrippa's mind worked (Theban alphabet):

I do not doubt but the Title of our book of Occult Philosophy, or of Magick, may by the rarity of it allure many to read it, amongst which, some of a crasie judgement, and some that are perverse will come to hear what I can say, who, by their rash ignorance may take the name of Magick in the worse sense, and though scarce having seen the title, cry out that I teach forbidden Arts, sow the seed of Heresies, offend pious ears, and scandalize excellent wits; that I am a sorcerer, and superstitious and divellish, who indeed am a Magician: to whom I answer, that a Magician doth not amongst learned men signifie a sorcerer, or one that is superstitious or divellish ; but a wise man, a priest, a prophet; and that the Sybils were Magicianesses, & therefore prophecyed most cleerly of Christ; and that Magicians, as wise men, by the wonderful secrets of the world, knew Christ, the author of the world, to be born, and came first of all to worship him; and that the name of Magicke was received by Phylosophers, commended by Divines, and not unacceptable to the Gospel.

Page 319: On Venus (Malachim alphabet):

Things are under Venus, amongst Elements, Aire, and Water; amongst humours, Flegm, with Blood, Spirit, and Seed; amongst tasts, those which are sweet, unctuous, and delectable.

Page 320: On Mars ("passing the river" alphabet):

> Things are Martiall, amongst Elements, Fire, together with all adust,
>
> and sharp things: Amongst humours, Choller; also bitter tasts, tart,
>
> and burning the tongue, and causing tears.

Page 321: General precept of "The Picatrix" ("passing the river" alphabet):

> The cautious Soul collaborates with the Astral action just as the
>
> skilled peasant collaborates with Nature when plowing and digging.

Page 322: Agrippa on the Sun (Zodiac alphabet):

> Things under the power of the Sun are, amongst Elements, the lucid
>
> flame; in the humours, the purer blood, and spirit of life; amongst
>
> tasts, that which is quick, mixed with sweetness.

John Dee

Page 324: Theorem 1:

> It is by the straight line and the circle that the first and most simple
>
> example and representation of all things may be demonstrated,
>
> whether such things be either non-existent or merely hidden under
>
> Nature's veils.

Pages 324 and 325: Theorem 2:

> Neither the circle without the line, nor the line without the point, can be artificially produced. It is, therefore, by virtue of the point and the Monad that all things commence to emerge in principle. That which is affected at the periphery, however large it may be, cannot in any way lack the support of the central point.

Pages 325 and 326: Theorem 3:

> Therefore, the central point which we see in the centre of the hieroglyphic Monad produces the Earth, round which the Sun, the Moon, and the other planets follow their respective paths. The Sun has the supreme dignity, and we represent him by a circle having a visible centre.

Bibliography

Books and Periodicals

Albani, Paolo, and Berlinghiero Buonarroti. *Aga magera difura dizionario delle lingue immaginarie*. Bologna: Zanichelli, 1994.

Belloc, Alexis. *La télégraphie historique depuis les temps les plus reculés jusqu'à nos jours*. Paris: Firmin Didot, 1894.

Bouleau, Charles. *The Painter's Secret Geometry*. New York: Harcourt, Brace & World, 1963.

Carcopino, Jérôme, *La basilique pythagoricienne de la porte majeure (The Pythagorean Basilica of the Porta Maggiore)*. Paris: L'artisan du livre, 1927.

Carrouges, Michel. *Les machines célibataires (Bachelor Machines)*. Paris: Chêne, 1976.

Castera, Michel. *Le compagnonage*. Paris: Presses Universitaires de France, 1988.

Copeland, B. Jack, ed. *The Essential Turing*. Oxford, UK: Clarendon Press, 2004.

Dach, Michel. *Le Désert de Retz à la lumière d'un angle particulier*. Rocquencourt, France: Michel Dach, 1995.

Daillez, Laurent. *Les Templiers et les Règles de l'Ordre du Temple*. Paris: Editions Pierre Belfond, 1972.

Davis, Martin. *Computability and Unsolvability*. New York: McGraw-Hill, 1958.

Desgris, Alain. *Organisation et vie des Templiers*. Paris: Guy Tredaniel Editeur, 1997.

Delclos, Marie, and Jean-Luc Caradeau. *L'ordre du temple (The Order of the Templar)*. Paris: Trajectoire, 2005.

Félibien des Avaux, André. *Entretiens susr les vies eet les ouvrages des plus excellents peintres anciens et modernes*. Paris: Sébastien Mabre Cramoisy, 2005.

Flournoy, Theodore. *From India to the Planet Mars: A Case of Multiple Personality with Imaginary Languages*. Princeton, N.J.: Princeton University Press, 1994.

Freudenthal, Hans. Lincos: *Design of a Language for Cosmic Intercourse*. Amsterdam: North-Holland Publishing, 1960.

Gannon, Paul. *Colossus: Bletchley Park's Greatest Secret*, London: Atlantic Books, 2006.

Ghyka, Matila C. *The Geometry of Art and Life*. New York: Dover, 1978.

Hambidge, Jay. *The Elements of Dynamic Symmetry*. New York: Brentano's, 1926.

Henry, Victor. *Le langage martien*. Paris: J. Maisonneuve, 1901.

Howard, Michael A. *The Runes and Other Magical Alphabets*. Wellingborough, UK: Thorsons Publishers, 1978.

Huntley, H. E. *The Divine Proportion: A Study in Mathematical Beauty*. New York: Dover, 1970.

Jusserand, J. J. *With Americans of Past and Present Days*. New York: Charles Scribner's Sons, 1917.

Kahn, David. *The Codebreakers*. London: Weidenfeld and Nicolson, 1966.

Le Rouge, Georges-Louis. *Détail des nouveaux jardins á la mode*. Paris, 1776–1787.

Martin, Jean-Jack. *Compagnons Charpentiers, ces derniers indiens*, Tours, France, 2006.

Montagné, Jean-Claude *Histoire des moyens de télécommunication de l'antiquité à la seconde guerre mondiale*. Bagneux, France: Jean-Claude Montagné, 1995.

Morrison, Philip, and Emily Morrison, eds. *Charles Babbage and His Calculating Engines*. New York: Dover, 1961.

Ollivier, Michel. "Comment naquit le monopole des télécommunications." *Le Monde*, May 3–4, 1987.

Pernoud, Régine. *Hildegard of Bingen: Inspired Conscience of the Twelfth Century*. New York: Marlowe & Company, 1998.

Renard, Pierre-Emile. *Chambourcy et le Désert de Retz*, Chambourcy, 1984.

Richter, Irma A. *The Notebooks of Leonardo da Vinci*. Oxford, UK: Oxford University Press, 1952.

Rougier, Louis. *La religion astrale des Pythagoriciens*. Paris: Presses Universitaires de France, 1959.

Scholem, Gershom. *Kabbalah and Its Symbolism*. New York: Shocken Books, 1969.

Seuphor, Michel, ed. *Cercle et carré*. Paris: Pierre Belfond, 1971.

Shugarts, David A. *Secrets of the Widow's Son*. New York: Sterling Publishing, 2005.

Singh, Simon. *The Code Book*. New York: Doubleday, 1999.

Vergez, Raoul. *La pendule à Salomon*. Paris: Juliard, 1970.

Wilson, Geoffrey. *The Old Telegraphs*. London: Phillimore, 1976.

Wolfe, James Raymond. *Secret Writing: The Craft of the Cryptographer*. New York: McGraw-Hill, 1970.

Yaguello, Marina. *Lunatic Lovers of Language: Imaginary Languages and Their Inventors*, London: Athlone Press, London, 1991.

Internet Sites

These links are referenced with the usual caution where the Internet is concerned. Their addresses are valid at the time I write these lines, but the sites may have moved or disappeared by the time you read this.

Artificial Language Lab	www.rickharrison.com/language/index.html (Rick Harrisson)
The Cincinnati of Pennsylvania	www.pasocietyofthecincinnati.org (state society)
Journeyman Stonecutters Association of North America	www.stonecarver.com/union.html
Mason marks	www.goldenageproject.org.uk/ 192masonsmarks.html
Minoan marks	www.mmtaylor.net/Holiday2000/index.html (Insup and Martin Taylor)
Norfolk Incredible Font Design	www.norfok.com/ (a Nug Soth free font)
Nu Isis Working Group	www.geocities.com/nu_isis/index_f.html (a site on rare fonts)

Ronald W. Kenyon — www.geocities.com/rwkenyon/chronology.htm

Betsy Ross and the flag — www.ushistory.org/betsy/flagtale.html

Villard de Honnecourt — www.villardman.net
(Carl F. Barnes)

Voynich font — www.voynich.nu/extra/eva.html
(rare Voynich fonts can be found on this site by René Zandbergen and Gabriel Landini)

The Voynich manuscript at Yale University — http://webtext.library.yale.edu/beinflat/pre1600.MS408.htm

Index

Note: Page numbers in *italics* indicate code solutions.

Active code. *See also* Computers
  fractals and, 70–72
  key events leading to, 226–235
  quantum leap to, 226
  today, 253
  trends of thought leading to, 226
Aeneas, 7–9
Aesthetic codes, described, 3–4
Agrippa, Heinrich Cornelius, 104, 111, 121, 124–126, 316–322, *337, 360–361*
Agrippa's Occultese, 316–322, *360–361*
Alberti, Leone Battista, 114–115, 159–160, 162–163, 164, 189–193, *338–339, 344*
Aleph-zero/aleph-one. *See* Infinity code, of Cantor
Alien languages, 274–294, *350–355*
  Conan Doyle's Dancing Men, 293–294, *355*
  Edgar Allan Poe, 290–292, *353–355*
  Hélène Smith's Alien Languages, 278–281, *350–351*
  Howard Phillips Lovecraft, 284–287, *352*
  J. R. R. Tolkien's Worlds of Words, 281–284, *351–352*
  Star Trek's Klingon, 287–289, *353*
  Thomas More, 275–277, *350*
Angelic mysticese, 307–326, *358–362*
  Agrippa's Occultese, 316–322, *360–361*
  Doctor Mirabilis's Ciphers, 312–314, *358–359*
  Geoffrey Chaucer, 314–316, *359*
  Hildegard's Coded Faith, 307–311, *358*
  John Dee, 322–326, *361–362*

Antoinette, Marie, 183–185, 214, *343*
Artificial intelligence, test for, 264

Babbage-Kasiski method, 193–195, *345–346*
Bachelard, Gaston, 226, 235
Bachelor machines, 229, 232, 234, 247, 249, 266
Bachelor machines theory, 233–234
Bacon, Roger, 158, 312–314, *358–359*
Becher, Johann Joachim, 297–298, *356*
Belaso-Vigenère system, 190–193, 243, 244, *345*
Benni, Stefano, 302–304, *357*
Bernard de Clairvaux, 79, 82
Berners-Lee, Tim, 174, 268
Blanc brothers, 24–25
Bride machine, 232, 266
Brotherhoods. *See also* Compagnon brotherhoods; Freemasons
  historical perspective, 130–131
  networks of inns, 132–133
  of Pythagoras. *See* Pythagoreans

Caesar, Augustus, 13
Caesar, Julius, 11–15
  accomplishments, 12
  breaking code of, 13–14
  as code of reference, 13–14
  codes to decode, 11, 12–13, *331*
  coding method of, 11–12
  death and deification of, 12–13
  landing on British soil, 11
  longevity of code, 13
  torch telegraphs at time of, 12
  Turing machine code of, 240–242, *349*
Cantor, Georg, 64–66, 265

Cantor sieve, 264–266
Carpenter's alphabet, 139–140
Carrouges grid, 234–235
Carrouges, Michel
  bachelor machines theory of, 233–234
  grid for checking machines, 234–235
Cato the Elder, 10, *330*
Cesariano, Cesare, 120–121
Chappe brothers' telegraph
  beam system, 20–21
  Blanc brothers exploiting, 24–25
  codebook, 19, 21–22
  codes to decode, 19, 22, *332–333*
  first network virus, 24–25
  French government supporting, 20–21
  glassman and ropeman for, 21–22
  inspiring Samuel Morse, 28–29
  military developments from, 22–26
  Napoleon closing, 23
  Polybius inspiring, 17
  shutter system, 18, 19–20
  tachygraph system, 18, 19
  tower operators, 21–22
Chappe, Claude, 16
Chaucer, Geoffrey, 158, 314–316, *359*
Cincinnati, Society of, 203–205
Cipher disks
  coupled with typewriter, 242–243, 244–246
  created by Thomas Jefferson, 242, 243–244
Cipher gallery, 273–328, *350–362*
  Agrippa's Occultese, 316–322, *360–361*
  alien languages, 274–294
  angelic mysticese, 307–326, *358–362*
  Bruno Munari, 305–306, *357–358*
  Conan Doyle's Dancing Men, 293–294, *355*
  Doctor Mirabilis's Ciphers, 312–314, *358–359*
  Edgar Allan Poe, 290–292, *353–355*
  Geoffrey Chaucer, 314–316, *359*
  Hans Freudenthal's Lincos, 328

Hélène Smith's Alien Languages, 278–281, *350–351*
Hildegard's Coded Faith, 307–311, *358*
Howard Phillips Lovecraft, 284–287, *352*
Johann Joachim Becher's Lingua Universalis, 297–298, *356*
John Dee, 322–326, *361–362*
J. R. R. Tolkien's Worlds of Words, 281–284, *351–352*
Palanc's Cream Lines, 298–300, *356*
The *Pioneer* Plaque, 327
Serefini's *Codex Seraphinianus*, 300–302
SETI@home, 327
space code, 326–328
Star Trek's Klingon, 287–289, *353*
Stefano Benni, 302–304, *357*
Thomas More, 275–277, *350*
Voynich manuscript exhibit, 295–296, *355–356*
Ciphers
  as conversations between three people, 3
  gallery of. *See* Cipher gallery
  looking like puzzles, 2–3
Codebooks
  of Aeneas, 7
  aesthetic, fractals, 70–72
  aesthetic, of Pythagoras, 33, 34–35, 46–47, 50. *See also* Golden mean; Pythagorean heritage
  Chappe system, 19, 21–22
  of New York telegraph, 27
  of Polybius, 8, 9
  sample format, 7
  used in Civil War, 188
  vulnerability of, 188
Codes
  balancing complexity and usefulness, 3
  E backdoor, 158–163, 184, 188–189, *338–339*
  letter frequency and, 158–161
  meanings of word "code," 2

paradox of, 1
prevalence today, 1–2
security systems and, 1–2
this book and, 2, 4
Codex Seraphinianus, 300–302
Compagnon brotherhoods, 130–145
    apprentice education, 132–133
    beam/timber talk, 140–142, *338*
    carpenter's alphabet, 139–140
    Christian rites and rebirth, 133–135
    codes and secrets of, 135
    codes to decode, 141–144, *338*
    facade alphabets, 140–145, *338*
    initiatory journey, 132–133
    marks of, 136–140
    mason's stone marks, 136–138
    networks of inns, 132–133
    Solomon's clock and, 139
    Solomon's temple and, 136
    song of, 135–136
    Templars and, 131–132
    tile talk, 142–144, *338*
Computers. *See also* Machines
    Alan Turing and, 249–250, 269–270. *See
        also* Turing machine
    bachelor machines theory and, 233–234
    blossoming of, 254–257
    Cantor sieve, 264–266
    Carrouges grid and, 234–235
    coding lives, 264–271
    definition over time, 254
    Diffie-Hellman-Merkle paradoxical key
        exchange, 261–263
    early prototype. *See* Turing machine
    end of Morse code era and, 30–31
    GENCODE, 174
    genesis of virtual Eden, 255
    hypertext, 174, 255
    interaction as fifth dimension, 267–268
    Internet explosion, 255–256

    Kabbalah connection, 257–260
    Konrad Zuse and, 247, 249
    markup technology, 174–175
    as multiplayer bride, 266
    mystical connection, 257–260
    "primordial net soup" of, 268–269
    privacy and secrecy, 260–263
    SGML and HTML, 174
    testing for artificial intelligence, 264
    virtual immigration with, 256–257
Conan Doyle's Dancing Men, 293–294, *355*
Cook, William Fothergill, 28
Crusades. *See* Knights Templar
Cursus velox, 13

Dali, Salvador, 46, 69, 232
The Da Vinci Code, 42, 85
Da Vinci, Leonardo, 100, 106–107, 116–119,
        168–171, 172–173, *336–337, 340–341*
De Crema, Simeone, 164–166, *339*
Dee, John, 127, 296, 301, 305, 313, 322–326,
        361–362
"Desert" revolution of Europe, 209–220
Diffie-Hellman-Merkle paradoxical key
        exchange, 261–263
Divine proportion, 116–119, *336–337*
Doctor Mirabilis's Ciphers, 312–314, *358–359*
Dreaming, lucid, 152–153
Duchamp, Marcel, 229–234, 240
Duke of Montmorency, 174–177, *341*
Dynamic symmetry (codes), 61–62, 70, 226

Eagle, of the Cincinnati, 203–205
E backdoor, 158–163, 184, 188–189, *338–339*
Edelcrantz, Abraham Nicola, 16, 22–23
Enigma, 246–248, 267
Euclid, 66, 117, 128

Fibonacci, 59–63, 72, *333*
Flags, pentagram, 200–201

Fort McHenry, 199
Fractals, 70–72
Freemasons. *See also* Compagnon brother-
    hoods
    American War of Independence and, 149
    apron of, 147, 149–150
    dealing with Christian persecution, 146–147
    death, resurrection and, 150–151
    earliest lodges, 145
    emergence of, 145–146
    freedom of thought and, 146
    guilt and, 130
    mythic journey of, 151–155
    in New World, 145–146
    obedience as weapon of, 147
    108° signature and, 50–51
    as paradox, 145
    political masterpiece of, 148–149
    Pythagoreans and, 50–51, 57–58, 74, 148–149
    rites of entry, 150–151
    secrecy of, 148
    Solomon's temple and, 147, 150
    stone talk, 145
    symbols of, 147–148, 149–150
    Taccola and, 112–113
    Templars and, 74, 84, 96, 129, 147
Freudenthal, Hans, 328

Gallery of ciphers. *See* Cipher gallery
Game codes, 232–233
GENCODE, 174
Giocondo, Giovanni, 119–120
Giorgi, Francesco, 121–122, 124, 127
Giorgio Martini, Francesco di, 113–114
Gödel (Kurt) numbers, 66–67, 236–237, 240,
    333
Golden mean, 34
    discovery and explanation, 47–50
    Fibonacci numbers and, 62–63
    Mondrian's portrait of, 67–68

obituary of, 69
Salvador Dali and, 69
true appeal of, 51–52
Vitruvius and, 111, 118–119
Golem, 228
Goujon, Jean, 123–124
Greek codes
    Doctor Mirabilis's Ciphers, 312–314,
        358–359
    of Polybius, 6–10
    scytale system, 14–15, *331–332*
Grout, Jonathan, 26

Hellman, Martin. *See* Diffie-Hellman-Merkle
    paradoxical key exchange
Henri II of France, 178–181, *342*
Henri III of France, 190–192, 193
Henri IV of France, 166, 185–188, 193,
    343–344
Hexagon numbers, 45
Hilbert, David, 236
Hildegard von Bingen, 102–104, 307–311,
    358
Homophones
    Alberti's wheels within wheels, 189–190,
        344
    Babbage-Kasiski breakthrough, 193–195
    Belaso breakthrough, 190–193, *345*
    breaking, 166–167
    cipher adulthood and, 164–183
    codes to decode, 162–163, 165, 168–171,
        172–173, 176–177, 180–181, 182–183,
        184–185, 186–187, 189–190, 193, 195,
        338–346
    defined, 157
    Duke of Montmorency and, 174–177, *341*
    earliest known document with, 164
    E backdoor and, 158–163, 184, 188–189,
        338–339
    etiquette weakening, 167

François Viète and, 166–167, 185, 186–187, *343–344*

Giambattista Palatino and, 172–173, *340–341*

Henri II of France and, 178–181, *342*

Henri III of France and, 190–192, 193

Henri IV of France and, 166, 185–188, 193, *343–344*

letter frequency and, 158–161

Marie Antoinette and, 183–185, *343*

Mary Stuart and, 182–183, *342–343*

Michele Steno and, 168–171, *340*

Simeone de Crema and, 164–166, *339*

tables vulnerability, 188

Infinity code, of Cantor, 64–66, 265–266

Internet
freedom from hierarchy, 256
genesis of virtual Eden, 255
military past of, 256
"primordial soup" of, 268–269
privacy and secrecy, 260–263

Jeanneret-Gris, Charles-Édouard, 68–69

Jefferson, Thomas
approving L'Enfant Capitol design, 220
cipher disks created by, 242, 243–244
ending L'Enfant's services, 222
as Freemason, 149
ovals of, 217–219

Julia, Gaston, 70, 71, 72

Kabbalah, computers and, 257–260

Kafka, Franz, 228–229

Karl XIII, King of Sweden, 22–23

Kasiski-Babbage method, 193–195, *345–346*

Kelley, Edward, 295, 296, 301, 323

King Solomon, proverb of, 144, *338*. *See also Solomon references*

Klingon, from *Star Trek*, 287–289, *353*

Knights Templar, 73–97
belief in physical transmission of faith, 75–76
Bernard de Clairvaux and, 79, 82
codes to decode, 89–93, *334–336*
communication codes, 88–93
compagnon masons/carpenters and, 131–132
creating, 78–79
Crusades overview and, 77–78
daily life, 82–83
fall of, 74, 81, 94–95
Freemasons and, 74, 84, 96, 129, 147
heritage of, 96
hierarchy and assemblies, 83–84
King Solomon's temple and, 79–80, 81, 132
Knights Hospitallers and, 79, 80, 132
Le Temple today, 97
losing Jerusalem, 95
millennial predictions and, 76
as mounted Pythagoreans, 84–85
oath and organization, 81–82
overview, 73–74
Peter the Hermit and, 78–79, 224
pilgrimages to Jerusalem and, 74–76
from "Poor" to Templar, 79–80
Solomon's seal and, 85–87, *334*
Teutonic Knights and, 80

Le Corbusier, 68–69

L'Enfant, Pierre Charles, 201–207
army engineer and artist, 202–203
design of U.S. capital and, 208–209, 217, 220–224
falling out of favor, 220–222
grand commissions, 205–207
inexact angles in D.C. and, 222–223
Monville desert and, 214
promising Garden of Eden for Washington, 210, 217

Society of the Cincinnati eagle and, 203–205
symbolism of name, 224
Letter frequency, 158–161
Life appearing on earth, 268–269
Lovecraft, Howard Phillips, 284–287, *352*

Machines. *See also* Computers
   bachelor machines, 229, 232, 234, 247, 249, 266
   bachelor machines theory, 233–234
   bride machine, 232, 266
   Carrouges grid for, 234–235
   Franz Kafka's penal code and, 228–229
   game codes and, 232–233
   the Golem and, 228
   Jefferson-Scherbius active cipher (Enigma), 242–248
   Mary Shelley's *Frankenstein* and, 226–228, 268, 269
   reproduction of characteristics of, 235
   Turing machine, 236–242
Mandelbrot, Benoît, 70, 71, 72
Martha's Vineyard to Boston telegraph, 26
Mary I, Queen of Scotts. *See* Stuart, Mary
Masons. *See* Freemasons
Medusa, 55
Merkle, Ralph. *See* Diffie-Hellman-Merkle paradoxical key exchange
Millennial predictions, 76
Miller, Stanley, 268, 269
Mondrian, portrait of the mean, 67–68
Monville, François Racine de, 211–212, 214, 215–217, 218
More, Thomas, 275–277, *350*
Morse code, 28–31, *333*
Morse, Samuel, 28–31
Munari, Bruno, 305–306, *357–358*
Musical harmony, 51
Mythic journey, 151–155

Napoleon, 3, 11, 23, 96–97, 202, 204
New Jersey to Staten Island to Manhattan telegraph, 27
Numbers
   comparing infinities, 64–66, 265–266
   families of, 44–45
   golden mean. *See* Golden mean
   hexagon, 45
   irrational, discovery of, 46–47
   musical harmony and, 51
   pentagon, 45
   spatial perfection and, 45–46
   symbolism of Pythagoreans, 41–44
   triangular, 44

108° Signature, 50–51. *See also* Washington, D.C.
Optical telegraphy, 5. *See also* Chappe brothers' telegraph
   early military developments, 23–26
   first system (of Aeneas), 7–9
   Martha's Vineyard to Boston, 26
   New Jersey to Staten Island to Manhattan, 27
   in New World, 26–28
   Roman system, 15–17
   San Francisco semaphore, 27–28
   torch/tower systems, 8–10, 12, 15–16

Pacioli, Luca, divine proportion of, 116–119, *336–337*
Palanc, Francis, 298–299, 302
Palanc's Cream Lines, 298–300, *356*
Palatino, Giambattista, 172–173, *340–341*
Penal code, of Franz Kafka, 228–229
Pentagon numbers, 45
Pentagram city. *See* Washington, D.C.
Pentagram flags, 200–201
Persistence, 270–271
Peter the Hermit, 78–79, 224

Pioneer Plaque, 327

Poe, Edgar Allan, 234, 290–292, *353–355*

Polybius, 6–10

   Cato the Elder, 10, *330*

   development of code, 7

   from Greece to Rome, 6–10

   Marie Antoinette and, 183–185, *343*

   methods of sending messages, 7–10

   Scipio Africanus, 6, 10, *330*

   Virgil, 10, *330*

Porta Maggiore, 54–58

Privacy and secrecy, 260–263

   balancing out secrecy, 260

   Diffie-Hellman-Merkle paradoxical key
      exchange, 261–263

   random numbers and, 263

Pythagoras, 2

   aesthetic codebook of, 33, 34–35, 46–47,
      50. *See also* Golden mean; Pythagorean
      heritage

   biographical overview, 35–38

   blue "eye" of, 219–220

   brotherhood of. *See* Pythagoreans

   codebook development, 34–35

   death of, 52

   as first coder, 34

   games, Christianity and, 153–154

   history of geometry and, 34–35

   as master, 37–38

   mythic journey and, 152–155

   square root of 2 and, 46, 65

   theorem of right-angle triangles, 35

Pythagorean heritage, 58–72

   Adolf Zeising and, 63–64

   Fibonacci and, 59–63, 72, *333*

   fractals and, 70–72

   Georg Cantor and, 64–66

   Gödel numbers and, 66–67, *333*

   Le Corbusier and, 68–69

   Mondrian's portrait of the mean and, 67–68

Salvador Dali and, 69

Vitruvius and, 58–59. *See also* Vitruvius,
   Marcus

Pythagoreans

   arranging numbers in families, 44–45

   astronomical explanations of, 52–54

   basis of success and originality, 46

   belief in transmigration of souls, 40

   comradeship of, 39

   discovery of irrational numbers, 46–47

   fascination with numbers, 40–41

   founding of, 38

   Freemasons and, 50–51, 57–58, 74, 148–149

   fundamental discovery by, 46–47

   golden mean of, 34, 47–50, 51–52, 59,
      61–64

   hierarchy within, 38–39

   Hildegard von Bingen and, 103–104

   Knights Templar acting as, 84–85

   lifestyle in, 39–40

   logic challenged, 46

   master ruling, 37–38

   Medusa and, 55

   musical harmony and, 51

   numbers as symbols, 41–44

   108° signature, 50–51

   persistence of, 270–271

   Plato receiving teachings of, 52

   Porta Maggiore basilica and, 54–58

   religious beliefs, 52–54, 55–58

   spatial perfection and, 45–46

   teaching method, 37–38

   tragic end of, 52

   Villard de Honnecourt and, 105–109

Romans

   Julius Caesar. *See* Caesar, Julius

   optical communications systems, 15–17

   Polybius code and, 6–10

Rotors of Enigma, 244–246

San Francisco semaphore, 27–28

Scherbius, Albert
coupling typewriter with cipher disks, 242–243, 244–246
rotors and German Enigma of, 244–248, 267

Scipio Africanus, 6, 10, *330*

Scytale system, 14–15, *331–332*

Serefini's *Codex Seraphinianus*, 300–302

SETI@home, 327

SGML (Standard Generalized Markup Language), 174

Shelley, Mary, 226–228, 268, 269

Smith, Hélène, alien languages, 278–281, *350–351*

Solomon's clock, 139

Solomon's seal, 85–87, *334*

Solomon's temple, 79–80, 81, 132, 136, 147, 150

Space code, 326–328
Hans Freudenthal's Lincos, 328
The *Pioneer* Plaque, 327
SETI@home, 327

Spatial perfection, 45–46

Stars, Pythagorean explanation of, 52–54

Star Trek's Klingon, 287–289, *353*

Steno, Michele, 168–171, *340*

Stone talk, 145

Stuart, Mary, 182–183, *342–343*

Sturgeon, William, 28

Taccola, 112–113

Tachygraph, 18, 19

Telegraph
in England, 23–26
first electric, 28
Morse Code and, 28–31
of Napoleon, 23
optical. *See* Optical telegraphy
vulnerability of, 242–243

Tolkien, J. R. R., Worlds of Words, 281–284, *351–352*

Torch codes, 12, 15–16

Torch tower systems, 8–10

Tory, Geofroy, 122–123

Trajan's Column and network, 15–17

Triangular numbers, 44

Turing, Alan, 225–251
bachelor machines theory and, 233–234
death of, 250
Franz Kafka's penal code and, 228–229
game codes and, 232–233
the Golem and, 228
key events leading to work of, 226–235
Marcel Duchamp and, 229–234, 240
Mary Shelley's *Frankenstein* and, 226–228
sparking quantum leap in code, 226
symbolism of life of, 250
Turing Caesar, 240–242, *349*
Turing Turing and, 226, 240
ultimate bachelor machine of, 249
vision and contribution to computer development, 249–250, 269–270. *See also* Turing machine

Turing machine, 236–242
codes to decode, 237–239, 240–241, *347–349*
composition of, 237
Gödel numbers and, 236–237, 240
question of decidability as basis of, 236–237
Turing 2 by 3, 237–239, *347–349*

Turing test 2.0, 264

Viète, François, 166–167, 185, 186–187, *343–344*

Vigenère, Blaise de, 190. *See also* Belaso-Vigenère system

Villard de Honnecourt, 104–109, 204–205

Virus (network), first, 24–25

Vitruvian saga, 99–128
  Cesare Cesariano and, 120–121
  Francesco di Giorgio Martini and, 113–114
  Francesco Giorgi and, 121–122, 124, 127
  Geofroy Tory and, 122–123
  Giovanni Giocondo and, 119–120
  Heinrich Cornelius Agrippa and, 104, 111,
    121, 124–126, 316–322, *337, 360–361*
  Hildegard von Bingen and, 102–104,
    307–311, *358*
  Jean Goujon and, 123–124
  John Dee and, 127, 296, 301, 305, 313,
    322–326, *361–362*
  Leonardo Da Vinci and, 100, 106–107,
    116–119
  Leone Battista Alberti and, 114–115,
    159–160, 162–163, 164, 189–193,
    338–339, 344
  Luca Pacioli's divine proportion and,
    116–119, *336–337*
  man, square, circle and, 100–102
  paradox of Vitruvian men, 127–128
  paragraph central to, 100–101, 111–112
  Poggio Bracciolini and, 109–110
  revival, 109–110
  square/circle template and, 100–102,
    111–112
  Taccola and, 112–113
  Villard de Honnecourt and, 104–109,
    204–205
Vitruvius, Marcus, 58–59
  biographical overview, 110
  book on architecture, 58–59
  golden mean and, 111, 118–119
  revival of thinking, 109–110
  works of, 110
Voynich manuscript exhibit, 295–296,
    355–356

Washington, D.C., 197–224
  Andrew Ellicott and, 222
  blue "eye" of Pythagoras, 219–220
  Désert de Retz and, 211–212
  design of, 208–209, 217, 220–224
  Eden on the Potomac, 217
  European "desert" revolution and, 209–220
  fallen angles, 222–223
  Fort McHenry and, 199
  guardian angles, 198–199
  108° angles and symbolism, 198–199,
    212–214, 219
  pentagram city, 198–201, 222–223
  pentagram flags and, 200–201
  Pierre Charles L'Enfant and. *See* L'Enfant,
    Pierre Charles
  Thomas Jefferson's ovals and, 217–219
  Versailles 108 and, 223–224
Washington, George
  as Freemason, 146, 149–150
  Freemason apron of, 149–150, 198, 217
  inauguration of, 207
  interest in ovals, 219
  Pierre Charles L'Enfant and, 202–203, 209,
    217, 220
  Society of the Cincinnati and, 203–204
Wheatstone, Charles, 28
Wheels within wheels, 189–190, *344*
World War II
  codebreaking, 246–248
  homophones broken during, 167
  machine vs. machine in, 246–247, 267
  rotors and German Enigma in, 244–248, 267
World War I, Jefferson-Scherbius active
    cipher and, 242–243

Zeising, Adolf, 63–64
Zuse, Konrad, 247, 249

Acknowledgments

I wish to thank the following people for their invaluable help:

Laurent Bastard
Ginny Bess
Jacques Borowczyk
Jean-Mary Couderc
Mike Dickman
Denis Dugas
Didier Guiserix
Meredith Hale
Jean-Jack Martin
Chrissy McIntyre
Stuart Miller
Guy Nouri
Pierre-Emile Renard

Picture Credits

pages 37, 54, 55, 56, and 57: Jérôme Carcopino, *La Basilique Pythagoricienne de la Porte Majeure* (*The Pythagorean Basilica of the Porta Maggiore*), © 1927 Choureau et Cie.

page 61 (top): Chris73, Wikimedia, Gnu Free Documentation license

page 68: Le Corbusier, *Le Modulor*, © F.L.C./Adagp, Paris 2008

page 69 (top): Salvador *Dali, La crucifixion* (*The Crucifixion*), © Salvador Dali, Fondation Gala-Salvador Dali/Adagp, Paris 2007/ARS, New York City

page 69 (bottom): Salvador Dali, *La Cène* (*The Last Supper*), © Salvador Dali, Fondation Gala-Salvador Dali/Adagp, Paris 2007/ARS, New York City

page 70: Eequor, *Julia Set*, Wikimedia Commons

page 71: Wolfgang Beyer, *Mandelbrot Set*, Wikimedia Commons

page 97 (top): Map of Paris, © Google

page 108 (upper left): Mauritz Escher, *Drawing Hands*, © M.C. Escher. Used with permission from the M.C. Escher Company.

page 132: Pierre d' Aubusson, *Histoire du Siège de Rhodes (History of the Siege of Rhodes),* Bibliothèque Nationale de France

pages 133 and 135: Jean-Jack Martin, *Compagnons Charpentiers (Carpenter Compagnons)*, Tours 2006, © Jean-Jack Martin

page 188: Union General Joseph Hooker's code book, National Security Agency

page 192 (top): Union Cipher Disk, National Security Agency

page 192 (bottom): Confederate Cipher Cylinder, National Security Agency

page 206: Collection of the New-York Historical Society, negative 50222d

page 207 (upper right): Library of Congress

pages 212 and 213 (top): Courtesy of Michael Drach

page 218: Thomas Jefferson, "Capitol, Pavilion ovals, circular plan," Massachusetts Historical Society

page 229 (bottom): Man Ray, *Rose Scelavy*, © Man Ray Trust/Adagp, Paris 2007/ARS, New York City

page 230: Marcel Duchamp, *Nu descendant un escalier (Nude Descending a Staircase)* © Marcel Duchamp/Adagp, Paris 2007/ARS, New York City, Philadelphia Museum of Art

page 231: Marcel Duchamp, *With Hidden Noise,* © Marcel Duchamp/Adagp, Paris 2007/ARS, New York City, Philadelphia Museum of Art

page 232: Marcel Duchamp, *La mariée mise à nu ...(le grand verre) (The Bride Stripped Bare by Her Bachelors, Even [The Large Glass]),* © Marcel Duchamp/Adagp, Paris 2007/ARS, New York City, (as broken by author)

page 233: Marcel, Duchamp, *Etant donné, seulement la porte extérieure...(Given, the Door Only)* © Marcel Duchamp/Adagp, Paris 2007/ARS, New York City, Philadelphia Museum of Art

page 243 (top): The US National Archives

page 243 (bottom): National Security Agency

page 248: Matt Crypto, Wikimedia Commons

page 326 (bottom): NASA

Code Font Credits

Unless indicated otherwise, all fonts used in codes were composed for this book by Pierre Berloquin & Denis Dugas.

page 285: Nug-Soth: urhixidur font, copyright Daniel U. Thibault

page 296 (bottom): EVA Hand 1, created by René Zandbergen and Gabriel Landini and displayed at http://www.voynich.nu/extra/eva.html. © René Zandbergen, 2004

page 301: Luigi Serafini, "Codex Seraphinianus," Franco Maria Ricci, 1981, © Luigi Serafini

page 302-304: Font by Denis Dugas, made with permission from Stefano Benni

pages 316-318: Theban, © Ben Whitmore 1998

page 319: NI MalachimB, freeware font created by the NU Isis Working Group, 2001

pages 323–326: NI Enochian, freeware font created by the NU Isis Working Group